Praise for *Out of the Shadows*

"In this fast-paced, engaging book, Emily Midorikawa shows that, for six nineteenth-century women, communicating with the dead was the best way of claiming a public voice. No stereotype of Victorian ladyhood survives. From Wall Street to presidential campaigns, from the courtroom to the stage, these women captivated their audiences and made serious claims about society in the process. Midorikawa tells their stories with sensitivity and grace, moving between the personal, the political, and the phantasmagoric with a sure step and a keen eye for detail."   —MO MOULTON,
author of *The Mutual Admiration Society:*
How Dorothy L. Sayers and Her Oxford Circle
Remade the World for Women

"I was captivated by Midorikawa's vivid portraits of Victorian-era women who used their Spiritualism to rise from obscurity and poverty to astonishing, often dizzying, social and political influence. *Out of the Shadows* brings to the fore the forgotten histories of these bold, radical, ambitious, and complicated women who campaigned for women's equal rights and suffrage, and even to become America's first female president—all while channeling the voices and guidance of the dead. Meticulously researched, engrossing, poignant, and often very humorous, *Out of the Shadows* does a huge service to feminist history."   —SUSAN BARKER,
author of *The Incarnations*

"Public speaking was a disreputable occupation for Victorian-era women—unless they were communicating with the dead, a skill that turned out to be much in demand and often quite lucrative. Emily Midorikawa's account of six women who were adept at working psychic miracles offers a fascinating new view of fame, belief, and feminism." —LAURA SHAPIRO,
author of *What She Ate: Six Remarkable Women and the Food that Tells Their Stories*

"This book is a treasure—a little-known history about forgotten movers and shakers, women who influenced our country in unimaginable and unseen (to say the least) ways. Reader: you need this book! Take it home with you and learn about a potent part of our history that you didn't know you needed to know. Writing with seamless clarity, Midorikawa has produced another true gem. I love this book." —MIRA PTACIN, author of
The In-Betweens: The Spiritualists, Mediums, and Legends of Camp Etna

OUT OF THE SHADOWS

ALSO BY EMILY MIDORIKAWA

A Secret Sisterhood: The Literary Friendships of Jane Austen,
Charlotte Brontë, George Eliot, and Virginia Woolf
with Emma Claire Sweeney

1871 image from *Frank Leslie's Illustrated Newspaper*, depicting political hopeful and Spiritualist Victoria Woodhull addressing Congress. *Photo courtesy of the Library of Congress*

Out of the Shadows

SIX VISIONARY VICTORIAN WOMEN IN SEARCH OF A PUBLIC VOICE

EMILY MIDORIKAWA

COUNTERPOINT
Berkeley, California

Library of Congress Cataloging-in-Publication Data
Names: Midorikawa, Emily, author.
Title: Out of the shadows : six visionary Victorian women in search of a public
  voice / Emily Midorikawa.
Description: First hardcover edition. | Berkeley, California : Counterpoint, 2021.
  | Includes bibliographical references.
Identifiers: LCCN 2020025301 | ISBN 9781640092303 (hardcover) | ISBN
  9781640092310 (ebook)
Subjects: LCSH: Women mediums—Biography. | Spiritualism—History—19th
  century. | Women—History—19th century. | Feminism—History—19th
  century.
Classification: LCC BF1281 .M53 2021 | DDC 133.9092/52—dc23
LC record available at https://lccn.loc.gov/2020025301

Jacket design by Lexi Earle
Book design by Jordan Koluch

COUNTERPOINT
2560 Ninth Street, Suite 318
Berkeley, CA 94710
www.counterpointpress.com

Printed in the United States of America
10 9 8 7 6 5 4 3 2 1

For Erica, another remarkable woman

CONTENTS

Seen and Not Heard / 3

Heard but Not Seen / 26

The Talk of the Town / 41

Dim Prophecies / 54

The Path of Light / 68

A Blaze of Glory / 87

The Little Queen / 108

A Valuable Asset / 125

The Devil's Wife / 144

Private Frustrations / 174

Ghastly Consequences / 194

Public Triumph / 210

End of an Era? / 233

In Remembrance / 255

Acknowledgments / 261

Notes / 265

Select Bibliography / 309

Index / 319

OUT OF THE SHADOWS

Seen and Not Heard

One warm spring evening in 1853, Queen Victoria was staying at Osborne House, her opulent holiday residence on the Isle of Wight, just off Britain's southern shore. She had arrived three weeks earlier, the era of rail travel allowing her party to journey from Buckingham Palace by royal train and yacht in a single day. Tonight, May 18, the thirty-three-year-old British monarch and her companions were in a relaxed mood. While the distant song of nightingales in the surrounding woodland drifted in on the breeze through the open windows, the group decided to have a go at a "wild" craze imported from the United States of America and now sweeping London's high-society drawing rooms.

The queen would record in her diary that her husband, Prince Albert, was the first of the group to place his hands at the rounded edges of an empty-topped table. One by one, the others—including senior courtiers and ladies-in-waiting—joined in, forming a circle, resting their hands in a similar fashion. As they did so, a strange thing happened. The table began to rotate, apparently of its own accord. Faster and faster it spun, seemingly rising off the floor. When the queen's close friend Lady Ely joined them, the table picked up speed still further, causing its surface to fairly slip away beneath their fingers, leaving the excited group chasing after it as it slid around the room. In Victoria's words, it really was a "very peculiar" sensation. She took issue with the skepticism of two military men present, who claimed that the movement must be caused by nothing more mysterious than the pressure of so many hands. In the queen's view, the explanation was much more likely to be electricity or magnetism. She could not believe that "so many hundreds, if not thousands,—high & low" could simply have "performed a trick!"

The hundreds, if not thousands, referred to by Queen Victoria hailed, indeed, from rich and poor backgrounds. They lived in major cities and tiny villages on both sides of the Atlantic Ocean. Some were highly educated. Others had known next to no schooling. They included people in lasting positions of power and celebrity, and those whose lives would leave only the lightest traces on written histories of the nineteenth century. Some individuals, like Her Majesty, seem to have regarded "table turning" and its associated practices, such as "spirit rapping" and "spirit writing," as intriguing yet harmless amusements. Others considered these activities frightening, even the work of the devil. To others still, they could be harnessed for profit, or serve as opportunities to wield otherwise unthinkable levels of political and cultural clout.

Five years earlier, and three thousand miles from the Italianate splendor of Osborne House, commotion gripped the hamlet of Hydesville—a rural community in Wayne County, New York. On March 31, 1848, Mary Redfield, a no-nonsense woman in her thirties, heard a knock on the door. Peering into the frosty evening darkness, she saw her neighbor John D. Fox, an older man aged about sixty, standing outside. John asked Mary to accompany him back to the small wood-frame house nearest to hers, where he'd recently moved with his wife, Margaret, and two young daughters, Margaretta and Catherine. According to John, strange noises had been troubling the family. His visible nervousness caused Mary some amusement.

This wasn't the first she had heard of these sounds. Some days before, Margaretta and Catherine—known as Maggie and Kate—had told her a similar tale. Mary had not taken the girls seriously then, and she did not take their father seriously now. Before setting off with him, she declared that if there was, as the family suspected, a ghost next door, she would "have a spree with it."

When the two arrived, they were met by Margaret and the girls, who all looked uncommonly pale. Maggie, a pretty, dark-haired fourteen-year-old, had none of her normal vivaciousness. The eyes of sprite-like eleven-year-old Kate seemed even more intense than usual.

Margaret was around fifty, and given to emotional outbursts. Over the three and a half months that the family had been living in Hydesville, she had come to respect her younger neighbor's usually unflappable nature. And so, thinking that Mary would surely have something sensible to say, Margaret asked, "Mrs. Redfield, what shall we do?" They had all been hearing this mysterious knocking for some time, and now it seemed that the ghost was attempting to converse with them. It had started answering "all of our questions, and we cannot account for it."

Leading Mary into the room where the whole family slept, Margaret invited her neighbor to sit down beside her on one of the beds. While Kate and Maggie hovered close by, Margaret asked the unseen presence to count to five, and then fifteen, both of which it did with the correct number of raps. More urgently, she implored it, "If you are an injured spirit manifest it by three raps."

Three raps answered in reply.

When Mary glanced at the two girls, the appearance they gave was one of genuine terror. Feeling unusually agitated herself by then, Mary decided to go back next door to fetch her husband, Charles. He in turn fetched several more neighbors. Soon a throng of men and women filled the Foxes' house, some too frightened to enter the bedroom, where the raps had last been heard. Others barged straight in and began asking their own questions of the invisible visitor, so that even John and Margaret found themselves pushed aside. Amid the chaos, their daughters Kate and Maggie took on that idealized youthful quality of being seen and not heard, leaving even less of an impression than their parents on the adults gathered.

Those crowding the house continued to interrogate the spirit, asking how long it had been since it was injured. About five years, apparently. Had it been murdered? More rapping affirmed this. They went through the names of various members of their little community on the banks of the Ganargua River to try, unsuccessfully, to establish a culprit. One of their group, William Duesler, thrust himself into the role of chief interrogator. He asked about several former occupants of the rented house, including John C. Bell, who had since moved away from Hydesville. At this point the spirit seemingly became animated, rapping out the loudest three knocks of the evening, making the bedstead shudder.

The spirit would go on to divulge that it had been murdered for money—for the considerable sum of $500, far more than most workingmen could hope to make in a year. Further raps would tell that while it slept someone had slashed its throat with a butcher's knife, that it had been taken down through the buttery the following night and buried in the cellar, and that Mrs. Bell was the one other person—till now—who knew what her husband had done.

On hearing this grim tale, Mary's husband, Charles, mustered the courage to descend to the cellar with a candle. William, continuing with his questioning from up above, had Charles stand in various spots while he asked whether this place or that was where the body was hidden. Knocking revealed that it had been buried in a specific area, ten feet below the cellar floor, and that it was the body of a man.

In a society where everyone knew each other, news traveled fast. As the evening wore on, more and more curious locals, many of whom had been braving the cold to go river fishing under a starlit sky, dropped by the Fox family's house. Since it must have seemed obvious that the spirit could hardly have once been one of their own close-knit community, William put forward the suggestion that it was that of a wandering peddler. Rapping confirmed this, but when he and the others tried to persuade the dead man to spell his name, by knocking each time William guessed a letter correctly, the noise died away.

Through further raps in answer to dramatic scenarios suggested by William, the spirit told them that, with no witnesses to the crime, there would be no chance for justice on earth, but that the murderer would be punished in the hereafter. The rapping sounds would continue intermittently until someone discovered the victim's bones, it said, after which the spirit would return to silence.

Having eventually exhausted all their questions, the party broke up at about midnight, with John Fox and Charles Redfield steeling their nerves to stay in the house while Margaret, Maggie, and Kate went elsewhere. In the morning, the family would find the place besieged. As the days passed, more people kept coming, including those from surrounding villages and towns, intrigued by what they had heard.

As Margaret would later tell in a sworn statement, she and her family had heard no knocking until late March 1848. But following the night some days later when so many of their neighbors descended on their house, the accepted story became more complex as others added their own twists and turns. The naming of John Bell as the murderer focused attention on Lucretia Pulver, a young woman now living a mile and a half away. She had boarded with and worked for the Bells during the winter when the killing supposedly took place. Lucretia recalled a peddler dressed in "a black frock coat, and light colored pants" who called at the house one afternoon. She had wanted to buy some things from him but had no money, and so he'd suggested that he could come again the next day. In the meantime, her mistress told the girl, then in her midteens, that she was going away for the night. Since Lucretia would not be needed for the time being, she was to go home until the Bells sent for her again. Her absence lasted only three days, but when she returned she noticed a few changes.

Mrs. Bell had acquired a couple of coats, which she wanted to cut down and refashion for her husband. She sought Lucretia's help with the task, and the girl saw that the coats were badly ripped. A while later, Mrs. Bell gave Lucretia a thimble that she said she'd bought from the peddler. Other things would appear from time to time, including a second thimble—a source of annoyance to Mrs. Bell, since she said that the man had tricked her, presenting it as pure silver when it had turned out merely to be nickel.

According to Lucretia, the peddler was never again seen, but she soon began to regularly hear raps similar to those now afflicting the Foxes. One day she thought she'd caught the sound of footsteps in the buttery when it should have been empty. On another occasion, she tripped over a patch of uneven floor in the cellar, which caused her to fall down and scream. She had expected sympathy from her employer, but instead Mrs. Bell had laughed and told her that rats must have disturbed the earth. The incident stayed in Lucretia's mind, perhaps especially because, a few days later, she'd seen the man of the house carrying "a lot of dirt" into the cellar. As Lucretia recalled to a journalist from the nearby town of Canandaigua, John Bell carried out this task "just at night" and had stayed down there for "some time."

E. E. Lewis, the enterprising lawyer turned reporter who interviewed Lucretia, had seen financial potential in the rumors from Hydesville and decided to produce a booklet of statements by local people. Lucretia's stories of her former employers naturally caught his attention, as did those of another trio who'd occupied the house between the departure of the Bells and the arrival of the Foxes. A couple named Weekman and their live-in help had tales of unexplained encounters of their own. The couple spoke of rappings and mysterious footsteps. Jane Lape, the hired help, recalled coming face-to-face with a strange male figure in the bedroom. Her account, notably given six days after Lucretia Pulver's statement, dwelled on the man's "grey pants, black frock coat and black cap." Jane would muse that she "knew of no person in that vicinity who wore a similar dress."

Many individuals seemed keen to air their views, and Lewis would include a total of twenty-one statements in his report. One of the shortest but possibly most damningly unequivocal, for those seeking hard evidence of murder, was made by two men who'd lived near the house in the summer of 1844. They recalled that "during that summer the water in that well was very offensive and bad."

On the other hand, the report also included a copy of a certificate circulated in the town of Arcadia, a mere two miles away, another place where John Bell had previously lived. The certificate, produced about a week after attention was first drawn to the Foxes' home, had been signed by forty-four people. They said they wanted to counteract the "foolish and superstitious reports" against this man, who—though he'd departed the immediate area—remained a resident of Wayne County. Those who signed the certificate wished to let it be known that they still thought him "a man of honest and upright character, incapable of committing crime."

Lewis clearly felt it important to acknowledge both sides of the argument, even though it risked widening the acrimonious gulf that had opened up between dwellers of two neighboring rural communities. He had gone to the trouble of interviewing not just those who seemed to have the most intimate knowledge of the noises but others whose involvement was less direct. Frustratingly, however, this early journalist on the scene managed to miss the real story. His decision not to formally interview Kate and Maggie leaves them voiceless at this stage. All we have are Mary Redfield's recollections that they were the first to speak openly of the noises.

It's possible that John and Margaret Fox had felt wary about allowing their daughters to talk with a journalist, although what would happen over the following months does not appear to bear this out. More likely, Lewis reasoned that, having interviewed the parents and neighbors, he had learned all he needed to know about the views of two young people, and girls at that, who could not be expected to know their own minds. Whatever his reasoning, it is certainly a pity, since, over the next four decades, it would be Maggie and Kate's personal narratives that became the most significantly entwined with the strange occurrences at Hydesville.

Lewis may have regarded Kate and Maggie as only minor players in the strange drama, but during the following weeks and months their parts would gradually transform into starring roles. That such a shift should have happened is due in large part to another member of their family—the girls' older sister, Ann Leah Fish.

Leah, who went by her second name, was a single parent, deserted by her husband years earlier. Now in her midthirties, old enough to be Maggie and Kate's mother, she was one of John and Margaret's four surviving adult children, after whom there'd been a significant gap before Kate and Maggie were born.

For largely self-serving reasons, Leah would later emphasize that, as her family had sent no word, she'd had no knowledge of the goings-on at her parents' home until more than a month after they had begun. Given the flinging of recriminations to come in the future, it's difficult to know whether Leah's claim can be true. The rumors from Hydesville had found their way into two papers, *The Western Argus*, based in Lyons, and *The Newark Herald*—both printed in towns in the immediate vicinity. (The *Argus* was printed in the town in which the accused, John Bell, now lived.) Still, it seems just about possible that the sense of excitement generated by the local press had not yet reached Leah forty miles away in Rochester, then an industrialized mill city and hub of radical ideas.

In the absence of a husband, Leah, an attractive, proudly independent woman, supported herself and her daughter, Elizabeth, by giving piano lessons. Elizabeth, known as Lizzie, was then in her late teens.

According to Leah's account, one day in May, when she was teaching at the home of the Little family, her students' mother, Jane, burst into the room. Jane Little was accompanied by a local printer, who had a proof sheet of a new pamphlet with him.

Jane, who knew that Leah's maiden name was Fox, hastily introduced the two strangers.

"Is your mother's name Margaret? Have you a brother David?" the printer asked Leah.

Leah, startled, stared at the man and cried out, "For mercy's sake, what has happened?"

He placed the early copy of E. E. Lewis's *Report of the Mysterious Noises Heard in the House of Mr. John D. Fox* into her hands. Leah began to read and then burst into tears.

Though she apparently found the wild tales within the booklet difficult to believe, she declared defiantly, "If my father, mother, and brother David have certified to such a statement, *it is true.*"

Distraught, Leah left the Littles' home to call on two friends. She told them that she needed to go to Hydesville. Each offered to accompany her and Lizzie on the night boat along the Erie Canal—that great system of waterways connecting New York City with the Great Lakes and the Atlantic Ocean, completed some twenty years earlier. The next morning, upon arrival in Newark, they took a carriage to Hydesville. But alighting at the wood-frame house by Mud Creek, as the locals referred to the Ganargua River, they found the scene deserted. Guessing that her sisters and parents must have gone to stay with David, Leah asked the driver to take them on down the lanes to her brother's farm, two miles away.

On seeing the group draw up, Leah's overwhelmed mother came out to greet her oldest living child with sighs and tears. The strain of the past weeks showed on Margaret's face. Although she and John had brought the family away from their rented home to escape the ghostly noises—"spirit raps," as they'd come to be known—the knocking had followed them to this new location. They all still frequently heard the sounds—although only, as they had begun to realize, when either Kate or Maggie was present.

Leah, Lizzie, and Leah's friends stayed at David's home for two weeks—a testing time for all concerned. Margaret remained, in Leah's words, "completely broken down by the recent events."

Even before these unexpected disturbances, the family's hopes on arriving in Hydesville had been put on hold. The cramped wood-frame structure where they'd been living had only ever been intended as a temporary residence, but John's plans to start work on a new house for his family had been delayed by the snowdrifts of an exceptionally harsh winter. Now that they'd had to flee the hamlet, not only had the planned building work been further delayed, but the spirit raps—apparently representing menace from beyond the grave—had followed them to David's farm.

What's more, a still greater terror may have lain at the root of Margaret's exhaustion—deep fear at the thought of standing out. Like the peddler, the Foxes had been relative strangers in Hydesville. And now, within just a few months of arriving, the two daughters had disrupted the calm of this quiet community through the perplexing sounds that their presence appeared to attract. Already, the wider local area was split over the question of the supposed killer John Bell's guilt, and now Margaret may have worried—rightly, as it would turn out—that blameful fingers might be pointed at her whole family.

In a region famous for its religious fervor, where old ideas about the supernatural continued to exist alongside new beliefs such as Shakerism and Mormonism, those who stood out could find themselves targets—especially if it seemed they were attracting malevolent spirits. And although 155 years had passed since the Salem witch trials in the bordering state of Massachusetts, those events still cast a long shadow. During that reign of hysteria, women and girls, in particular, who distinguished themselves from the crowd were the most likely to end up as victims.

Having discussed her fears with Leah, on whom she tended to lean, Margaret agreed to let her eldest daughter take the youngest, Kate, back to Rochester with her. Leah had suggested that by separating Kate from Maggie they might "put a stop to the disturbance."

But it was not to be. At least in Leah's telling of the story, on the canal ride raps similar to the ones they'd hoped to leave behind at David's farm began once more. When Leah and her party took their place at the boat's dining table, the knocking became livelier still—the spirit presences, apparently emboldened, lifting up one table end at intervals, upsetting the water in people's glasses. Thankfully, the typical noises of a busy crossing muffled the sounds, so that only those in their own small group noticed anything suspicious. Leah's recollections, published in a book she authored almost forty years later, do not record whether any among them asked Kate if she was somehow doing the knocking herself. Certainly, in Leah's case, the course she may even then have mapped out for all three sisters could have discouraged her from seeking answers to these kinds of questions.

Leah's memoirs would go on to explain how, once they'd reached Rochester, the spirit disturbances continued. On the first night back, Leah decided that they should all go to bed early, but neither Kate nor Leah's late-adolescent daughter could fall asleep. Moments after Leah had put out the lamps, she heard screams. A terrified Lizzie had felt a cold hand moving over her face, she cried, and another running down her back. But this was only the start of the night's activities. A Bible, which Leah had placed out of harm's way under her pillow, dislodged itself and flew up; a box of matches began to rattle of its own accord. Not until just before dawn did the interruptions cease, and only then did the three sleep.

They rose late in the morning, the June sun bathing the garden of 11 Mechanics' Square in bright light. As birdsong floated from the trees, Leah delighted in the colors of the newly blooming roses and decided to put aside all thought of these troublesome spirits.

But this was not the end of the matter. That night the company was roused from its slumbers once more by what Leah would recall as "the most frightful manifestations," which plunged the house into an uproar. There was something almost performance-like about it this time. Many different spirits seemed to be engaged in the spectacle, one of whom sounded as if it were dancing in clogs. When it had finished its musical turn, an invisible round of applause from the unseen presences rang out.

Shortly after this peculiar incident, Leah made the decision to move. The three took up residence on Prospect Street, in a property never before inhabited, Leah insisting that there would be less chance of its being haunted. But if escaping proximity to death was her aim, it seems unfortunate that Leah did not pay greater attention to the old cemetery at the rear of the house, known as the Buffalo Burying Ground.

The new house had extra bedrooms—particularly handy since Leah had written to her mother to tell her that the rapping sounds had followed them to Rochester, and Margaret had immediately agreed to come and stay, bringing fourteen-year-old Maggie with her.

With Maggie and Kate reunited in the bustling city, the disturbances took off like never before, "shuffling, giggling, and whispering," shaking the beds the first night. In the morning, Margaret asked Calvin Brown, a local man, to come and stay at the house and protect them. Calvin—who had lived for a time with the Foxes when he was a child, during a period when the family had lived in Rochester—was upset to see Margaret in such distress. He assured her that "he would conquer" the spirits "or die in the attempt." But, if anything, his presence only seemed to encourage them. When Leah called upon the spirits to behave themselves, one answered by stamping loudly on the floor and even keeping time to the rhythms of a Highland fling. Later, according to Leah, invisible hands raised Calvin's bed clean off the floor, pelted him with slippers, and struck him with his own fashionable walking stick.

During all this turmoil, Maggie and Kate's father, John Fox, chose to remain at his son, David's, farm. Unlike John's wife, Margaret, who seemed fully committed to the idea that the raps were caused by spirits, the family patriarch remained more skeptical. A heavy drinker in the early days of his marriage, he had left all that behind when he committed himself fully to his Methodist faith before Kate and Maggie were born. As steadfastly religious as any of his new neighbors, he did not hold with old superstitions. Though his decision not to reunite with his family may seem strange, John perhaps felt that younger and fitter men like Calvin could be more help, and that the sooner he could build a permanent home for his family, the sooner they could put this oddness behind them.

In addition to Calvin, in Rochester Leah had other close friends to whom she could turn for support. Amy Post, a radical Quaker, was part of the city's thriving community of politically engaged progressives. She and her husband, Isaac, were both women's rights campaigners and abolitionists. The social reformer Frederick Douglass, a former slave, lived nearby, and the Posts had joined him in helping men and women who had been enslaved to escape along the Underground Railroad.

Isaac and Amy Post initially felt merely amused by Leah's tales and made little effort to hide their belief that her family was "suffering under some psychological delusion." Still, they invited Kate and Maggie into their home and became curious when, in the girls' presence, they too seemed to experience the spirit manifestations. Perhaps the possibility of communicating with the dead held some appeal for a couple, who, not unusually for the era, had suffered the death of a child. In addition, Isaac had lost his first wife and a child from that former marriage. Other friends of Leah's, including wealthy Methodists Lyman and Elisabeth Granger, also showed a strong interest early on. Elisabeth was one of the friends who'd accompanied Leah and Lizzie on their recent visit to Hydesville. Like Amy and Isaac Post, she knew the pain of bereavement.

The death of the Grangers' daughter Harriet continued to exert a particular agony. Elisabeth and Lyman believed that the young woman had been murdered. A postmortem had revealed the presence of poison in Harriet's body, her husband had been tried but acquitted, and the case remained unsolved. During a session held in Rochester at which the murdered peddler from the Hydesville house appeared to make contact via Kate and Maggie, Harriet also made her presence known by rapping yes or no answers to the group's questions. It transpired that she wanted to warn her parents that her husband meant to destroy them. The alarmed couple took some comfort in their late daughter's assurance that she intended to watch over them and see that they came to no harm.

Over the following weeks, more and more of the Posts' circle of reformer friends grew interested in the wondrous feats that Kate and Maggie's company so often brought, many of these well-educated men and women becoming invested in the sense of possibility that the girls' apparent powers presented. Although the likes of the Posts and the Grangers may seem unduly gullible when viewed through jaded modern eyes, it's worth remembering that the mid-nineteenth century was full of new discoveries and inventions, the mechanics of which were not understood by most people. Thanks to the electrical telegraph, it was now possible for those with access to one of these machines to communicate almost instantaneously across previously unthinkable distances. In 1844, Samuel Morse had summed up the feeling of awe and mystique the new technology inspired when he transmitted the biblical message "What hath God wrought!" across a breathtaking thirty-eight miles of wire from Capitol Hill to the Mount Clare rail depot in Baltimore. And so it was not really such a great leap to view spirit communication in the same light as other marvels, such as Morse code or early daguerreotype photography, recently achieved by enterprising humans.

Despite living in an age of technological wonder, however, the socially progressive goals of the Posts and their ilk—such as the extension of voting rights and the abolition of slavery—remained frustratingly out of reach. Therefore, the Fox sisters' ghostly manifestations had an additional encouraging dimension for those engaged in political struggle. After all, if two seemingly ordinary country girls like Maggie and Kate Fox could cross so easily into the realm of the dead, what feats might individuals such as themselves still achieve in the world of the living?

While some of the Fox sisters' observers had seen incredible potential in the spirit rapping, others appeared ground down already by the frequency of the ghostly appearances. The day after the incident with the Grangers' deceased daughter, Leah's only child, Lizzie, staged a dramatic protest.

An initially skeptical clergyman friend of Lyman Granger had witnessed the knocks supposedly made by the deceased Harriet. The Reverend Lemuel Clark accompanied the couple to Leah's house on Prospect Street the following evening for a follow-up session. Several months later, he would pen a private letter, giving a harrowing account of the proceedings.

After they had all had tea, the group began their questioning. But, unusually, no sounds came in response. Leah's eyes traveled around the room, alighting on Kate and Maggie, their mother, Margaret, the Grangers, and Lemuel, before coming to rest on Leah's daughter, Lizzie.

"You are the cause of this silence," Leah declared. "You have been a very wicked girl today. You have grieved the Spirit."

Almost immediately, a rap sounded. Lemuel thought that it came from the vacant rocking chair in the corner of the parlor.

"That's it!" someone said, the others joining Leah in heaping accusations on Lizzie, demanding that she repent so that she might placate the slighted spirit.

Lemuel, who could not understand what Lizzie had done wrong, felt his blood boiling "with indignant emotion" on behalf of the young woman. It would transpire that Lizzie, now weeping convulsively, had recently spoken out against the spirit, arguing that to remain in contact with it would "be an injury" to the family. Other people, Lizzie said, would come to believe that the girls were "performing tricks to deceive" the public. Though Lemuel thought that these concerns were sound and wise, he decided that rather than making his feelings known just yet he would ask the supposed ghostly presence some questions of his own. Bit by bit, he too became convinced that Lizzie was in the wrong, particularly when the spirit told this religious man that she had sinned against God by speaking out against it. Eventually, Lizzie fell to her knees to ask the Almighty for his forgiveness.

Things began going more smoothly, with the singing of songs around the parlor piano in addition to all the spirit communing. But not long after that evening, Leah, perhaps feeling that her daughter was a liability, sent Lizzie to live elsewhere—an act that gives weight to the accusations of brutal coldness that would one day be directed at Leah.

Late in July 1848, a sizable group of the Fox sisters' progressive friends from Rochester made the journey with them to the Hydesville house. Attempts in April to dig down beneath the now locally infamous cellar had been hampered by water from the high river. Now, temperatures had risen considerably and the snow that once covered the ground had long melted away. Leah doubted whether any of the gentlemen she had brought with her from Rochester "had ever used the pickaxe and spade before." Nonetheless, spurred on by the thought that the body of some poor man lay buried beneath the ground, each came determined to put his back into the task. According to Leah's later recollections, by the time the friends arrived in Hydesville that summer, the communications of the peddler's spirit had become more explicit. It had begun to insist, presumably through its usual method of knocking, that its body had been buried along with a bowl in which the murderer had caught his victim's blood. At night, the sisters had even been plagued by the sound of blood "dropping slower and slower, until at last it ceased entirely; and then the sound would come as if the bowl were thrown and broken in pieces."

The group was able to stay at Leah's brother, David's, home. Perhaps wary of how his neighbors would react, David had needed some convincing to take part in the dig. But eventually, persuaded by more spirit rapping, he'd relented and even roped in a few other men to help. On the day that work was due to commence, the Rochester party, which seems to have included Leah but not Kate and Maggie, set off from David's farm. They took with them a plentiful supply of chickens, pies, puddings, cakes, and sweetmeats, all supplied by David's wife, Elizabeth. The mostly inexperienced team worked uncomplainingly until noon, battling against the unyielding soil of the cellar.

At around midday, they hit a layer of charcoal and traces of lime. Further excitement ensued when they uncovered some reddish hair and a few teeth. Leah's account of the dig would state that it proved conclusively that the earth had "at some time, and for some purpose, been disturbed," but many would write the finds off as the remains of farm animals. The afternoon brought no new discoveries, and that evening they went back to David's farm, set among grain and peppermint fields. In the morning, the party returned in a procession of several wagons, attracting a good deal of attention along the way.

From the roadside, hordes of locals—no doubt disconcerted to see such a throng, many of them strangers—directed mocking comments and laughter at them. A crowd soon formed outside the Foxes' house, while inside, Leah and the other women from Rochester, candles in hand, formed a protective ring around the men toiling in the dark cellar.

Suddenly one man exclaimed, "Great God! here are the pieces of a broken bowl!"

More indisputable proof, in Leah's eyes—but once again, not everyone was persuaded. When the group later unearthed some fragments of bone, a few pounced on the notion that they *must* be human—but it would not be enough to convince future doubters. All the while, the ominous sound of the crowd up above added to the rising tension. Every so often, a few men would break in and rush down to the cellar to antagonize the diggers, sometimes spitting on them.

Eventually, the prospect of violence raised its head. Years later, Leah would recall the shouts of "Drag out the women . . . drag out the men!" Thankfully, the threats came to nothing. But probably feeling lucky to get away unharmed, her friends from Rochester departed the next day.

Leah's younger sisters and mother might not have played a part in the cellar dig, but, having stayed on with her at David's farmhouse, they were there to witness a terrifying spectacle a few days later. Alerted to danger by the frightened barking of their dog, the family had taken refuge in the parlor. Huddled together, they could make out the sounds of gunfire, rowdy shouting, and the clatter of wagons approaching. As a mob surrounded the building, one of their number, a woman in hoopskirts, managed to jump through a kitchen window, which the panicked family besieged indoors had neglected to close. David left his sisters and mother on their knees, praying in the parlor, to calmly inform the woman that, if only she had knocked at the door, he would have let her in. Then he went outside and told the agitated throng that they could come in and search the house if they wished, provided they do it respectfully.

To which their flabbergasted leader replied, "No, we won't come in now. We'll go home and dress ourselves and come another time."

A potentially perilous situation had been averted, but it must have seemed to Margaret that it was time for her and her daughters to leave. Margaret's husband, John, remained—still a minor actor in the family's strange unfolding story. As in similar stories to come over the next forty years, the key roles in this mysterious new community created by the Fox sisters were often filled by women.

Not so in the wider world, however. The inaugural women's rights convention, held at Seneca Falls that same month, had come about in response to growing frustrations that women's voices were being ignored. Campaigners Lucretia Mott and Elizabeth Cady Stanton had done a good job of attracting three hundred reform-minded women and men to the mill village some twenty miles northeast of Hydesville. Stanton herself lived in Seneca Falls. The assembled company was far from united in its aims, however. Divisions swiftly emerged among those gathered for the two-day event at the redbrick Wesleyan Chapel. Disagreements centered on the issue of the vote. Frederick Douglass and others argued that the convention's resolutions, drafted by Stanton, should retain words emphasizing the delegates' support for extending the franchise to women. Still others felt that such language would be seen as inflammatory and ought to be dropped from the final version. Their fear was that potential supporters, ready to decry the general lack of rights granted to women—property-holding, wages—might feel that female suffrage went a step too far.

The lack of consensus kept both sides arguing for many hours.

Luckily, weary attendees looking for a diversion from these frictions could turn to the by then well-known story of the ghostly rappings at Hydesville. Some among the delegates, like Amy Post, already claimed to have direct experience of the manifestations. Others— such as Douglass and journalist Eliab Wilkinson Capron, who had yet to make his name—had no personal experience but would find themselves increasingly caught up over the coming months in the circus surrounding the Fox sisters. By that autumn, yet others who'd taken part in the Women's Rights Convention would be talking of raps heard in Elizabeth Cady Stanton's home, and even upon the very table on which she had drafted the convention's Declaration of Sentiments.

The sisters' expanding cohort of radical supporters must have been delighted when, in the months after Seneca Falls, the messages they received from the spirit world began to become more political. Rather than continuing to rely on raps to signal yeses and nos to their questions, the Foxes had worked out a way of attaining more complex answers by having those dead men and women they channeled spell out words by giving specific sequences of knocks that corresponded with different letters of the alphabet. Once, in the presence of their friend Isaac Post, a bold new message came through.

"Dear friends," it spelled out, "you must proclaim these truths to the world. This is the dawning of a new era; and you must not try to conceal it any longer. When you do your duty, God will protect you; and good spirits will watch over you."

But what exactly was the sisters' duty to be? Hints were dropped about "a mission to perform" and the need to "make ready for the work." In the summer of 1849, the youngest, Kate, then aged around thirteen, was invited to stay in the town of Auburn, sixty miles southeast of Rochester. Her host was the journalist Eliab

Capron, who'd been present at Seneca Falls the previous year and had become intrigued by stories about the Fox family. Although the Hydesville rappings had already been covered by E. E. Lewis's initial *Report* and in various local newspapers, Eliab clearly saw greater potential in the story. In Auburn, he subjected the child—often regarded as the sister most finely attuned with the spirits—to a series of rigorous and presumably harrowing tests, administered by other women staying at the boardinghouse where he lived with his wife. In order to make sure that the child had no items on her person, the ladies stripped her to her underwear. They discovered nothing, and a satisfied Eliab became a prominent advocate for the Fox sisters.

One evening that autumn, after Margaret had departed from Rochester and finally returned to her husband in Hydesville, the spirits apparently began to issue clear directives for the duty they expected. With Kate still away, Leah and Maggie should hold meetings in the homes of several prominent local progressives and invite an audience of other well-known persons. The spirits even supplied a list. On it were "lawyers, editors, and doctors" and also Frederick Douglass. Whether motivated more by genuine fascination or a wish to placate his friends the Posts, at whose house the first meeting was held, Douglass dutifully turned up for this public demonstration, along with all but one of those invited.

Given the presence of celebrated figures such as Douglass, one wonders whether Maggie and Leah ever pinched themselves and marveled at the sway they now held with members of some of the city's most illustrious circles. As the spirits would soon make clear, the potential for even greater influence now lay within the Foxes' grasp. During one of these sessions, loud raps informed the gathered company that the mysterious unseen presences had a further audacious challenge to propose. In order to relay their message to greater numbers still, Maggie and Leah should take the bold step of booking Corinthian Hall.

This, the largest civic venue in Rochester, had opened to great fanfare earlier that year. It seated well over a thousand people. Here, as must have been immediately apparent to the listeners, the sisters would have a tantalizing opportunity to publicly cement their reputation. But attention on this scale would have its share of potential pitfalls. Such a move risked exposing the Foxes to further scrutiny, greater hostility, and ever more threatening physical danger.

Heard but Not Seen

During that series of meetings in Rochester in late 1849, the spirits had asked that just Leah and Maggie Fox demonstrate their powers at Corinthian Hall. With Kate currently absent from the city, this was in a sense convenient, but it could also have caused something of a problem. Until now at least, only the youngest two sisters, Kate and Maggie, had seemed able to summon the knocking sounds. But neither Kate's absence nor her own requested inclusion seemed to trouble the enterprising Leah, and so the Corinthian Hall booking went ahead as planned.

The spirits had named Lyman Granger, two other prominent local Methodists, and one Quaker, plus another person to appear onstage with the sisters to create a show of support. Three of the named individuals were male and two female, giving the impression of balance. But it was the men who, outwardly at least, played the more active roles in presenting Maggie and Leah to the audience: manning the door, overseeing the management of the evening, and speaking on the sisters' behalf. In contrast, the accompanying women, and indeed Leah and Maggie themselves, would sit quietly on the podium, their muteness allowing them to be cast in more acceptably ladylike roles.

Ahead of the performance, the local press carried announcements of the forthcoming evening of "WONDERFUL PHENOMENA," which would give attendees an "opportunity of hearing a full explanation of the nature and history of the '*mysterious noises*'" whose fame had spread throughout the region. The wording framed the event as one of scientific inquiry, letting people know that after the demonstration, "a committee of *five persons* may be chosen by the audience." Their task would be to congregate in the morning to conduct their own examination and "report at the next evening's lecture whether there is collusion or deception." "*Come and investigate,*" the notice implored its readers.

On November 14, 1849, four hundred people took up the challenge and paid the twenty-five cents—fifty cents admitted "a gentleman and two ladies"—into the mock-Grecian Corinthian Hall, with its two columns modeled on the Monument of Lysicrates flanking the back of the red-curtained stage. Excitement filled the air. The audience—some no doubt wanting to believe, others doubting—waited to see what would unfold.

The party's arrival on the stage brought a frisson of anticipation. Maggie is said to have worn a long dress made of soft blue wool, a striking contrast against her dark hair. The older Leah, a fine-looking woman herself, also gave a pleasing first impression in her dark green outfit. Eliab Capron, the journalist at whose boardinghouse Kate had been staying, had arrived in Rochester to take part in the onstage demonstration. Interestingly, he had left the youngest Fox sister behind. This raises the possibility that, either owing to fears about the girl's safety or for other, less altruistic reasons, her elder siblings had thought it better to keep her out of the way. Eliab

opened the proceedings with a long lecture, which incited only boredom for a reporter from the *Rochester Advertiser*. The highlights of
the speech, for this journalist at least, seem to have been the background raps that echoed intermittently through the hall, breaking
up Eliab's drone.

The editor of a religious newspaper spoke next. Like Eliab, he
said that the sounds were spiritual in nature. Rather than sanctioned
by God, however, as the Fox sisters' supporters believed, he warned
that they were the work of the devil. The thought that a struggle between good and evil might be at work, right here inside Corinthian
Hall, must have concentrated the collective mind of the audience.
Now, all that remained was to appoint five members to the committee that would carry out further investigations.

Five suitable men were duly appointed. Many within the audience, perhaps rattled by the words of that last speaker, headed off
into the night assuming that the committee's findings would do the
sisters no good. The *Rochester Daily Democrat* decided to get ahead
of the game by preparing a scathing report of the committee's findings before its reporter had even had a chance to hear them aired.
But when the *Democrat*'s reporter returned to Corinthian Hall the
next evening to take his place among an even larger crowd, he was
astounded to hear that, after many experiments on Leah and Maggie, the five men had failed to discover any means by which the pair
could be responsible for producing the rapping noises.

This was not good enough for the audience, many of whom
had arrived convinced that they were about to see two cunning female confidence tricksters unmasked. Disgruntled words rumbled
around the auditorium, intimations that the committee had not
been thorough enough. Reluctantly, the sisters consented to further
examinations.

This time, the new committee of men—all distinguished local figures—was decidedly rougher. They made Maggie and Leah stand up on a table so that they could inspect them better, tying ropes around the usually private area of the sisters' hips to restrict the movement of their feet, which they felt might be producing the knocking sounds. Leah later labeled the behavior of one physician member of the group "very insulting and even violent." But, once again, no evidence of deception was uncovered. And so a third committee was appointed.

The following evening, the size of the audience at Corinthian Hall had swelled once again, and it seemed some had come with the sole intention of making trouble. In an age when even the discussion of intimate body parts remained beyond the pale, Maggie and Leah had submitted not only to be bound by rope once more but also strip-searched by a subsidiary committee of women. Both sisters are said to have wept through the ordeal, their rising sobs echoing through the walls until eventually their friend Amy Post, unable to stand their anguished cries, rushed into the room and forced a halt to the investigations. Despite the extreme rigor of the ladies' committee, the crowd's reaction this time was even more aggressive than on the previous evenings.

At this last of the Corinthian Hall demonstrations, the sisters watched in terror from the stage as the rowdiest section of the audience transformed into a baying mob. On hearing the verdict of the final committee, a man later identified as their ringleader stormed the stage, brandishing a long, heavy stick—the signal for his well-prepared friends to start bombarding Leah and Maggie with smoking hand grenades. Afterward, it was rumored that some among the armed men had even brought warmed tar, which they'd stowed in a cupboard just outside the auditorium. Though it was not used, its meaning to the Fox sisters must have been only too clear. Calling attention to yourself carried a severe risk, especially if, as in their cases, your voices were deemed unworthy of hearing.

In the wake of the attacks at Corinthian Hall, Leah and Maggie beat a retreat from the public stage, withdrawing first to the home of their radical friends Isaac and Amy Post and then to Leah's new cottage, on Troup Street. This most recent move, to a location in Rochester's fashionable Third Ward, had demonstrated Leah's improved financial circumstances.

As autumn turned to winter and the last golden leaves disappeared from Rochester's tree-lined thoroughfares, the sisters continued to give readings for private groups, capitalizing on their newfound fame by charging set fees for their services. Within these smaller, more controlled settings, Maggie and Leah seem to have been comfortable with the idea of calling on the younger Kate for help. The thirteen-year-old had recently returned from the Caprons' boardinghouse in Auburn and could therefore take part in the lucrative spirit summonings. The sisters' mother, too, had rejoined her daughters. On hearing of the indignities and violent threats suffered by Maggie and Leah during the recent demonstrations and committees, Margaret Fox had reacted with maternal horror, insisting that such things would not have happened if she had been there.

Eliab may have bid Kate goodbye for now, but his interest in all three sisters remained strong. Having introduced Maggie and Leah at Corinthian Hall, he sought to extend his unofficial role as their manager by keeping news of the mysterious rappings in the public consciousness. On December 8, 1849, he and George Willets—a cousin of Isaac Post—published a summary of the Rochester committees' findings in the *New-York Weekly Tribune*. With a circulation of almost twenty-eight thousand, this well-established newspaper, based three hundred miles away, spread the fame of the unnamed "ladies" of the newspaper's report far beyond Rochester's immediate vicinity.

In New York's expanding urban heart, the *Tribune* article caused quite a stir. Many a reader, rustling the pages of that Saturday's copy, thrilled to descriptions of the unexplained knockings and mulled over the question posed by its authors: Would these "remarkable phenomena . . . pass away with the present generation," or did the events represent "a new era of spiritual influx"?

As at Corinthian Hall, not everyone took the mysterious rappings seriously. Skeptical response pieces followed in other newspapers. Even the *Weekly*'s sister title, the *New-York Semi-Weekly Tribune*, seemed doubtful of the story's merit. In an article published on the same day, it stated that "we really cannot see that these singular revelations have, so far, amounted to much." Expressing surprise that anyone might be convinced, the paper pointed out that, even if the spirits were real, "it is certain also that crowds of people would never be got together, nor would Committees of respectable gentlemen be appointed to investigate the process employed by a child or an idiot in thumping the wall with a stick or a hammer; and it is difficult to understand why spirits, who not with as little reason as children or idiots, should be treated with any more consideration."

Many of those in Rochester predisposed to believe in the sisters' abilities were attracted primarily by the wonder of the spectacle. For others, the manifestations offered a tantalizing opportunity to rekindle bonds with departed loved ones. Still others may have felt that any association with the Foxes might somehow lead to exciting opportunities for themselves.

In February 1850, Maggie and Kate were called to the home of Nathaniel and Rachel Draper, local farmers. The Drapers, who had been following news about the knockings since the previous summer, wished to have a go at contacting the dead themselves. As Nathaniel would later tell a local newspaper, his wife was "susceptible to magnetic influence." Ideas about animal magnetism had been doing the rounds since the eighteenth century, when the German doctor Franz Mesmer put forward the theory that all living beings contained an invisible force, which a mesmerist could harness to put a person into a trance. The Drapers had apparently induced a trance in Rachel with ease. They said that from deep within her altered state Rachel had connected with a spirit—and not just any old spirit either, but one of the Founding Fathers of the United States, Benjamin Franklin.

Rachel channeled Franklin's spirit and, perhaps using an alphabet method like that established by the Fox sisters, was able to discern that he wanted her to assemble a group of people already familiar with the ghostly rappings, including "two of those young ladies about whom there is so much excitement in your city." She and Nathaniel invited a small crowd to their house, divulging nothing of the reason for the meeting, they would claim, to either Kate or Maggie.

Despite allegedly having no idea why their presence had been requested, the pair and their mother, Margaret, seemed happy enough to turn up at the Drapers' home on a cold day in mid-February. Rachel, who'd slipped into a trance again, allowed the unseen presence working through her to direct Kate and Margaret to a room at the far end of the house, along with a male member of the party who would take notes. The rest of the group, including Maggie, remained in the parlor, with another male note-taker present. This move perhaps illustrates the fact that—excepting prominent examples to the contrary, such as Queen Victoria, whose diaries would be preserved for posterity—the written testimony of male witnesses was considered more valuable than that of women.

The still apparently semiconscious Rachel directed the assembled party to two different parts of the house. Those in each of the two rooms began to hear knocks, which Nathaniel likened to the sounds heard in one of the era's new telegraph offices.

Franklin's ghost, however, was a relatively reserved presence that day. Using language that brought to mind his lifetime experiments with electricity, he explained that he was just "trying the batteries." After about ten minutes, he called the proceedings to a halt, insisting—via the Fox sisters—that Rachel be woken up. In words rapped out on an alphabet board, he went on to say that the Drapers had not followed his instructions carefully enough. They had directed an incorrect number of people to each room. He wanted them all to meet again, on the following Wednesday afternoon, at four o'clock.

When the group reassembled at the appointed date and time, proceedings went off much more smoothly. No sooner had Rachel entered a trance state than loud knocks rang out. In the parlor, where she waited in the company of Maggie and three others, a series of raps began to spell words.

In phrasing strikingly reminiscent of that heard some months earlier in the presence of Isaac Post—not here for today's proceedings—Franklin's ghost let it be known that "now I am ready, my friends. There will be great changes in the nineteenth century. Things that now look dark and mysterious to you will be laid plain before your sight. Mysteries are going to be revealed. The world will be enlightened."

He added that they should "not go into the other room." They did not have to wait long, however, to discover what had transpired on the other side of the house, where Kate and her party waited.

That group's note-taker soon came in, explaining to Maggie and those in the parlor that the knocking sounds in his room had encouraged him to join them. To everyone's astonishment, they discovered that Franklin had conveyed identical messages to the company in either part of the Drapers' home. This proved too much of a coincidence for those present to feel any lingering doubt. They all swiftly agreed that they really had been in the presence of the great Benjamin Franklin, who had been dead sixty years.

The wider population of Rochester, on the other hand, remained divided between skeptics and believers. Frederick Douglass, again a guest at a gathering at the home of Amy and Isaac Post, made himself a lone doubting voice among supporters when he demanded the spirits answer a question that they had so far ignored, which he said was the only one that could have tested "the intelligence of the agents by which the rapping was made."

Repeatedly fobbed off, Douglass became incensed. He branded the knocking "atrocious," much to the horror of Amy and Isaac, who stayed steadfast in their backing of the Fox sisters.

Afterward, Douglass wrote to Amy to apologize, saying that he had "meant no disrespect" to either her or her husband. In the years to come, he would remain on good terms with the Posts, but he'd never come close to embracing their wholehearted trust in the powers of Kate, Maggie, and Leah. Isaac, in contrast, did not waver and would ultimately discover mediumistic abilities of his own. He went on to pen a book, *Voices from the Spirit World*, which included details of messages he'd received from the departed souls of Benjamin Franklin (again), Thomas Jefferson, George Washington, Voltaire, and others.

Another local who, like Douglass, wanted to scrutinize the evidence was schoolteacher Mary B. Allen. Miss Allen was well-respected in the community, independent-minded, and sharp-witted. Admitted to one of the Troup Street gatherings—occasions so popular that people packed the rooms of Leah's cottage, colonizing even the stairs—Miss Allen let it be known that she would like to speak with the spirit of her beloved grandmother.

Was there a particular question?

"Yes, I am interested in education, and I would like to know about methods in the other world," came Miss Allen's answer. "Spelling, for example. How does my grandmother now spell the word 'scissors'?"

A patterns of raps, which the Foxes interpreted, rang out its response: "s-i-s-s-e-r-s."

Miss Allen pounced in triumph: "That is just the way Katy Fox spelled 'scissors' when she was a scholar in my school!" she exclaimed.

Kate's response goes sadly unrecorded, but the incident—recollected by a local man—highlights two wider issues. Typically for the era into which they'd been born, none of the sisters had enjoyed an extensive education. Leah had left childhood behind when she married at fourteen, and her younger sisters, though still unwed, had received similarly rudimentary schooling. As time went on, older men who came into Maggie's and Kate's lives would lament their lack of book learning and urge them to enroll in further study. In terms of their current situations, a larger problem illuminated by the encounter with Miss Allen was that many locals had been acquainted with the Foxes before they became well-known figures. To some of their new supporters, such as Eliab Capron, taking the Foxes away from Rochester seemed the best way of avoiding possible future awkwardness. Over the course of that winter, he and a friend, Henry D. Barron, had been working on a substantial pamphlet about the spirit rappings, and Eliab had been pushing Margaret to allow her youngest two daughters, especially Kate—whose talents, in Eliab's eyes, remained the most potent—to embark on a public tour.

Initially, Margaret refused. Not to be put off, Eliab tried using his powers of persuasion, arguing that men of "science and influence" in New York City were eager to learn more of these manifestations. "It would be of great advantage to your family to have such men satisfied," he claimed, and would "*forever* clear all who are now being ridiculed and lied about, from all charges of fraud." If Margaret would spare him Kate again, Eliab said, he and his wife could act as chaperones. Moreover, he added, going away would be a "delightful" trip for the girl. He even stated, rather unconvincingly, that Margaret "would hardly realize" Kate's absence.

Eliab's letter of February 1850 identified the oldest Fox daughter as a key figure of influence in Margaret's decision-making process: "I think if Leah would only say yes," Kate "might come right away." Certainly, it was due in large part to Leah's influence that the sounds that appeared to follow the sisters had gone from being a local curiosity to a profit-making enterprise, one that had begun to attract national attention. In an age when it was thought proper for a woman to concern herself almost entirely with her husband and children, there was something breathtaking—and at times extraordinarily hard-nosed—about the scope of Leah's ambition. This had seen her willing to put herself and Maggie in humiliating and dangerous positions, not to mention sending her own daughter, Lizzie, away for threatening to derail the Fox sisters' fledgling careers. But despite her entrepreneurial streak, on this occasion Leah remained hesitant. Scarred, perhaps, by what had transpired at Corinthian Hall, she seemed disinclined to leave the safety of the lucrative household sessions, which the trio continued to run in Rochester. At this stage, Leah was still listed in the *Directory of the City* as a music teacher, but by the following year her official occupation would be given as a "mysterious knocker." Although individual audience members, like Frederick Douglass and Mary Allen, might bring about awkward moments, this was nothing in comparison to the threat of a raging mob.

While Leah mulled over the best way forward, well-publicized critical opinions continued to compete with the glowing accounts of converted eyewitnesses. In February 1850, Eliab Capron and Henry D. Barron published *Singular Revelations*, their work devoted to the subject. Eliab and his coauthor, who had stayed at his house during Kate's visit in the autumn, argued that the knockings should be placed within a natural, rather than *super*natural, context. The much heard but unseen phenomenon, the pair implied, ought to be studied within the same framework as any other new field of scientific inquiry. Over the past decade or so, advances had included the beginnings of commercial telegraphy, major developments in steam technology, and the coining of the word "dinosaur" to describe the prehistoric beings whose fossils were now being discovered at a significant rate.

Just weeks after the publication of *Singular Revelations*, another new pamphlet came out. In *History of the Strange Sounds or Rappings, Heard in Rochester and Western New-York, and Usually Called the Mysterious Noises!*, the Rochester-based author D. M. Dewey stated that he did "not undertake to argue, pro or con, in regard to the sounds being made by disembodied spirits." Instead—and notably assuming a solely male readership—the author said that he would "leave every man to decide for himself" based on the many statements he'd collected from "gentlemen whose word upon any other subject would not be questioned for a moment, by any person acquainted with them."

The *Rochester Daily American* took a more combative approach, remarking incredulously, "That so large a portion of the community have suffered themselves to be humbugged, is more wonderful than any of the spirits' pretended performances." The *Northern Christian Advocate*, based sixty miles away in Auburn, declared to its readers that "not being overstocked with gullibility, and having very little taste for the low marvels which furnish entertainment to some people," they would not engage with the Foxes' story. And, in a piece titled "Those Rochester Knockings," the *New-York Commercial Advertiser* wrote the whole thing off as a great money spinner. At a time when an unskilled laborer often earned less than a dollar per day, the paper suggested that the sisters' and their mother's combined daily takings totaled somewhere between $50 and $100. The *Commercial Advertiser*'s shocked tone amply demonstrates how much attention an entrepreneurial woman might attract by launching herself, however unusually, into the world of business.

Eliab Capron found himself taken to task, too, for stoking the flames of publicity. Enraged, he fired off a furious response. His letter, included in a self-justifying passage in one of his future books, attacked the newspaper for shoddy journalism, taking particular issue with its presentation of him as a scheming "journeyman printer." Pointing out that he "had never set a line of type in my life," Eliab said that this fact alone should give the public some idea of the trustworthiness of the *Commercial Advertiser*. But its editor declined to print Eliab's letter, for the moment depriving readers of the opportunity to draw his preferred conclusion.

With so many theories swirling, a smarting Eliab must have been even further convinced of the need for a public tour. As luck would have it, Leah had changed her mind about the benefits of such a venture. Later she'd write of being "directed (by the spirits) to 'go forth and let the truth be known.'" But, rather than allowing Kate to travel alone with the Caprons, it was decided—by Leah presumably—that a better course of action would be for Maggie, Kate, herself, and their mother to rely on a business manager, notably not Eliab, plus their old family friend Calvin Brown as their escort. Calvin, who had tried in vain to control the spirits that had made such mischief at Leah's old home on Mechanics' Square, was an obvious choice for this role. Eliab may have been demoted because Leah felt that he had become too involved in the family's affairs and that this had diminished her own supervisory role.

In preparation for the tour, the sisters, now including Kate, would test public reactions by staging another demonstration in

Rochester in April 1850. This time, things went well. Although pro-ceedings ended, once again, with people rushing the stage, now it was excited supporters, wishing to herald the accomplishments of the women, rather than aggressors armed with grenades.

One wonders how Eliab reacted to the decision to limit his in-fluence still further by having a Universalist minister from Albany, rather than himself, introduce the Foxes to the audience. The Rev-erend R. P. Ambler had attended a private reading given by the sis-ters earlier that month and left a believer. Having set the tone for a successful event in Rochester, he must have seemed a better bet than Eliab to open proceedings at their first event in his home city.

In 1850, Albany was a bustling hub for manufacturing, a major rail stop and port at the north end of the Hudson River, and a termi-nus of the Erie Canal. Goods flowed in and out of the state capital. Since colonial times, Albany had been a center of the fur trade, and the city now counted lumber and cast iron among its main exports. Over the past decade, steam-powered sawmills and foundries belch-ing out smoke had sprung up at a clip. Publishing was another key industry. In the mid-nineteenth century, the city ranked second only to Boston in number of books produced. Albany was a place from which ideas spread—an ideal start for the Fox sisters' tour.

The Albany *Weekly Argus* heralded their arrival in tones of cyn-icism, remarking that these "quite pretty young ladies" had already knocked the citizens of Rochester "almost out of their senses" and "furnished food for about four hundred columns of editorials." More seriously, one man of God mounted a grave accusation by pub-licly accusing them again of blasphemy. Others, however, welcomed these strikingly modern women who, without a fine background or good marriage to their names, had risen to fame propelled by their unusual talent. Such was the public's fascination that many were happy to part with considerable sums for the privilege of experiencing the sisters at work. Leah would later record that the trio regularly charged one dollar to those attending the group sessions at their hotel room and five dollars to those who requested a private reading. Clearly enjoying their earning power, they took a suite at the prestigious Delavan House and, according to Leah's future memoirs, racked up staggering expenses of $150 per week.

After about three weeks, they moved on to Troy, another prosperous city, eight miles north up the Hudson. Although their arrival there caused excitement, even more vociferous accusations dogged them, Leah later recalling that the women of the city raised "cruel and unchristianlike" objections to their presence. The three apparently managed to turn things around, since she would also paint a picture of a warm farewell, with a band playing in front of their hotel and the sisters out on the balcony looking down at a cheering crowd, who removed their hats as a mark of respect. But all in all, Troy had given them a mixed reception, and so it must surely have been with some sense of foreboding that they returned to Albany to catch the night boat that would take them to their tour's chief destination—New York City.

The Talk of the Town

For the likes of Kate, Maggie, and Leah Fox—whose rare talents had already brought them extraordinary opportunities for earning—steamboat travel in the mid-nineteenth century would have been a luxurious affair. Their cruise along the Hudson River, through waters busy with boats and plentiful fish, would leave an impression of meandering beauty, which no doubt helped to put their nerves at ease. Passengers such as the sisters and their party, able to afford the higher fares, could enjoy fine dining in the elegant restaurant or sit on sofas in one of the lounges, complete with richly carpeted floors and elaborate hanging lamps. For others in a less fortunate financial position, the same journey would have been a very different experience. Those belowdecks could expect to find themselves crammed in with the cargo, suffocated by dirt and heat from the boilers, the squalling cries of livestock on board, and the odors of many human bodies packed together.

On sailing into New York City around the beginning of June 1850, the Foxes took rooms at Barnum's Hotel, situated on the busy corner of Broadway and Maiden Lane. Over the past months, people had speculated that these three mysterious knockers from Rochester might eventually join forces with P. T. Barnum, whose American Museum—displaying scientific exhibits alongside freak show performances—lay only a five-minute walk through the burgeoning entertainment district. Regardless of whether the Foxes had this in mind when they selected this hotel—owned by a cousin of the famous promoter—it wouldn't be long before the trio found themselves generating the kind of publicity that rivaled the showman's own.

Thanks to all the recent press attention, Leah, Maggie, and Kate had come to New York City as objects of intense interest. As had been the case in Albany, a steady daily stream of visitors soon began at their hotel. An early caller was Horace Greeley, the thirty-nine-year-old editor of the *New-York Daily Tribune*, as well as its weekly and semiweekly titles. Greeley had been responsible for publishing the article by Eliab Capron and George Willets that brought the events at Rochester's Corinthian Hall to a huge urban readership.

Most other newspapermen viewed the women's activities with a mixture of suspicion and amusement—although a ticket to guaranteed high sales. Greeley, in contrast, retained an open mind, feeling that so little was known about the natural world that it would be unwise to "determine at a glance" what was or was not "supernatural." Rather than writing off potential miracles out of hand, he preferred to admit to himself "that things do occur which are decidedly superusual" and "rest in the fact without being able, or feeling required, to explain it." His approach here feels rational and objective, and yet Greeley's personal circumstances also played a part. Like several of the Foxes' earliest supporters in Rochester, he and his wife, Mary, had known the pain of losing several children. Only a year prior to the sisters' arrival in the city, the couple had buried their darling five-year-old son, Arthur—known as Pickie—whose mischievous, golden-haired presence continued to haunt his parents' imaginations.

Greeley first called at Barnum's Hotel with a friend on the afternoon of June 4. The sisters' official hours for receiving visitors had ended, but after some negotiation the pair was admitted to the Foxes' parlor. On its door, the men would have noticed a list of "rules and regulations," designed, perhaps somewhat optimistically, to preserve the "atmosphere of a solemn religious ceremony." These included the requirement that callers sit in the seats assigned to them by the sisters, and that they refrain from discussing the spirits' answers while the session was in progress.

Greeley surveyed the women seated side by side on a large sofa with a long, cloth-covered table in front of them. He took the youthful-looking Leah, who was just two years his junior, to be around twenty-five. He found her "pleasing and intelligent countenance" appealing, but the appearances of Maggie and Kate, at eighteen and fourteen, worked a stronger spell. Greeley was much taken by their strikingly dark eyes and "transparent paleness." Their manner, he felt, was "quiet and refined," their conduct decidedly proper.

The two men were assigned seats across from the women. They did not have to wait long for the knocking to begin, ringing out on both the floor and the table between them. Try as they might, neither man could work out the source of these sounds. Seeing their confusion, the Foxes—by all appearances none the wiser themselves—invited the two men to move to the sofa and sit beside them. This was meant to prove that the sisters were not surreptitiously rocking the table.

Leah let Greeley know that a spirit, now with them, was willing to talk.

He asked, "Are you a friend? Are you a relative?" Two firm

knocks thudded on the floor beneath his feet, signifying a definite yes.

Greeley asked more questions, about the gender of the deceased and the age at which this person had passed away. Both these answers seemed to suggest to Greeley that this was a particular distant member of his family who had been dead for a decade. Following this train of thought, he then requested that the spirit confirm the place of death. The unseen presence indicated that it would be willing to spell out the word using the alphabet method.

A number of raps gave the first letter correctly, but then there came a pause.

The spirit, apparently disinclined to demonstrate its spelling prowess, suddenly went quiet.

Greeley's friend went next, but it seems the Fox sisters' success had run its course. Of his six questions, a different spirit answered only five correctly and then a stubborn silence ensued. Under further questioning from the women, more knocks let it be known that, rather than continue to communicate now, the spirits preferred to meet with the men at a future appointed time.

Greeley left intrigued, not least by the three deafening thumps that heralded the men's exit, and which he felt certain came from a chest of drawers by which the sisters innocently stood. They explained that this kind of commotion followed them everywhere, with knocks ringing out "in the steamboats, on the railroad, in carriages and even on the marble floor of the hall of the hotel." The trio presented Greeley with an infuriating puzzle. He could find no clear reason to doubt them as frank and sincere, but neither could he quite shake the nagging feeling that all three were "in some way cognizant" of the manner in which the sounds were produced.

Contrary to the majority of earlier reports—which had assumed Kate, the youngest, to have the strongest connection with the spirits—Greeley's first impression was that Leah was the most familiar with the sounds. His perception illuminates the fact that, since spring 1848, the oldest Fox sister had gone from someone who observed her sisters' talents on the sidelines, to an active participant, to the person who took the central role in directing what had become a major public spectacle.

Throughout the hot summer of 1850, the Foxes continued to give paid readings at their hotel. They scheduled three sessions daily: from ten in the morning until noon, three to five, and then eight till ten in the evening. During these hours, parties of people, paying the set fee of a dollar each, crowded into the Foxes' parlor. But outside of advertised times, private callers—like Greeley—often showed up, and were generally shown in to meet the sisters, even in the hours before breakfast.

Each night, the three would fall into their beds, exhausted. But overcome by the excitement and stresses of the day, they'd then find it a battle to sleep. Maggie, overwhelmed with fatigue, fell ill and struggled to shake off her symptoms. Their mother found it all quite a trial and fretted about the negative ways in which many perceived her daughters. Margaret disapproved of the committees of women, here in New York too, who insisted on undressing the Foxes, searching for instruments that might be making the knocks, hidden beneath their clothes.

With all the activity at Barnum's Hotel, there remained little time for taking in the sights of the city. But in people's homes, out on the streets, and at entertainment venues, the sisters were ever-present. The Olympic Theatre, nearby on Broadway, mounted a farce, *Mysterious Knockings*—followed, sadly not unusually for the era, by a blackface version, staged at Chanfrau's National Theatre—and the popular stage star Mary Taylor sang a song about the Foxes, "The Rochester Knockings at Barnum's Hotel." The sisters' apparent feats, and the verdicts of those who decried them, added news stories daily—paraded first in bold captions on advertising boards and then delivered, via smudged columns of print, to readers throughout the city.

The daily drama of the Foxes, although of utmost seriousness to some, may well have been looked on by others as much-needed relief during a turbulent year. The ugly issue of slavery continued to fill newspaper columns, and the prospect of civil war seemed never far away. The terms of the Compromise of 1850 were still being debated in the Senate. The legislation promised, on one hand, to tip the balance of power in favor of free states—the admittance of California increasing their number. On the other, it threatened to tighten the grip of masters on those they enslaved by decreeing that escapees be returned to their owners, and that even those in free states cooperate to ensure this. In July, President Zachary Taylor died suddenly from an intestinal condition, plunging negotiations into even greater uncertainty.

Horace Greeley continued to visit the Foxes, sometimes with his wife, Mary. He and one of the *Daily Tribune*'s most popular reporters, literary critic George Ripley, were among guests at a gathering on June 6, 1850, at the home of the author Rufus W. Griswold. According to Ripley's report of the evening, published in the *Tribune* two days later, the male members of the party had been selected on the basis of their "intelligence and probity," so that they would not be "deluded by hasty impressions" of the sisters. Other attendees included luminaries of the city's cultural scene—including James Fenimore Cooper, author of *The Last of the Mohicans*, and poet and *Evening Post* editor William Cullen Bryant—plus military men, medical men, and at least one member of the clergy.

Leah, Maggie, and Kate arrived at eight in the evening. For the first half hour, nothing happened. Just as people were beginning to

show signs of impatience, the sisters, now seated at a table, beckoned for the guests to gather in a tight circle around them.

Soon afterward, faint knocks began. As the minutes slipped by,
the volume and frequency of the raps increased until their force overwhelmed the room. It would take some time to convince the spirits
to converse with anyone, but eventually they assented to answer
some questions. The esteemed company put a series of inquiries to
the invisible throng, each man addressing a single spirit at a time.

In one instance, a spirit was asked his nationality. "American?
Was he an Englishman? Was he a Scotchman?"

A battery of loud knocks replied.

"Was he a merchant? Was he a lawyer? Was he an author?"

More loud knocks.

"Was he a poet?"

Further knocks.

Then, quite thrillingly, via the alphabet method adopted by the
sisters, the spirit began to spell out his name: "b-u-r —"

At this, one man, unable to contain his excitement, cried out,
"Robert Burns!"

To this, the celebrated Scot—dead for over half a century—
answered in assent. Sadly, however, for those who might have
wished to learn more of the poet's existence in the afterlife, that was
the end of the conversation.

While Maggie, Kate, and Leah would be given just one collective line of dialogue in Ripley's report in the *Tribune*—"Will the
spirits converse with anyone present?"—they come across as fully
defined, unlikely women and girls to be granted attention thanks to
the knocking sounds that answered the venerated men's questions
at the gathering. Margaret Fox, also in attendance, was described
as "the mother of the 'ghost-seers.'" The four women had been escorted there by "a couple of gentlemen from Rochester" whose iden-

tities no one seemed to trouble themselves to discover. It is striking that, unlike the sisters, both Margaret and the Rochester gentlemen fade out of the reader's view as the article progresses. Unable to summon the words of dead spirits, the actions of these other three are deemed unimportant.

The witnesses had departed that evening perplexed. The Foxes, they had to admit, gave a favorable impression. According to Ripley, these apparently harmless countrywomen had "no theories to offer in explanation," preferring—perhaps more tactically than he could guess—to allow the learned men to come to their own conclusions. But if there really had been spirits among them that night, what was the purpose of it all? Why would departed souls come on "such an unusual journey, on an unprofitable errand?"

Whatever the explanation might be, the Foxes certainly left their mark on this literary critic, who would visit them several times during their stay in the city and describe them affectionately as "the lions of New York." As for his editor, in later years Greeley would play down the level of attention he paid the sisters, claiming that he remained acquainted with them simply for the sake of his grieving wife. But his well-publicized comments in the summer of 1850 tell a different story. The newspapers he owned were famously support-ive, and Greeley took a personal interest in the Foxes—especially Kate, the youngest, to whom he felt a sense of responsibility.

At the end of their time at Barnum's Hotel, Greeley invited the family to stay at his home on Nineteenth Street, where the flow of callers curious to hear the spirit rappings continued. Not long afterward, he and Mary Greeley suggested that Kate stay for a lon-ger duration with them, presenting it as a chance for the girl to benefit from a period of quality schooling. The couple also viewed it as an opportunity for them to try to establish a connection with their dead son Pickie, and this is indeed what transpired. During one such session, the boy's ghost recalled a time when he had disturbed Greeley in his study and been asked to leave the room. This memory saddened Mary, but the forgiving child said that his hardworking father had been justified in his actions.

This contact with the much-missed boy must have brought great comfort to the Greeleys, but for their young guest in their gloomy household the days felt long and empty. The powerful editor, obsessed with his work, rarely spent much time there. When Kate was not attending classes, she had to stay cooped up with the depressed Mary, broken by the deaths of so many children.

The bleakness of Kate's days in the Greeley home was interrupted one day by a visit from the opera singer Jenny Lind—already wildly popular in Europe and a favorite of Queen Victoria. The British monarch had attended Jenny's 1847 debut performance on the London stage and been so taken by the woman known as the Swedish Nightingale that she broke with established protocol to throw a bouquet at the singer's feet. In her diary, the queen would record that Jenny—then aged twenty-six—was "absolutely perfection," and that at the end of the performance she "was called before the curtain 3 times being received with cheers & waving of handkerchiefs." Given the sensation that Jenny had caused across the Atlantic, it's no surprise that P. T. Barnum should have wanted to bring her to the United States for a tour. In September 1850, she had arrived in the country to considerable fanfare, including in Greeley's newspapers. When Greeley himself called on Jenny, she expressed an interest in that other current favorite newspaper topic, spirit manifestations, and asked how she might learn more about them. Greeley suggested she visit his home, where the youngest Fox sister was staying.

Jenny thus turned up at Greeley's Nineteenth Street address, accompanied by an entourage of hangers-on whom Greeley had not invited. The young Kate, too, may well have been caught off guard, but, though still in her early teens, she was experienced enough—after her months in the city with her sisters, and the daily spirit readings she'd since endured with Mary Greeley—to get down to business. She soon had Jenny and her friends seated around a table, and, sure enough, not long afterward the knocking sounds began.

A child among adults, all listening in earnest, Kate observed the puzzled Jenny casting a critical eye around the room. It landed on her but then settled on Greeley, whom she addressed with what he'd recall as "the tone and manner of an indifferently bold archduchess."

"Take your hands from under the table!" Jenny commanded her baffled host.

"What?"

"Take your hands from under the table!" she repeated, to which a shocked Greeley raised his hands above his head and kept them there until the session was over.

Interestingly, it seems that, although the raps continued to ring out well after Greeley had adopted this pose, Jenny's suspicions did not fall upon Kate. Perhaps the tender age of the youngest Fox sister made it unthinkable for Jenny to believe that the child could be the mastermind of the brazen trickery she suspected.

During Kate's lonely stay with the Greeleys, she wrote her sister Leah a letter—now lost—perhaps asking permission to leave that miserable house. But when Leah delayed replying, Kate penned another desperate missive to a friend back in Rochester. She wrote that, although her studies were going well, she found living with Mary "impossable." She had "cried my self almost sick," she said, and longed to see Maggie and Leah.

In Rochester by then, the older two had been welcomed back by their friends, many of whom were looking ahead to the first National Women's Rights Convention—inspired by the Seneca Falls conference of 1848. It would take place in Worcester, Massachusetts, in October 1850. At the same time, emotions ran high over the passing of the Fugitive Slave Act that September, part of the Compromise of 1850. In addition to requiring those in free states to return enslaved men and women to their masters, other draconian measures enshrined by the law slapped the prospect of heavy penalties on those, like Amy and Isaac Post, who aided runaways in their perilous journeys along the Underground Railroad.

Leah, much involved in her busy life in Rochester, seems to have more or less disregarded Kate's pleas in her letter, feeling perhaps that the girl would get over her loneliness, and that maintaining a bond with the Greeleys was more important than the feelings of any individual family member. Leah's past conduct, for instance in the shunning of her own daughter, Lizzie—from whom she remained estranged—shows that she could be remarkably unbending. However, just weeks afterward, in November 1850, the middle sister of the famous trio would be placed in a position so dangerous that it spurred Leah into immediate action.

It seems that, while Leah remained where she was, a decision had been made that Maggie should return to Troy—a troublesome point on the Foxes' first tour. Given their past treatment in the city, it is unclear why the sisters should have felt it advisable for Maggie to return. But, following the fond farewell they had received, not to mention the success of their past months in New York City, they may have felt that now was a safe time to consolidate their standing in Troy. As Maggie would soon discover, however, in the months since their departure from the city, resentment against them had not quelled. And whereas Leah's earlier complaints had centered on the behavior of Troy's women, this time it was to be the men who mounted the greatest threat.

Not long after Maggie's departure, Leah received a distressing letter from her sister's host family. "A most determined murderous mob" had besieged their property, throwing stones and firing bullets through the windows. More urgent messages followed, this time by telegraph, explaining that they had been unable to subdue the agitators or whisk Maggie away to safety.

Leah set off from Rochester at once, taking an eastbound train some two hundred miles to Schenectady. Here she changed services for Troy, and on this new train she felt a sense of danger herself. A group of men came aboard and began to question her roughly about where she was going. Leah wondered—correctly, as it turned out— if they might be associated with the mob that had her sister under siege. Eventually, they moved on and let her be. She would learn later that her youthful appearance threw them off the scent, as they had come looking for an older woman.

Arriving in Troy at about eight that same evening, Leah stepped down in the dark onto the platform. A carriage stood waiting in front of the hotel opposite—the scene of the sisters' farewell back in May when some of those who'd welcomed their presence in the city had gathered with the band to cheer them off. Now, a group of "disorderly persons" swarmed her, and Leah could only hope that the waiting horse-drawn cab was the one that had been ordered to meet her.

Just then, two well-dressed men approached, each with a drawn revolver.

"I am right, it is Leah," one of them said. "I know you by your resemblance to Maggie."

Reassuring her that he and his companion had come to protect her, they ushered her into the waiting carriage, doing their best to shoo away the agitated crowd. As the horses set off, the group made chase on foot, following Leah and her companions along that first stretch of road.

The cab, of course, outran its pursuers, but when Leah's party arrived at their destination, they found that a mob still surrounded the house. Luckily, a plan was already in place. As Leah's armed escorts had outlined to her on the journey, they should wait for the appearance of three men who would suddenly rush from the building's door, reach into the carriage, and carry her inside to what she hoped would be safety.

Once within the house, Leah discovered her terrified sister "sick and nearly paralyzed with fright" from the experiences of the past days. For the moment, relative calm ensued, but this would not last. Ten minutes later, the quiet was shattered by the sound of breaking glass as rocks and bullets sailed in through the windows. The sisters got down on the floor beneath the furniture to escape. This clearly was no time for reflection, but Leah would later look back and feel certain that the telegraph operator who transcribed the urgent messages between Rochester and Troy must have leaked the information about when she'd be arriving in the city. Summarizing the attacks in a book he'd write about the spread of interest in spirit manifestations, Eliab Capron suggested that the attacking men had been Irish Catholics, incensed that these three women were committing heresy by preaching a "new doctrine." According to Eliab, the men had hoped that by destroying Maggie and Leah "the whole matter would be put to rest."

Although the sisters escaped this attack, fleeing to the Delavan House in Albany, the coming years brought further threats. The level of support they received also grew dramatically. Conservative estimates of the number of Americans convinced that the living could commune with the dead would reach over a million as the movement that had exploded out of the hamlet of Hydesville spread across North America and over the ocean, sparking a transatlantic craze.

Dim Prophecies

Emma Hardinge Britten, whose words would come to represent this era-defining phenomenon, once said that she was "never young, joyous, or happy, like other children." Instead, as a girl she liked to "steal away alone" and "wander in churchyards, cathedral cloisters, and old monastic ruins." In these enchanted places, mysterious sounds would ring in her ears, "sometimes in the form of exquisite music, suggesting new compositions and pathetic songs, sometimes in voices uttering dim prophecies of future events, especially in coming misfortunes." Unsurprisingly, a decade or so before those first spirit rappings at Hydesville, Emma's talk of such baffling noises had mystified those around her, causing her own age group to shy away and even her mother to anxiously wonder whether her daughter might be headed for an asylum.

Born in London in 1823, the child christened Emma Floyd spent her earliest years in Bethnal Green in the capital's East End, then a poor area that lived up to its name, with clusters of houses surrounded by fields. In due course, the Floyds relocated westward, eventually settling in Bristol—a port city made rich on the triangular slave trade between Africa, the Americas, and Europe. The death of the family patriarch in 1834 pushed his widow and children into potentially ruinous financial hardship. And so Emma, who had shown an aptitude for singing from an early age, helped to make ends meet by taking work as an apprentice music teacher, or "pupil-teacher." Such a position would likely have had some rewards. Working under the guidance of a senior educator, pupil-teachers typically continued their studies while schooling less advanced students. However, looking back on this period decades into the future, Emma would recall that she went about this work "with a breaking heart."

A searing memory from this time locates her standing in the darkness on the banks of Bristol's River Avon, looking down on the deep, black waters. Bereft of her beloved father, Emma found she could think of nothing she would rather do than jump into the icy depths to join Ebenezer Floyd in the afterlife. But just then she heard the former seafarer's voice calling her away from the river and back to the school where she worked. A moment later, she felt the kindly grip of his hand, guiding her up across the slope of the banks and back to the safety of the land.

It was a seminal moment. Emma would later insist that a part of her died by the Avon that night and, shortly afterward, was reborn. Whatever one makes of this story, honed by the passage of time, what is clear is that Emma would inhabit numerous incarnations during her earthly life.

Bristol in the mid-1830s was a prosperous city, its port and waterways making it a major manufacturing and trading hub. The Great Western Railway, designed by the famed engineer Isambard Kingdom Brunel and by then under construction, would soon connect it directly with the British capital. Nonetheless, the city, with its strong and politicized working class, bore the scars of the Queen

Square riots of 1831, when huge numbers of citizens had taken to the streets in protest of Parliament's reluctance to overhaul the country's highly irregular voting system. Over three days, several hundred protesters stormed the streets, attacking private and public property, including the Mansion House and the city's prisons. At least twelve people were killed and dozens more injured; untold others may have burned to death in the resulting raging fires. The disturbances, which had terrified Britain's establishment, contributed significantly to the passage of the Great Reform Act of 1832. This extended the franchise to many more men—but not women—and ironed out some of the most serious issues with parliamentary representation. However, those swaths of the population still without a vote would not remain silent for long.

It was against this backdrop of agitation and change that a "Miss Floyd" made her entrance into surviving city records. Emma's precocious talents as a musician and her fierce, can-do attitude meant that more glamorous opportunities would eventually present themselves than a career as a school music teacher. In November 1838, at the age of fifteen, her name appeared in an advertisement in *The Bristol Mercury*, aimed at the "Nobility and Gentry" of the city. In this, "her first appearance in public," Emma would be performing in a mixed musical program at a fundraising benefit at the Assembly Rooms. This was followed by at least one other musical performance, mentioned in the same newspaper a few months later. Then, in May 1843, she was billed in the cast list of a "fairy extravaganza," acting the part of Prince Placid in *The White Cat*. Following British burlesque conventions, all the princely roles would be taken by young women, whose shapely legs could be shown to their best advantage when encased in tight-fitting breeches. Although it may be that there is simply a gap in the record, extant newspaper articles suggest that between her earliest musical appearances and her acting role in *The White Cat*, Emma was absent from Bristol's theatrical scene for several years—something seemingly confirmed by her own recollections.

Exact chronological details are hazy, but in her *Autobiography*—published posthumously at the beginning of the twentieth century—Emma suggests that she spent considerable time in the late 1830s and early 1840s honing her soprano voice in Bristol and also eventually London and Paris. Despite her lack of wealth, she had high hopes of making it as an opera singer. And, flitting about the edges of high society thanks to her musical performances, for a time this seemed to be something that she might reasonably hope to achieve. At some point, the composer Thomas Welsh, who routinely took on poorer students with a view to profiting from their future careers, became her music teacher. She had other influential backers too. Pierre Erard—appointed pianoforte maker to Her Majesty, Queen Victoria in 1839—gave Emma the use of one of his coveted musical instruments in exchange for playing daily to customers in his showrooms in Paris. In old age, she would reminisce about time spent in France's first city: "Endless were the great and notable personages who came to Erard's to hear the child pianiste."

Emma's artistry, however, was not the only draw. The stunning "magnetic abilities" that had caused such alarm in her childhood now caught the attention of these Parisian sophisticates. A decade or more before the Fox sisters first made their name through the mysterious knocks that followed them around, Emma could apparently captivate her audiences by demonstrating that, with nothing more than a wave of a hand above her head, she could play any piece they desired. One can imagine the frisson in that elegant showroom as the refined crowd—men in frockcoats, women fashionably dressed in cloaks and bonnets—moved in closer to try to comprehend her powers. Only the face of her mother, Ann Sophia, looking on from the sidelines, may have registered any deep alarm. So panicked was she by this quirk in her daughter's personality that, still fearing lunacy or some satanic influence, she is said to have consulted a doctor.

If Emma's rise from humble beginnings feels as improbable as that of Leah, Maggie, and Kate Fox—whose activities were also thought by some to be the work of the devil—it is worth noting that Emma herself acknowledged the unlikeliness of her life's path. In a letter to the American diplomat and abolitionist Charles Edwards Lester, published in the magazine *Banner of Light* in 1869, Emma wrote: "The career of struggle, romantic adventure, and fearful effort I led in England, is too much of the wild and wonderful for print." Her missive mentions her time at London's famous Adelphi Theatre, where from 1844 she performed in numerous productions, including *The Phantom Dancers*. In this spoof of the Romantic ballet *Giselle*, Emma appeared in a gauzy, bell-skirted costume as the Queen of the Wilis—mythical creatures, said to be the spirits of jilted young women. Other Adelphi roles that embraced the vogue for the supernatural were her parts in *Number Nip and the Spirit Bride* and *The Chimes*—a tale about goblins, adapted from the novella by Charles Dickens.

Emma also spoke of composing music under the masculine pseudonym Ernest Reinhold—and there was indeed a composer of this name whose works were being performed in Bristol in the 1840s and 1850s. Less easy to back up with surviving evidence are her assertions that she penned theatricals, sermons for preachers, and even speeches for members of Parliament. On the other hand, each of these accomplishments—playwriting, sermon writing, and political discourse—would have direct parallels with the unexpected career Emma went on to forge for herself in the years to come. Even her claim about working in secret for parliamentarians is not necessarily implausible. By the 1850s, Emma—who, were it not for her considerable and varied gifts, might have slipped into destitution—had been moving for years among mighty company, which included members of Parliament.

At some time during Emma's impoverished youth, a group of wealthy individuals, whom she'd later guardedly refer to as the Orphic Circle, drew her into their shadowy world. She named Philip Henry, the fourth Earl Stanhope, and bestselling author Edward Bulwer Lytton as members of this mysterious clan, "far above her in rank and educational culture," as one contemporary put it. Both men, known to have been interested in "occult science," were among the elite who gathered regularly at Gore House, home of notorious society hostess Marguerite Gardiner, Countess of Blessington. Lady Blessington's infamous soirées often involved the pursuit of trance-induced visions of the future achieved by gazing into a spherical rock crystal consecrated to Michael, the archangel of the sun. Another member of the Orphic Circle identified by Emma was Richard James Morrison—the astrologer known as Zadkiel. He predicted future events based on patterns in the night sky and would acquire Lady Blessington's treasured crystal after her death. Those within this so-called Orphic Circle appear to have paid for Emma's musical training at a time when her future career as an opera singer seemed written in the stars. But as with her customers in that Parisian piano showroom, it was other qualities that appear to have particularly attracted these men.

According to a central story she stuck to throughout her life, Emma recalled that members of the circle sought her out by means she had to swear never to reveal in public, and that over "a period of several years, I, and many other young persons, assisted at their private sessions in the quality of somnambulists, or mesmeric subjects." How exactly they assisted Emma did not say—unsurprisingly, perhaps, given that she had apparently been bound to lifelong secrecy by figures whose influence continued to exert a firm hold over British politics and culture. Hints can be gleaned, however, from her 1876 book *Ghost Land*, which contains several mentions of an Orphic Circle, described as a masculine society that met to conduct experiments "through the mirror and crystal," helped by various "young ladies" who would be in a state of trance for the duration of these tests.

If the power imbalance expressed in such an arrangement is discomforting, a further cause for alarm comes from a statement in Emma's *Autobiography* suggesting that, at around this time in her life, she experienced some kind of unspeakable trauma. She recalls that during her time as a music scholar, she became impelled to repeatedly "rise from her bed in her sleep" and go out into the street to "preach, recite and enact fearful scenes." Her "wild cries and screams" must surely have alarmed her mother, with whom she still lived. In the end, the exertion put so much pressure on Emma's vocal cords that she ended up destroying her soprano voice and her chance for an operatic career.

What might have caused this nightmarish disorder? A possibility is what she once referred to as a youthful marriage to a "gentleman." Owing to the lack of evidence of any legal ceremony, past scholars have suggested that her description of herself as married is euphemistic, lending credence to a longstanding rumor that a member of the Orphic Circle tricked a barely conscious Emma into a temporary "mystic marriage." The story goes that on waking and realizing that theirs was not an official union, and feeling that she had no legal recourse, Emma chose to adopt a version of the man's surname to force him to acknowledge the abuse she had suffered at his hands. Although no conclusive proof of her motivation has come to light, it is certainly the case that during her time at the Adelphi Theatre in London in the mid-1840s, she abruptly changed her name to Miss Emma Harding—an unusual move for someone who had already established something of a theatrical reputation under the moniker Miss Floyd.

It has been suggested that the man who caused Emma such suffering was a member of the aristocratic Hardinge family, which counted among their number the British military commander Viscount Hardinge of Lahore. But Emma's claim that she used to write music under the name Ernest Reinhold opens up an alternative trail of possible clues that leads, via her performing days in the city of Bristol, all the way to the notorious milieu of Lady Blessington's gatherings, frequented by members of the so-called Orphic Circle. A reference in *The Bristol Mercury* from 1849 mentions a performance of a "sacred cantata" by the enigmatic Reinhold, dedicated by the composer to the Honourable Francis Henry Fitzhardinge Berkeley, the member of Parliament for Bristol. On another occasion, in 1852, the paper notes that the MP has specifically requested a performance of a "very capital" glee by Reinhold, entitled "They rest not here." The brother of this prominent local politician was the Honourable George Charles Grantley Fitzhardinge Berkeley—a fellow parliamentarian and generally disreputable character, infamous for beating up the publisher of *Fraser's Magazine*, which had featured a scathing review of his historical romance *Berkeley Castle*. This brother, like the Earl Stanhope and Edward Bulwer Lytton, was a frequent visitor to Lady Blessington's gatherings at Gore House. And so a member of this family, too, could have been among the powerful players who made up the Orphic Circle—and, therefore, a further plausible candidate for Emma's "husband."

Whether the man referred to by Emma in these terms was even called Hardinge or Fitzhardinge remains a niggling question. Less debatable is the fact that, over time, she would come to regard this period of her life as one of serious exploitation. As an elderly woman,

Emma would remain understandably bitter about the pressures so often heaped on poor struggling actresses by a "vicious aristocracy," singling out one "cruel and remorseless persecutor" for particular criticism. This anonymous "millionaire" and "baffled sensualist" had, she said, pressured theater managers into withdrawing offers of roles, hoping that, with nowhere else to turn, she'd have been forced to rely on the "terrible taboo" of his "*kind* protection."

As luck would have it, at this difficult juncture in her life Emma received an invitation from the Anglo-American theatrical entrepreneur James W. Wallack. Though usually based on Broadway, he was putting together a British company for a run of Shakespearean drama in Paris. And so, in need of a fresh start, Emma and her mother set off again for France. Little did they know that, once they'd arrived, Emma would receive another most unexpected and life-changing offer.

Sailing away from the white cliffs of Dover, with the foaming spray that gathered around the boat's stern trailing choppy lines behind the vessel, the dejected woman, now in her thirties, had a chance to contemplate her current circumstances. A stint with a new group of performers and the opportunity to reacquaint herself with old friends in the French city must have been welcome. And yet, having worked in Britain's capital for so long, she surely considered the route forward precarious. As the ship made its way across the English Channel, puffing out clouds of steam, Emma gradually began to feel all that she had known these past years slipping from her reach. In words that have echoes of her night as a child by the river in Bristol, she would one day recall that somewhere on the waters between the two nations her sense of identity as a London stage performer died a death.

She arrived in Paris as "a new being," but it wouldn't take her long to learn the truth about the Wallack Company's dire financial circumstances and the unlikelihood of ongoing work. Despite a determination to enjoy herself, Emma's future seemed veiled in a "dim haze" from which she could find no way out. She spent her evenings performing at the theater, and many a morning at Erard's piano rooms, where her magnetic powers drew much the same attention as before. "Tempting offers of engagements" based on these talents came in, but her wary mother rejected them, leaving Emma with no prospects to speak of. But then on the last night of the Wallack Company's run, after Emma had played "a little character piece" she'd written herself, a gleam of light appeared in the form of an offer of nine months' work at the Broadway Theatre in New York City.

Although she didn't know it at the time, the Broadway's manager, E. A. Marshall, had watched several of Emma's performances with the company. He approached her mother, Ann Sophia, to try to tempt her and her daughter across the Atlantic, offering them their ship's passage and what seemed to Emma an "excellent salary." Still, she felt unsure and would commit only to considering his offer. Marshall was having none of it. He was to depart for the United States the next day and needed an answer at once. And while Emma remained conflicted, Ann Sophia—perhaps fearful for her daughter's other options—encouraged her to accept the offer. Thus, the three adjourned to an office and swiftly drew up an agreement. And so, with only the narrowest notion in her mind of the United States and Americans, Emma signed the necessary paperwork, as she put it, before "the clocks of Paris struck twelve on that—to me—most momentous night."

Soon afterward, the two women returned to Britain to prepare for departure from Liverpool. Having traveled by the American steamship *Pacific*, they arrived in New York City in late August 1855. In the pungent heat and clamor of the metropolis, they were greeted with nothing like the luxury laid on for the Fox sisters during their stay at Barnum's Hotel five years before. Adrift in an unfamiliar city, Emma and Ann Sophia accepted the invitation of a fellow passenger they'd befriended en route and went to board at his home.

A new environment, a new climate, and what would turn out to be some uncomfortable living conditions all played havoc with Emma's health, leading her to fall ill. The Broadway Theatre's doctor, deeming her current situation unsatisfactory, arranged for mother and daughter to move to a boardinghouse, after which Emma appears to have swiftly recovered. Other problems were less easy to solve. In London—at least prior to the episode with the "baffled sensualist"—she had worked regularly as an actress and dancer. In September 1855, Horace Greeley's *New-York Tribune* noted her arrival from London, while *The New York Herald* remarked that this was part of a summer's drive to recruit "actors of repute and popularity," and that Emma would be taking the part of Mrs. Bracegirdle in John Oxenford's comedy *The Tragedy Queen*. But Emma's run of luck at the theater would not last. She and the manager, who'd seemed so keen to bring her to the United States, clashed with each other from the start. She would perform only intermittently with this new company and soon find herself confined once again to second-tier roles.

Emma could at least take some pleasure in decent press notices. In June 1856, for instance, the *Herald* would comment that she had played these minor characters with "a good deal of success" and had "created a desire on the part of the public to see more of her." She was still getting paid, too, and—unlike the Fox sisters before her—could not complain of excessive busyness or exhaustion. But she felt constantly frustrated by the attitude of the theater and at a loss to know how to spend her evenings of enforced idleness at the boardinghouse.

In the meantime, she continued to make friends, with members of the Broadway Theatre's company and—as had long seemed to be her knack—with several prominent citizens. One such outwardly refined woman became so incensed by the manager's treatment of Emma that she made what the recent arrival termed a "noble offer" to come down and thrash him. At Emma's new lodgings—where meals were served at a large communal table—she and her mother became acquainted with a married couple, who, although undoubtedly "nice" and "respectable," had an alarming habit of speaking about their personal encounters with the spirits of the dead.

Despite, or perhaps because of, Emma's prior involvement with that secretive London cabal she'd termed the Orphic Circle, she and Ann Sophia initially recoiled. But on making further inquiries, Emma learned that the landlady of the establishment considered this couple to be two of her "best" boarders. If only Emma would talk with them in private, the landlady felt certain her new tenant would change her mind about them.

At the theater, too, the fashion for all things ghostly pervaded the backstage areas just as strongly as the thick scents of the gaslights and greasepaint. Augustus Fenno, a cast member with whom Emma got on particularly well, was "perpetually talking to all who would listen about the Spirits—the wonderful things they could do, and the wonderful intelligence they could and did communicate."

The city's many newspapers, and those beyond its limits, continued to fuel the appetites of eager readers with stories of the seemingly unstoppable phenomenon associated most prominently with the Fox sisters. Kate, Maggie, and Leah, all now living in the city, continued to garner much attention. Although the Corinthian Hall committees of 1849 had been followed by further critiques of their methods, their careers had escaped irreparable harm. An extensive inquiry in 1851, carried out by three academics, had resulted in a critical report in the *Buffalo Commercial Advertiser*. In the interests, it said, of saving the *Advertiser*'s readers "time, money and credulity," this team of medics and scientists had accused the sisters of producing the knocking sounds with their knee joints. Leah, though, had seized the opportunity to respond, mounting a hostile press campaign of her own.

Numerous skeptics remained, but it had been more than enough to convince the sisters' supporters that mounting evidence reinforced the claims of this exciting new movement—now known as Modern Spiritualism, a term usually attributed to *Tribune* editor Horace Greeley. As an example of the degree to which Modern Spiritualism had entered the public consciousness, in 1854 a "Spiritualist Memorial" was presented to Congress. Among its fifteen thousand signatories was Nathaniel P. Tallmadge, who had served both as a U.S. senator from New York and as governor of the Wisconsin Territory. The petition called for a public investigation into the apparent recent increase in mysterious wonders. However, the action it called for was denied. The Fox sisters' early supporter Eliab Capron wrote about the defeat with an air of resigned inevitability. "The carpenters and fishermen of the world are the ones to investigate new truths," he said. "It is vain to look for the reception or respect of new truths by men in high places."

With her time in New York City coming to an end, Emma's curiosity, piqued by the couple at their boardinghouse, won out. She agreed to accompany a "worthy Canadian gentleman" and self-proclaimed Spiritualist—as followers of Modern Spiritualism were known—to a rundown house on Canal Street, a crime-ridden area built on a covered sewer. In this disreputable part of the city, the two climbed several flights of narrow stairs that led to a poorly furnished room filled with people seated around a wooden table that rocked disconcertingly "to and fro."

Mr. Ranney, Emma's Canadian friend, informed her that the gathered circle was in the midst of receiving a spirit communication. At the appropriate moment, they too could join the group, once they had paid the required fee. From their vantage point in the corner, Emma trained her attention on a "thin, sad-faced looking man" calling out letters of the alphabet "in a monotonous tone" while another member of the assembled company wrote them down.

Eventually, the speaker stopped and the other man began to read out the transcribed message—words to the effect of "The Spirit answers, Immortality would be a mere fiction were there no evidence of it than Bible teaching."

This, apparently, was enough for Emma. Whether shaken by the conflation of the group's strange activities with the teachings of the Bible, or barely suppressed memories of her nights with the Orphic Circle, she could seemingly take it no more. Presumably leaving a shocked Mr. Ranney trailing in her wake, this thirty-two-year-old British woman who had arrived in New York so full of hope rushed out down those flights of steps into the street and back to the safety of her boardinghouse.

It would be some time, she'd later recall, before she recovered from the shock. But, ever enterprising, she began to wonder how she might benefit from the experience. She understood the world of professional writing and could imagine a British editor clamoring for a piece that exposed this "Yankee humbug." With just a few weeks of her theatrical contract to go and no sense of what she would do when it ended, she came up with a new plan—to commit herself to researching all she could about séances and turn what she discovered to personal profit. She would "learn sufficient about the 'horrid stuff,'" she decided, to write a scathing article all about these ridiculous *"American fooleries."*

The Path of Light

The kind of contemptuous firsthand account envisaged by the thirty-two-year-old Emma Harding would surely have found a keen readership in Britain. By early 1856, the Modern Spiritualist movement begun by the Fox sisters had gained a foothold in British society, attracting both fascination and scorn.

Some years earlier, in late 1852—while Emma was still regularly treading the boards of London's Adelphi Theatre—an American spirit medium, Maria Hayden, had begun to give séances in the city. Maria had traveled from her Connecticut home with her husband, the journalist William R. Hayden, and a friend, George W. Stone. William was a former editor of *The Boston Daily Atlas*, a staunch supporter of abolition and women's rights. Stone worked as a doctor and "electro-biologist," using copper-zinc discs to induce trances to treat his patients' ailments. An American national who'd settled in London, Stone had recently returned to the United States for a lecture tour on this much-publicized medical technique. There he'd encountered Maria's talents at spirit rapping, the method popularized by Kate, Maggie, and Leah Fox.

Highly impressed, Stone invited the Haydens back to his home in London, with the plan of acting as their business manager. From his own address initially and then the Haydens' rented quarters on Cavendish Square, he advertised entry to Maria's séances at a cost of one guinea per person—the hefty price for witnessing these "beautiful manifestations" putting them completely out of the budget of the average man or woman. (A street stallholder, for instance, could expect to earn less than this in a week.) Nonetheless, with London's wealthy soon calling at her door, Maria's table rapping became the talk of the town, winning influential converts. These included the well-known social reformer Robert Dale Owen—who, some years into the future, would become an important friend of Kate Fox and seek to endow her reputation with some intellectual credibility.

In the same period of Maria's monthslong residence, another American import arrived on British shores. Table turning—a method seemingly easier to effect than the ghostly rapping heard in the presence of the Fox sisters or Maria—involved a group of believers placing their hands on a table and waiting for it to move, apparently under the influence of spirits. Table turning particularly caught on among working people in the Yorkshire town of Keighley, with its history of social and political radicalism, as well as with the leisured classes residing in the nation's capital. In this climate of intense interest, it's unsurprising that even Queen Victoria and Prince Albert should have become intrigued and given the practice a go on that warm spring evening in 1853, while holidaying at Osborne House.

Although the queen may have ruled out widespread trickery as an explanation for spectacles such as the one her party had witnessed that night, others felt very differently. George Henry Lewes, the editor of *The Leader* and the future romantic partner of George Eliot, had attended one of Maria's séances two months earlier and tricked her into answering yes to a hidden question he had written on a card. As he'd gleefully informed his readers, his words were "Is Mrs. Hayden an imposter?"

Other publications, too, such as the popular *Household Words*—edited by Charles Dickens—encouraged skepticism of the "miserable delusion." Dickens enjoyed a good ghost story as much anyone but had little use for the work of spirit rappers. And yet mesmerism, as practiced by George W. Stone, was another matter, widely thought to be a "masculine" pursuit and therefore more readily regarded as science. Dickens had hovered on the edges of the coterie that met regularly at Gore House, including members of Emma's Orphic Circle, and took an active interest in the powers of trance. Having become somewhat skilled as a practitioner, he is known to have sometimes put his own family members into half-waking states, simply as a matter of curiosity or with the aim of curing minor medical conditions. Long after his death, Emma would refer to Dickens publicly as an "old friend." While no record exists of him ever speaking of her in such warm terms, her name can be found in an 1854 letter from him to the newspaper editor W. H. Wills, Dickens's trusted confidant, suggesting that some kind of relationship did indeed once exist between them.

Emma seems to have initially taken as skeptical a view of spirit rapping as Dickens. Careful to stress that she had always been in a "somnambulic condition" during her early clairvoyant experiences with the group she referred to as the Orphic Circle, she had—at least she claimed—never remembered anything on waking and so had no awareness of any encounters with spirits of the departed. How she squared this belief with her childhood memory of hearing her dead father's voice in the darkness by the River Avon is unclear.

Whatever the case, the experience on Canal Street of a Spiritualist séance apparently deeply unsettled her. At the Broadway Theatre, she shared her feelings with her actor friend Augustus Fenno, whose talk of Spiritualism had done so much to ignite her interest. A man who liked a challenge, Augustus proposed that she accompany him on a visit to a different medium—an acquaintance from whom she would "hear and witness nothing less than irrevocable truth."

And so, with the thought of the mocking article she planned to write still in mind, Emma found herself back on Canal Street, this time with Augustus. Together they climbed the narrow wooden staircase of a different house. They were greeted by a young woman who would one day become well known as the famous medium Mrs. Ada Foye. When asked if she could give them a reading, Ada welcomed them in and ushered them into a sparsely furnished room. She exchanged pleasantries with Augustus but paid little outward attention to Emma. Looking back on the episode, Emma would recall that she took the opportunity to appraise Ada's appearance—decidedly un-witchlike, she concluded, the opposite of what she had expected.

Ada motioned for Emma to sit at the table. There was no cloth draped over the top—giving the impression that everything was out in the open. This openness would become particularly important moments later, when a battery of raps rang out, it seemed, on the underside of the wood.

Emma started in surprise, but Ada showed no signs of shock. "Oh! there they are," she called, as if she'd been expecting the sounds. Turning to Augustus, she added—referring to Emma—that this friend of his must be "a great Medium herself." Pushing a card marked with the alphabet in Emma's direction, Ada asked Emma to point to its letters with a pencil. The spirits, Ada said, would "rap to those they want to spell out words with."

The knocks came "loud and furious." Emma lifted one side of the table to check that there really was nothing concealed beneath. In an instant, the same noises left their immediate vicinity and began ringing out on the floor, the wall, the mantelpiece, and the door. Emma stood up from her chair to search for any hidden devices that might be making the sounds. Dropping to her knees, she placed her hands on the floorboards. At last she sank back into a seat, nonplussed.

Ada regarded her with a sympathetic look. Repeating that Emma was "a great Medium" through whom the spirits had "a mighty work to perform," she added, "Now, be calm." Emma should take up the pencil again, and Augustus would transcribe the letters signified by the raps of the spirits.

Years later, Emma would remember—"Oh, Heavens!"—dead friends and foes from her past suddenly filling the room with their knocks, spelling out "names, ages, places of life and death" and "secrets buried deep" in Emma's heart—secrets known only by her and the deceased. Dearest of these visiting spirits was her brother, Tom, a sailor who had died overseas when Emma was a young woman and whose absence she still felt keenly.

Hardly daring to hope that it could really be him, an eager Emma said, "If that is you, Tom, tell me the name of the ship you went away in."

No knock came in reply, but before Emma could despair, Ada held up a piece of paper on which she had been writing: "*Sailed away in H.M.S. the manifestation of a cross girl.*"

To Emma, the words made perfect sense. "*Sailed away in Her Majesty's Ship Vixen*," she explained, for the benefit of her companions, "but oh, Tom, why do you speak in such enigmas?"

To the accompaniment of further raps, Ada began writing again: "I gave those words only to signify the meaning of my ship's name,

Vixen, because in after years no one should say that my answers were *mind reading.*" Before bidding his astounded sister goodbye, he added that she should return to her mother.

It was almost too much. As Emma's initial suspicions of Ada slid away, only gratitude remained. She fell upon the woman with kisses, looking into Ada's tearful gaze through her own wet eyes. Later, back outside, it seemed to Emma that this grimy quarter of New York City had been entirely transformed. She had arrived at the house on Canal Street a skeptic, she said, but had come out into a "new though invisible world, peopled by living beings of whom mankind had no knowledge, beings deemed dead . . . but in reality all alive and thronging around us," their presence filling the "streets, cities, earth, air, and skies."

Further confirmation was yet to come when, back at the boardinghouse, she discovered her mother in a state of happy excitement. Opening a bundle of her son's old letters, she told Emma, she had come across something in the tin box in which she'd found them. At this, Ann Sophia held up a little pencil sketch of the young man whose life they both so mourned.

The two shared a thankful kiss, but when Emma told her mother that she'd just come from a séance, Ann Sophia's mood soured. The cautious woman declared that, although she had followed her daughter "over the wide world," if Emma should continue to investigate "this horrible and blasphemous subject," she must prepare for Ann Sophia's departure back to Britain on "the next ship." She could not stay, she said, "beneath the roof where such abominations were practised."

But Ann Sophia seems to have been unable to stop herself asking for details of what had happened in the medium's presence. And what Emma told her led to a complete turnaround in her mother's stance. On hearing of the communications Emma had received from her late father and brother, Ann Sophia fetched a small table on which she and Emma might lay their hands to see if, here at the boardinghouse, they too could learn to contact the spirits.

With Emma now largely free of theatrical engagements, she had plenty of time for practice. She, Ann Sophia, and a fellow female lodger began rushing up to these rooms each evening as soon as dinner was over. Here, by Emma's account, the three managed to get the table to turn—not simply in the running, spinning motion effected by Queen Victoria and her party but to hurl itself into the women's laps and even make faltering attempts to rise in the air. The spirits that had taken control of the table were apparently fond of music, too: when Emma played the piano they would sometimes keep time by "dancing" along to the melody.

As Emma's fascination with this new world deepened, her circle of New York friends expanded to include many more Spiritualists. These men and women were only too keen to assist her along what she'd later term this "path of light," one suggesting that she should seek the advice of an established medium who might help Emma to develop her innate gift. By 1856, there really was no shortage of people in New York City to choose from. Spirit circles had sprung up among members of every social class, magazines aimed specifically at the Spiritualist market flourished, and articles concerning the famous Fox sisters and their ilk continued to regularly appear in the newspapers. Mrs. Kellogg, the woman who took on the role of Emma's first teacher, encouraged her to set aside time daily to sit with her alphabet board and await the knocking messages of the spirits.

Emma's conversion to Spiritualism happened to coincide with the aftermath of a mysterious event in early 1856 that had excited both Spiritualists and the public at large. The SS *Pacific*, the same steamship that brought Emma to New York City in the summer of 1855, had set off safely from Liverpool on January 23. It had been spotted just off the coast of Ireland but had not been seen or heard from since. By February 7, *The New York Herald* was reporting that the *Pacific* was overdue—something that at first seemed like nothing more than a minor irritation to that daily publication's editors. The *Herald*'s readers would have to be denied any news from Europe for the time being since, thanks to the delay, a consignment of the latest papers included in the *Pacific*'s cargo had not yet come ashore.

Within days, however, the story had gained a note of urgency and changed to that of a missing vessel. Other ships set off in search of it as fears increased on both sides of the ocean. On February 29, *The Daily Post* (Liverpool) reported that a boat passing by Newfoundland had spotted "a large quantity of broken ice" on which was perched "a quantity of broken cabin furniture, fine ornamental doors, with white or glass handles, a lady's workbox, and some other articles, such as would be in use in the cabin of a first-class ship or steamer." With no clear sense of what had happened, speculation flourished. American Spiritualist publications such as the *Spiritual Telegraph* and the *Christian Spiritualist* carried stories—some of which had also been covered in the mainstream press—about grieving relatives of lost passengers who believed they had managed to make contact with the ghosts of loved ones. Spirit mediums, typically for a fee, could interpret words knocked out in the darkness or the motions of a tipping table.

In later years, Emma would mark the official start of her life as a spirit medium from the loss of the SS *Pacific*, recalling in detail how she had learned of its sinking even before the disaster was publicly known. According to her, a chill ran through her one evening, accompanied by a "sensation as if water was streaming over me" and the sudden filling of the rooms at her boardinghouse with Arctic breezes. A lost passenger had also supposedly communicated the message that everyone aboard had "perished" and that the ship and its crew would "never be heard from more."

Colorful and immediate as this story is, published in her *Autobiography* half a century later, it has at least one glaring discrepancy. Emma gives February 20, 1856, as the date of these occurrences. But a trawl through the daily papers of the time quickly reveals that the press had begun widely reporting the *Pacific* as missing over a week before this. As for news of the vessel itself, no official conclusions have ever been reached. In 1861, however—five years after its disappearance—a message in a bottle washed up in the Scottish Hebrides. Apparently hastily written by someone on board, it told that the ship, surrounded by looming icebergs, was going down.

In the New York City of 1856, Emma continued to practice her craft, engaging in "researches and experiments in every available quarter, high or low—in circles in cellars and garrets, saloons and woods." With her lack of theatrical prospects in the United States and Britain and the need to keep supporting herself and her mother, Emma yielded—or so she said—to the words of spirit guides, including Benjamin Franklin. Given his earlier messages to the Fox sisters, Franklin was seemingly a fan of the séance. Now, or at least according to Emma, he proposed that she and Ann Sophia move in with the well-known medium E. J. French, who had recently arrived in New York City from Pittsburgh, Pennsylvania. The psychic readings she offered daily from her new address on Broadway dealt with "all morbid conditions of the human organism delineated and prescribed for with an accuracy hitherto unknown in the annals of Mesmeric Phenomena."

Mrs. French, with whom Emma and her mother ended up boarding for several years, introduced her new lodger to many luminaries of the early American séance scene. They encouraged her to abandon what was left of her stage career and become a lecturer who promoted Spiritualism.

Given the nineteenth-century attitude toward women speaking in public, it is perhaps unsurprising that, even when looking back on this period in old age, Emma was apt to emphasize how shocked she was by the notion that she, *"a young English lady,"* should "go out like a bold, strong-minded woman to preach!" Unlike her current theatrical prospects, however, work of this kind had the potential to bring lucrative rewards, and even fame, and this surely served as a means of enticement.

Influential supporters, such as the wealthy rubber merchant Horace H. Day, were ready to commit serious funds. Day had set up the Society for the Diffusion of Spiritual Knowledge (SDSK) at 553 Broadway. Part of the building was dedicated to the production and printing of the society's magazine, the *Christian Spiritualist*, which Emma—drawing perhaps on her experience with London magazines—would soon start writing for and editing. Day set aside other rooms for mediums to give readings, the most sought-after being those by Kate Fox. Then in her late teens, Kate occupied the spacious back drawing room. For the handsome salary of $1,200 per year, paid by Day, she gave free readings to the public each morning.

On the surface, Day, who allowed the novice Emma to take rooms rent-free for her own activities as a medium, may have seemed generous indeed. The society's headquarters provided a space where, as Emma put it, like-minded "friends and strangers could assemble together, interchange ideas and greetings, read the papers, buy or borrow all the spiritual literature of the day, and attend the circles held in different apartments of the building." However, as she would also note, Day seemed to have a political agenda. In the lead-up to the fiercely fought 1856 presidential election, spirit gatherings "held in that house," wrote Emma, would go on to exert their influence on "every State in the Union."

Election campaigning took place, once again, against the back-drop of the divisive issue of slavery. Tensions between those for and against the continuation of the brutal practice had eased somewhat since the Compromise of 1850 but now flared up again. Day—who some sixteen years later would thrust himself forward as a presidential hopeful—had put his weight this time behind the Democratic Party candidate, James Buchanan. Buchanan would ultimately emerge triumphant in November 1856, with Emma later claiming that "long months prior to their public issue, *State documents, and Congressional ordinances existed in the secret archives of an unconsidered spirit circle.*" She meant within the walls of 553 Broadway. Here, "the wires of the national machinery," she recalled with approval, had been "pulled by invisible hands." Although Emma was talking about unseen spirit intervention, with the society's board membership including former New York senator and governor of Wisconsin Nathaniel P. Tallmadge, one chief justice, three judges, one military general, plus many other figures of influence, "invisible hands" could have referred just as easily to the powerful men who met at these headquarters.

How much Kate Fox knew of such goings-on is unclear. Unlike her enterprising older sister Leah, or even—to a lesser extent at this stage—Emma herself, the youngest Fox sibling often found herself swept along by events. Since their first exhausting public tour of 1850, relations between Leah and her sisters had grown strained. Although the trio still presented a united front in public, their personal ambitions had diverged.

Maggie had become romantically involved with the celebrated Arctic explorer Elisha Kent Kane—a man she would go on to claim she had married in secret. Painfully aware of his loathing of her profession, which he considered fraudulent, Maggie had become increasingly reluctant to take part in séances.

There had been changes in Leah's relationship status, too. In 1851, their old family friend Calvin Brown had suddenly taken ill with a pulmonary hemorrhage. On hearing from doctors that his situation was hopeless, Calvin had asked Leah to marry him. Reminding her that he had always thought of her as a "dear sister," he informed her that the best future protection he could leave her with was the new identity of a respectable widow. Leah appears to have agreed, and so they were married when he was on what was supposed to be his deathbed. But, rather than passing away as she'd expected, Calvin had rallied and lived another twenty months before conferring the position of widowhood upon her. Now Leah was living independently again and earning a good income from the spirit circles she held at her Ludlow Place address, on the corner of West Houston and Sullivan Streets. Unsurprisingly, she resented Elisha's influence and its effect on her management of her sisters. With Maggie slipping ever further out of Leah's grasp, Kate, who remained single and thus easier to control, found the heaviest burden falling upon her.

This was something that Emma would witness firsthand during her months at 553 Broadway. Each morning, she set off from her lodgings at ten o'clock, "with all the punctuality of an official," arriving at the society's premises to find Kate already "in the midst of a captious, grumbling crowd" that invariably had arrived with specific expectations. In the spacious drawing room, the youngest Fox sister would have to sit for hours, spelling out names, ages, and dates with the aid of an alphabet board while under spirit influence. Emma would usually tarry in the doorway a while, helplessly observing the stress and indignities Kate so clearly suffered. What Emma perhaps didn't know is that such pressures had already pushed the young woman into the early stages of an alcohol addiction, which would end up leading to many future woes.

If the right moment arose, Emma would sometimes approach

Kate with some sympathetic words before heading, accompanied by "a furious thunder of rapping," upstairs to her own quarters. "Every nook and corner" of the building, she later recalled, seemed "charged ... with magnetic power."

The society had a great many ways of spreading the word about its cause. Not only did Emma give readings in her room upstairs, which was equipped with a musical organ, she also wrote songs for the New York Spiritualists' choir and rehearsed with them there once a week. The group's regular performances were so well received that people would come simply to hear the music. The bonus for the Spiritualists was that they would leave satisfied by the songs, having also been given a plentiful dose of what was by now becoming a kind of religion.

On April 24, 1857, after several frenetic weeks of rehearsal, Emma's group of fifty singers performed a cantata written by her but apparently imparted, amid the sunrise of a misty dawn, "by a power that worked through my organism." The event was billed as a Spiritualist performance, and members of the press flocked to the venue—New York's Academy Hall, at the junction of Broadway and Bond Street—no doubt expecting to be mightily amused. In fact, they couldn't help but leave impressed. The audience rose many times for encores. Even *The New York Herald*, which usually poked fun at the Spiritualists, had to admit that "whoever the Spirits that controlled Emma Hardinge might be, they could at least make good music, and the only pity was that she did not give up the shadow and take to the substance of life, when she would assuredly be one of the leading musicians and composers of the age."

The paper's addition of an *e* to the name Emma Harding was not a mistake. The official program billed her as "Miss Emma Hardinge," and during this period Emma began to use both spellings. In time, the Miss would become a Mrs., most likely—as in the case of the oldest Fox sister, Leah—to give her greater respectability. By presenting herself as a widow, Emma would be able to suggest to her growing future audiences that, despite her commanding spot in the limelight, she was still someone feminine enough to have submitted to the yoke of a Victorian marriage.

Even by that summer, people who'd witnessed her work with the choir and SDSK had started to encourage Emma to go out into the wider world to share her talents. Her medium friend and landlady Mrs. French—through whom the spirit of Benjamin Franklin, yet again, allegedly offered his approval—suggested that Emma embark on a public series of lectures. Another acquaintance, Gen. Edward F. Bullard, a vice president of the society, lived upstate in Troy—the city where the Fox sisters had previously experienced such difficulties. Whether General Bullard was aware of this history or not, he still felt that, as things stood in 1857, his hometown would make for an ideal place for Emma to begin her speaking engagements. Next week, he could send a friend to chaperone her and Ann Sophia on the steamer along the Hudson River. From there, he and his wife would accompany the two women to the general's house, where they could reside during their stay.

In the days leading up to the first of these appearances, Emma found herself overwhelmed with nerves. While supposedly under the influence of spirits, she had delivered small-scale talks at 553 Broadway. Leading large public lectures, however, presented a far greater test. In preparation, she spent many hours making notes for her performance on sheets of paper—words that, according to her, she would never speak aloud.

Finally, on that "miserable Sunday" in the heat of July, Emma found herself at Harmony Hall in Troy being led up to the lecture hall platform. In later life, she would recall her surroundings swirling about her in vague shapes and her faint sense of the quartet of chorists known as the Troy Harmonists filling the room with song.

When she looked down at her notes, she struggled to decipher her own writing. A feeling of "standing outside of myself" came over her, and then suddenly she was standing beside her late father—the seafarer she had lost over two decades before. As the quartet's sweet voices continued in the background, Emma found her fear of the podium dissipating. It did not matter that she could make no sense of what was written on the paper sheets gripped in her hands. Apparently guided by spirits, bold new words formed in her mouth and burst forth into the air—as much a surprise to her as to her audience.

From this first Sunday in Troy to so many future occasions over her long career, Emma came to think of her speaking self as "two individuals": one whose lips would be "uttering a succession of sentences," sometimes familiar but more often "new and strange," and a second, fully conscious individual, looking on and listening to these "unpremeditated" words.

What exactly was going on here? If one finds oneself unable to quite believe that, from the throes of a trance, Emma channeled the words of departed spirits, might there be another explanation? As time went on Emma would increasingly become known for controversial topics that focused on the "unladylike" themes of politics, female emancipation, and the need to look with sympathy on the plight of "fallen women." In the case of the latter, her own experiences as a vulnerable young actress and somnambulist may have provided the spark that fired her anger. Even so, the thought that *she* might talk publicly about so shocking a subject could have been too much for her to admit. It could well have seemed easier to console herself that she was merely an earthly mouthpiece for the views of dead—usually male—spirits.

General Bullard had seemingly been right in his judgment that Troy would be a good place for Emma to begin her lecture touring profession. Unlike the early mixed receptions to the Fox sisters,

Emma's first talk went so well that she was invited back multiple times. On a regular basis over the next couple of years, she continued to speak in Troy, New York City, Philadelphia, and other locations in easy reach of Mrs. French's home, building a thoroughly modern career as a female speaker, one profitable enough to support Ann Sophia and herself.

Emma continued to give private readings, too, becoming more and more entrenched in New York City's Spiritualist scene. This included attending elegant receptions at the home of Leah Underhill, the name by which the oldest of the famous Fox sisters had been known since marrying a third time.

In 1858, by then in her forties, the widowed Leah had wed the fire insurance businessman Daniel Underhill, who had also lost a spouse. Leah's new husband's wealth allowed the couple to live in style on West Thirty-Seventh Street, in a house fashionably decorated with plenty of gilt, velvet, and lace, its ornately carved furniture polished to a pleasing shine. They even had an indoor aviary, designed to capture the sun all year round, and filled with birdsong and the scents of blooming flowers. In what Emma described as one of the "splendid" drawing rooms, over several visits to the house, she and Ann Sophia had the pleasure of meeting such New York stalwarts as *Tribune* editor Horace Greeley; the writer of "Rip Van Winkle," Washington Irving; and author James Fenimore Cooper, who, like Greeley, had attended one of the Fox sisters' early séances in the city. Leah's newly acquired wealth had allowed her to give up paid readings entirely, although she continued to hold small private circles for family and friends. Having had many a brush with danger during her public career as a spirit medium, she would surely have sympathized with Emma over the aggression she sometimes faced from a hostile public.

One of the most serious examples came in the year of Leah's

marriage to Daniel Underhill, when Emma decided to embark on a short trip to Canada. She had received an invitation from a man in Montreal who wished to stage "an *experiment*." He offered to pay her round-trip rail fare, but her generous $100 fee for a series of three lectures would be dependent on Emma's level of success with her audiences. If she could not convince the crowds to listen to her, she must leave with only her travel expenses. On hearing of the high stakes, concerned friends tried to talk her out of going, arguing, among other things, that these coldest Canadian months could prove too much for her constitution.

Despite any misgivings, Emma agreed to the terms. As with her first experience of "trance lecturing" at Troy, when looking back on her decision, she would invoke an image of herself as two separate entities. The spirits had drawn an invisible line, she said, down the middle of her face. One side was "portentous and stormy," the other "triumphant and glorious."

Following a long journey north, Emma arrived at a rail terminal close to the Canadian border one day in February 1858. From here she was bundled up in buffalo robes by bear-coated sleigh drivers for a chilly ride across the frozen Saint Lawrence River.

After a night's stay at a Montreal hotel, Emma was taken to the packed Buona Venture Hall. Despite the fact that she had become an old hand at such talks, she surely felt apprehensive. But to her surprise those assembled in the rows of seats listened respectfully to her speech. The trouble began when she invited questions. Then, as she would later recall, "the long pent-up feeling of hostility" she'd sensed broke out in "full sway."

One person called on Emma to let her know if her grandmother's spirit was present, while another shrieked, "Tell me my mother's middle name or I won't believe!" Others still demanded that Emma weigh in on various biblical matters: the question of how the Lord was able to create the earth in six days, how God made Eve out of a single rib, and why serpents today could no longer converse as they once had in the Garden of Eden. One audience member sternly reminded Emma of St. Paul's command that women—even those who seemed to merely act as a mouthpiece for the thoughts of dead men—should not speak before a male audience. Somehow Emma found the strength to hold her nerve and suggest that, when she lectured here the following night, the audience should select a "committee of five gentlemen" to choose a topic for her to deliver while channeling the words of the spirits.

The group, including a rabbi versed in the Hebrew Bible who took on the role of chief interrogator, selected "The Geological Formation of the Earth and Its Ultimate Destiny"—a subject on which they must have felt confident a woman would have little to say, making it ideal as a tool for catching her out. As usual, once the lecture was over, Emma would claim to have no recollection of what had occurred. Happily, newspaper reports of the time—stowed for posterity by Ann Sophia—could fill in the blanks.

Before a company that included "priests, lawyers, doctors of various orders, and reporters," the apparently entranced Emma submitted to the men's questions. To a woman in her thirties with little formal education, this must have been daunting indeed. As a former actress, she was used to performing onstage, but to be publicly scrutinized by this formidable panel and not lose her nerve required a constitution of steel. When Maggie and Leah Fox had appeared at Corinthian Hall they could at least be thankful that there were two of them, not to mention the respectable and supportive men and women who accompanied them onstage. Emma, on the other hand, stood alone, but she ended up more than holding her own.

In fact, she answered with such success that the rabbi called her out as a fraud, suggesting that she must have devoted her life to the study of Hebrew. Emma denied that she had done any such thing, but "very shortly after," she was reported to have "tripped him on a point relating to that language, and reasoned him down until he acknowledged his error." It was this, the supportive *Spiritual Telegraph* said, that signaled her triumph: "At the close of the session, the victory remained triumphantly with the inspired but unconscious speaker."

After her series of talks came to a close, Emma would leave Montreal with her full fee as well as many gifts from new admirers. These included bunches of hothouse flowers that can hardly have been expected to survive long in the Canadian winter. Wrapped up once more in buffalo furs for the frozen sleigh ride to the station, Emma departed with the warm wishes of supporters ringing in her ears, but also the memory of the opposition she had faced.

The Spiritualist press might have been impressed, but other newspapers, particularly those with a traditional religious bent, looked on her performances far less favorably. *The True Witness and Catholic Chronicle* counseled its readers not to be taken in by Emma's "very respectable *physique*" and her "gift of the gab very galloping." It likened parts of her delivery to "the ranting of a Methodist minister at a protracted meeting" and warned that Modern Spiritualism was just the "latest development of Protestantism." with Emma its "real living Pythoness, or Apostless." And, of course, these words in print were nothing in comparison to some of the anger she had faced in person that first night.

By now Emma had already had many months to dwell on the precariousness of her new life as a public speaker. Just in case a reminder was needed, however, Montreal had left her with a scene in her mind that she could not erase. Decades later, she could still summon the memory of the audience shouting and hissing, and that phrase so many there had roared: "Down with the witch!"

A Blaze of Glory

The years to come would see Emma Hardinge's career constantly evolving, with aspects of her role almost coming to resemble that of a male member of the clergy. She'd continue with her Sunday lectures, and be asked to name babies and officiate at funerals, and she was even invited into the prison cells of condemned men to offer up the assurance that, if they truly repented, they too might share in a glorious afterlife.

Public perceptions about Emma's religious beliefs, however, often caused consternation, for although she maintained that she was devoted to God, by the late 1850s she had become openly critical of organized faith. In 1858, apparently at "the command of the Spirits," she delivered a series of talks, "Origin of All Religious Faiths." Her descriptions of ancient customs of "Solar, Sex, and Fire worship" proved too much for the usually supportive Spiritualists who attended gatherings at New York City's Dodworth's Hall, never mind a more hostile wider audience. "In the best interests of religion," wrote *The New York Herald*, Emma should "shut up" and be banned from speaking in public again until she committed to leave such subjects alone.

As much as criticism of this kind must have stung the thirty-five-year-old, other interactions with the public caused far greater alarm. According to her memoirs, one day that same year a letter arrived for her at the spirit medium Mrs. French's boardinghouse in New York City—where Emma still lodged with her mother when she wasn't working away from home. The sender, John Gallagher, whose name Emma did not recognize, addressed her most inappropriately by her first name and used intimate language she felt "no human being then in America had the right" to use with her. She initially tried to ignore the letter, but another turned up days later, swiftly followed by another.

Not wishing to worry her mother, Emma confided instead in Mrs. French. When further letters containing outpourings about Emma's pleasing appearance arrived, noting specific details about dresses she'd worn and things she had said at recent lectures, she decided to go to the authorities. A newly established Metropolitan Police had replaced the Municipal Police following a summer of tensions, most spectacularly the Great Police Riot of June 16, 1857, during which members of rival law enforcement bodies had come to blows outside—and even inside—city hall.

When Emma approached the police, here and eventually further afield, she found them sympathetic. But, in a situation that mirrors that of many modern victims of stalking, they made no progress in tracing Emma's obsessed pursuer. It was down to two men she consulted directly—a police magistrate and a lawyer friend—to point out that this John Gallagher was a repeat offender, his name known within the system. He usually posted letters from Massachusetts, but the details he gave of Emma's New York talks suggested that he must have been very much closer on the dates of her recent lectures.

The correspondence did not abate when Emma left to go on

tour. In fact, it continued with alarming regularity over the next two years. Continually on guard, Emma began to "sense the near approach of these hateful letters, first by a feeling of cold chills, and not unfrequently by the realization of some evil presence around me." At times, she said, "these perceptions were so powerful that I felt involuntarily impressed to place my chair close up against the wall, *lest the dreadful thing which I knew had entered the room should get behind me.*" Although one interpretation for her response could be psychic ability, another is that she was experiencing the hyperalert state of vigilance familiar to anyone who has endured a campaign of sustained harassment.

During a stay in Providence, Rhode Island, she was invited to give an evening lecture in the nearby town of Pawtucket. On the cold journey home, the driver of her covered carriage, struggling through the dark, drew up at an isolated inn he knew to rest his horses. The friends who'd accompanied her to the talk followed the driver inside, but an exhausted Emma remained in the carriage.

All alone, without even the glow of a lantern to break up the night, Emma's thoughts began to whirr. When the horses suddenly reared, she began to fear that someone lingered close. As those familiar chills ran through her body, she grew convinced that it must be her usual tormenter and that—although she couldn't see him anywhere—he might even have entered the carriage. Her panicked shouts soon sent her friends rushing out to help. Although Emma insisted that there had been an intruder, they could see no one.

In this fearful state of mind, it must have been with great difficulty that Emma continued her lecturing engagements, especially since this was not the only man who would become fixated with her over the years. In his case, she ultimately received an answer of sorts to the mystery behind his missives, although one may feel that it raises as many questions as it settles.

While staying in Boston, where many of the letters had been posted, two strangers—a mother and her adult daughter—arrived at Emma's accommodation. They had come, the younger woman said, on "a most singular and embarrassing errand." She then went on to introduce her mother as Mrs. Gallagher.

At the sound of the name, Emma flinched.

The daughter asked, "Do you know my brother, Mr. John Gallagher?"

"Not personally," Emma said, adding, "I have had some dreadful letters from an individual signing himself thus."

The older woman broke down in tears and explained that, although she and her daughter were both Spiritualists, her son had originally been a skeptic. Many months ago, however, he'd agreed to accompany them to one of Emma's lectures. It had proven a transformative experience. Gallagher not only withdrew his cynicism; he swiftly became obsessed with the woman he'd seen on the podium. According to his sister and mother, he had then fallen under the influence of a dangerous medium who'd convinced him that Emma was his spiritual "affinity," put him on a fasting "régime of fruit and vegetables," and taught him "abominable Vaudoo arts." These, if one took the women at their word, allowed Gallagher to "go out of his body" and visit Emma "as a Spirit." He had apparently recorded his observations about these visits in a book, which the women now produced.

Horrified, Emma flipped through the pages of Gallagher's ramblings, sickened to recognize many accurate details about her activities over the past two years. Nonetheless, she insisted that the women go back to Gallagher and tell him that everything he had written was entirely false. This, she hoped, would offer a short, sharp shock to his system. But to her great distress, she learned later that it had precipitated a full mental breakdown. The last Emma heard of the man, he had been committed to a lunatic asylum.

Some years into the future, Emma would speak publicly of this episode, but to do so at the time might have been more than she could bear, especially since it would have risked adding to existing public perceptions that there was something indecent at the heart of the Modern Spiritualist phenomenon. Like the oldest Fox sister, Leah—now living a luxurious lifestyle with her affluent husband in New York City—Emma wished to emphasize the movement's respectability. In her case, this was even more of a necessity. Unlike the semi-retired Leah, Emma was very much part of the public lecture circuit. And since the content of many of her speeches proved so controversial, giving the outward appearance of gentility may have felt like a matter of professional survival.

In February 1859, Emma gave a lecture, *The Place and Mission of Woman*, which—like many of her popular talks—was noted down and reproduced in pamphlet form. One Sunday afternoon, she took to the podium of Boston's Melodeon concert hall to argue that humankind had reached a moment in its history when genuine change for women was possible. The notion that the topics on which she spoke were ordained by the spirits may have softened her words; but Emma's demands were forthright. In the past, she said, the average woman had been not as much "the helpmeet for man, so much as an appendage upon the condition of man." That is, women's supposedly natural position as sources of support for their men had been dictated by the stage they had reached in human development. Whereas this may have made sense in eras gone by, Emma argued, now that "progress has been forced upward, as it were, from the plane of physical strength to intellect, and from intellect to spirituality," the status quo could not be allowed to stand. She spoke of the need for equality between men and women, arguing that the so-called fairer sex must be allowed to "govern her person, her property, her children." She should, Emma said, have "the right to enter into schools, and the associations of commerce and trade," and, most shockingly of all, "to hold positions in the government." At a time when there had never been a female member of Congress, and the vast majority of women did not have the right to vote, Emma's views were years ahead of popular thinking.

Nonetheless, many of these ideas, as Emma acknowledged herself, aligned with those already being espoused by some of the era's best-known proponents of female emancipation. Since the Seneca Falls convention, women's rights activists had maintained their momentum by continuing to hold regular gatherings. The first national convention in 1850 had been followed by another every year throughout the decade—memorable speakers having included famous escapees from the tyranny of slavery Frederick Douglass and Sojourner Truth, as well as other campaigners for greater equality, such as Lucretia Mott and Susan B. Anthony. Although the question of female enfranchisement remained the key preoccupation at these conferences, discussions also focused on women's lack of employment and property rights, and even the shocking subject of free love—the loosely defined belief that the state should not govern sexual relations between individuals.

As time went on, the close alignment of the abolitionist, women's rights, and Spiritualist movements invariably brought all three into alignment with notions of free love, associated by many with promiscuity. Emma, ever aware of the need for respectability, strongly resisted any link between Spiritualism and free love, though others did not. In a November 1859 letter to the *Daily Memphis Enquirer*, which had taken a strong dislike to her public lectures, she would insist that her own beliefs and those of free lovers represented "the north and south poles of morality." She added that those who knew the Spiritualism she taught "know also that it is *the death of Free Love.*"

These impassioned words, written during Emma's first tour of the American South, may have done little to convince skeptical readers of the *Enquirer*. One subscriber had already written to the editors to suggest that Emma was an "Infidel" lecturer "from the North." It was, he continued, "bad enough to hear Infidelity preached by men, but how humiliating to hear it from the lips of *woman*." His advice was that "this *woman* go home and attend to the duties assigned her by the laws of God and man; and let us have no more such importations to corrupt the morals of our youth." Another local paper, *The Memphis Daily Appeal*, lamented that Emma did not have a "judicious husband" who could prevent her from speaking in public. Although Emma had her supporters in the South, during that tour of 1859–1860 she found herself frequently castigated in the region's press. In addition to suspicions of her sexual morals and religious beliefs, as the United States inched closer to the outbreak of Civil War in 1861, her support for the abolition of slavery also caused much anger.

During Emma's opening Sunday lecture in Memphis, she was standing on a podium in the upstairs room of an elegant hall when a rock came crashing through the window. Pandemonium ensued. Some audience members rushed out to try to find the culprit, while others surrounded her onstage to check that she was not hurt. She remembered later that the rock had sailed through the air and landed at her feet, only just having missed "crushing them to pieces by its weight" because "it fell on the flounce of my extra long silk dress." She continued her talk without stopping for a moment, she said, apparently without the merest alteration to her composure, and within a few minutes "no one present would have known that such an act had been perpetrated had it not been so universally witnessed."

This highly unusual and determined Englishwoman had arrived in Memphis at a time when growing fears about the spread of Modern Spiritualism permeated the South. As in other parts of the United States, the phenomenon was associated with older local legends and lore. In the South, personal knowledge of spirits was linked in the minds of many with African beliefs in Hoodoo folk magic and thereby associated with white fears of slave resistance. For this reason, Emma and her ilk drew additional suspicion in this part of the country. In her case, once she had witnessed the brutality of slavery firsthand, her new understanding of "its wickedness both to God and man" found its way into the content of her speeches.

On arriving in Alabama by steamship in January 1860, Emma stepped off the boat to the sight of a huge placard bearing a copy of an order by the state legislature, banning her or any other Spiritualist from lecturing in public places. Undeterred, she would hold private spirit circles within people's houses instead. She also visited the State House in Montgomery, to stand in the hallowed hall where the bill had been passed. According to an account she published ten years later, no sooner had she reached the center of the legislative hall than she became overwhelmed by a ghostly presence that soon had her speaking in full voice.

"Woe, woe to thee, Alabama! Fair land of rest, thy peace shall depart, thy glory be shorn, and the proud bigots, tyrants, and cowards, who have driven God's angels back from thy cities, even in this chamber, have sealed thy doom, and their own together." Presumably to the startled alarm of passersby, Emma continued, "Thy sons shall be slain, thy legislators mocked and bound with the chains thou hast fastened on others"—sentiments that she would later describe as having been a prophecy of the bloody military conflict now only fifteen months away.

After returning to the North that year, Emma continued to combine speeches that focused explicitly on spreading the word about Modern Spiritualism with others, aimed at a wider audience, with an

increasingly politicized message. In June 1860, she wrote to the social reformer Caroline Healey Dall, who had given three influential
lectures in Boston in November 1859—nine months after Emma's
celebrated *Place and Mission of Woman* speech in the same city.
Dall's lecture series, *A Woman's Right to Labor, or, Low Wages
and Hard Work*, had highlighted the need for wealthier women to
open their eyes to the suffering of their poorer sisters. The opening
talk began with an image of Boston's "delicate ladies on Beacon
Street" who ordered "ices and creams flavored with vanilla or pear-
juice," oblivious to the backbreaking toil that went into producing
these delicacies. "Bituminous coal, rope-ends and creosote," Dall
said, furnished "a larger proportion of the piquant seasoning than
the blossoming bean or the orchard tree." Addressing the ladies of
Beacon Street directly, she implored them to turn their eyes "to the
most repulsive side of human life" and realize that "the 'perishing
classes' are made of men and women like yourselves."

Having touched on the struggles of working women who eked
out a living producing and laundering garments for meager wages,
she moved on to the decidedly unladylike subject of prostitution.
Now she put forward the sympathetic—and then novel—view that
women who sold sex were driven to do so by dire economic circumstances. "Poor pay," she said, "strikes as heavy a blow as a husband's right arm." Although she had felt it tactical to concentrate on
examples from Britain and New York City rather than those closer
to home, she insisted that even right here in Boston, she could "tell
you of ruin wrought under my own eyes."

Dall's lectures, like Emma's *Place and Mission of Woman* talk,
had been collected and published. In her June letter, Emma thanked
Dall for her pamphlet and suggested that the two of them work
together for the benefit of some of the most desperate of the female
population. In time, Emma would outline a plan for a Home for

Outcast Women, which she hoped that Dall, with her many connections in Boston, could help to establish in that city. Dall agreed,
and Emma produced an official report of what she envisaged: a
self-sustaining institution where "the fallen," or those at risk of
falling, could acquire new and useful employment—in the field of
horticulture—and regain their self-respect.

Unusually for the era, such nurturing would not take place
within a religious environment, and the regime would be far from
punitive. The only requirements expected were "order, cleanliness,
temperance, industry, and strict abstinence from stimulating drinks,
and harsh language." Each day, Emma proposed, "shall begin and
end with music and reading of an elevating character," and every
night, "each member shall be exhorted to forget and forgive each
other the trespasses of the day, making present duties and future
aims the only theme of conversation." The report made no suggestion that Spiritualist beliefs would be pushed either. Emma would
have rightly felt that this could put off potential donors, perhaps
even Dall herself. And it may also illustrate again the extent to which
Emma had begun to carve out a public image that was starting to
feel increasingly separate from her Spiritualist persona.

The two reformers pushed hard to make their Home for Outcast
Women a reality, but this progressive endeavor—aimed at "righting
some of these terrible wrongs" over which their "woman's hearts"
were "already bleeding"—was never realized. Many philanthropists
had begun focusing their attention instead on the growing likelihood
of a war that would split the country apart. Despite this setback,
both women continued to highlight the plight of women driven to
prostitution, a characteristic that would ultimately earn Emma the
nickname "the outcast's friend."

In August of 1861, in a talk at Dodworth's Hall called *America
and Her Destiny*, Emma took the opportunity to remind her audi-

ence that six thousand such outcasts languished in New York City alone. "Where are the six thousand men?" Emma cried. "In your saloons, and halls of legislature, your offices of trust, and places of honor, chanting the hymn of model America's 'FRATERNITY,' while gibing demons cry 'Amen.'" Perhaps surprisingly for a still fairly recent arrival in the country, Emma's speech mixed flamboyant tones of patriotism for her adopted homeland with moments of bold criticism. Although she heaped praise on the United States as a blessed rising nation, she chided listeners, saying that "the liberty hymn" could "never be chanted to the burden of the crack of the slave-whip." She spoke, too, of the condition of those who were free but desperately poor. The very notion of equality was a myth, she said, "when pointing with the skeleton finger of gaunt poverty, from the crowded tenant-house dens of ill-paid operatives, to the golden palaces of their aristocratic employers."

As had become customary, this speech of hers was said to have been given "extemporaneously," "Through Emma Hardinge, by The Spirits"—something that continued to open her up to public ridicule in some quarters. On this occasion, the *Ladies' Repository*—a Methodist journal based in Cincinnati—curtly remarked: "We advise 'Emma' to 'let the spirits alone,' get married and 'go to housekeeping.'" However, billing her speeches as spirit-led also allowed Emma to keep on abdicating much of the responsibility for her incendiary words, especially now that she had begun adopting the kind of "masculine," combative tone displayed to great effect in this address.

Two years later, her increasing renown would earn her yet another long public tour, this time without her mother. In October 1863, while the Civil War raged, she boarded the steamship *North Star*, run by the mighty Vanderbilt Line and originally designed as an immense private yacht for the aging tycoon Cornelius Vanderbilt and his family. Arriving at Aspinwall—present-day Colón in Panama—Emma delighted in the sight of monkeys wandering freely among the crowd of gauzily dressed locals who gathered to watch the boat's arrival. From here, the ship's passengers continued by rail to Panama City, where Emma's attention was captured this time by the alarming sight of huge, log-like alligators along the roadsides and the splendor of radiant blossoms and overhanging fruit.

From Panama they set sail again for San Francisco, then a rough-edged mining city, disembarking in early November. It was just as well that Emma had enjoyed the voyage, because she was immediately greeted by two discouraging pieces of news. A local medium, J. V. Mansfield—famous for accurately answering sealed letters to the spirits—handed over a loan of three twenty-dollar gold pieces to Emma, explaining that, in these times of war, government-endorsed "greenbacks" were not accepted anywhere in California. In addition to this unforeseen complication, Mansfield—the "Spirit postmaster," as he was known—warned Emma that she had her work cut out for her in California. Earlier "worthless adventurers" who'd arrived in the region, he said, had given Spiritualism a bad name.

Daunted but not cowed, Emma immediately decided to use a "considerable instalment" of her gold coins to advertise her forthcoming lectures in all four San Francisco papers and hire Platt's Hall, "the largest and finest" building in the city, capable of accommodating an audience of several thousand. By now a veteran at facing down difficult crowds, she soon won them over and had them listening in rapt attention. Buoyed by the welcome she'd received, Emma announced that she would return there the following Sunday.

She ended up staying in San Francisco for ten months, lecturing three times a week and making many new friends. Despite the city's busy pace and hectic spirit of adventure, she enjoyed living in quiet rooms and even came to feel affection for the packs of stray dogs that roamed the streets around her lodgings. Eventually, the increasingly independent Emma moved on to Virginia City, journeying, in the absence of a rail line, in a series of stagecoaches across the Sierra Nevada. In Nevada Territory—not quite yet a state—she discovered an untamed land carpeted in miles of gray sagebrush, the only plant that seemed able to survive the ravages of the desert climate.

In Nevada, Emma soon fell into her usual round of activity, dedicating her weeknight earnings to raising money for the United States Sanitary Commission (USSC), which supported Union soldiers and their families, reserving money left over from her Sunday lectures to send home to her mother. As a skilled public speaker, Emma acted as an auctioneer at USSC's merry Sanitary Fairs, enthusiastically helping to sell "all we could lay our hands on, good, bad, and indifferent."

She would come to look back on her fifteen-month tour of the Southwest and West Coast as a "constant scene of new and strange adventure." It also culminated in one of the most celebrated episodes of her remarkable life, which began in San Francisco. She'd returned from Nevada in 1864 at what should have been the end of her tour. Before a packed audience of thousands, once again at Platt's Hall, Emma threw her weight behind the campaign to re-elect Abraham Lincoln as president by delivering a speech entitled "The Coming Man; or the Next President of the United States." She would remark in its immediate aftermath that it drew "cheers and tears, warm pressures of hands, and showers of blessings" from her audience.

The next day, a few staunch supporters of the president arrived at her lodgings to ask if she would "stump the State for Lincoln," but only unofficially. As Emma scornfully noted, "The Union State Central Committee, whose campaign orators were clergymen, Congressmen, men of the highest place, wealth and talent, but always *men*, could not for a moment condescend to the indignity of employing a professional speaker, and that speaker *a woman*."

These patronizing terms aside, the committee seems to have failed to realize quite what an unattractive prospect campaigning so extensively might be for a female speaker, even one as experienced as Emma. She'd endured her fair share of aggression over the past few years, but—although her talks had become more and more political during this time—she still feared that entering a male-dominated arena in such an obvious way would open her up to "the choicest phrases of abuse that vocabulary of slang could supply" and a whole new level of harassment. In the end, the treasurer of the Union State Central Committee of California paid a visit and convinced her to agree to a more formal arrangement with the party: a series of thirty-two lectures, which they would organize, in the run-up to the November election. Although the treasurer offered to pay her a fee, Emma chose to ask only for expenses, recalling years later that she had feared the public would not trust her endorsement of the candidate if she took any more than that for her efforts.

These talks obliged her to journey "in the most oppressive heat and suffocating dust, from twenty to forty miles each day." She was "often stopped on the road by assembled multitudes, and compelled, in my travelling costume, heavy with dust, to deliver a speech from my carriage or a roadside rostrum by the way side." Her unusual status as the "Female Campaign Orator" proved even more novel than that of someone who channeled the thoughts of dead men and ensured that huge numbers poured into her official talks, causing "windows, doors, and even the frame walls" of buildings to be removed and scaffolding erected. Sometimes, the people of towns she visited lit celebratory bonfires and set off fireworks or even a small cannon salute. Emma would look back fondly on street processions lit by the glow of flaming paper lanterns while Union flags flapped in the breeze and marching bands played patriotic songs. In contrast to her worst fears, Emma's campaign was so successful that the Union Committee assured her that her work had been crucial in ensuring Lincoln's resounding victory in California.

Five months later, on April 15, 1865, Emma was back in New York City when news came over the telegraph wire that the president had been assassinated. Soon afterward, she received an invitation to deliver a eulogy—the first to be given in the city. That a woman, not American-born, was afforded this honor demonstrates the heights to which the former player of bit parts on Broadway had risen in less than a decade.

The forty-one-year-old Emma delivered her *Great Funeral Oration on Abraham Lincoln* that Sunday, just one day after the president's death, at the Cooper Union for the Advancement of Science and Art, an Italianate brownstone on Eighth Street. Five years before, Lincoln himself had given a historic address there. Before an audience of over three thousand, Emma lauded the late president as "strong, brave and immovable in the hour of trial and calamity" and praised him for the way in which, she said, he had, in the war's aftermath, united "again in one fraternal grasp the severed hands of North and South." Overly generous this may have been, but Emma must have judged it necessary to strike a conciliatory chord. Although she blamed Lincoln's death squarely on the Southern institution of slavery, she also reminded her audience that "there are men who sit beneath the Southern orange and magnolia and weep for him as we weep."

Talk of the spirits did not feature at all in this speech—another wise decision, perhaps, although the president's wife, Mary Todd Lincoln, might have been sympathetic. As a bereaved mother to William Wallace Lincoln—known as Willie—who had died of typhus during her husband's first term in office, she is said to have held several séances at the White House, which the president also attended. Seven years after her husband's death, in 1872, she would sit for photographer William H. Mumler, famous for his spirit photographs. During this session, Mumler duly captured the dark-cloaked Mrs. Lincoln in the foreground of the image with the white, airy figure of her late husband apparently standing behind her, his pale hands resting protectively upon her shoulders. Although Lincoln's wife wanted desperately to believe in the ability of spirits to remain in contact with the living, there exists no firm evidence that the president himself had been convinced. For Emma, however, there was seemingly no doubt. She might have left the subject alone at the time, but in her *Autobiography*, written toward the end of her life, she showed no such reticence. On the matter of whether Abraham Lincoln was a Spiritualist, she would write that she considered the question "quite unnecessary, as Mr. Lincoln's interest in the cause of Spiritualism and frequent interviews with spirit mediums were items of knowledge too well known to need any other confirmation than common report."

Later that year, Emma and her mother decided to return to Britain for a lengthy visit. Over the past decade, Emma's fame in the United States had grown to such an extent that *The New York Herald* devoted several column inches to her departure by steamship in August 1865. In the past, she had endured a tumultuous relationship with the *Herald*—which was generally critical of Spiritualism and Spiritualists—but its tone now was enthusiastic, perhaps even reverent. "Miss Hardinge," it said, had "devoted her life and best energies for the benefit of different benevolent and charitable enterprises." The paper particularly highlighted her campaigning on behalf of "fallen women," her recent reputation as a speaker on political subjects, and her tireless work toward the election of President Lincoln. She was, according to the *Herald*, "a writer and speaker, who has done good and is calculated to do good in the world."

She was leaving, the newspaper suggested, "for the purpose of looking after a legacy which has been left her by a relative." Emma's memoirs, on the other hand, would cite her mother Ann Sophia's homesickness as the chief reason. Another possibility is that the pair left for career reasons. Perhaps Emma's awareness of her growing transatlantic reputation—her recent work having begun to be covered not just in Britain's Spiritualist periodicals but by its mainstream press as well—had made her keen to cement this standing in her homeland. Whatever her main motivation for embarking on this trip at a time when her American career was going so well, her lifelong habit of hard work and enterprise makes it hard to take seriously her future claim that her intention had been to "retire into private life" once she'd reached Britain's shores.

And, of course, it was not to be. In London, the pair took lodgings in Chelsea—then a haven for artists, intellectuals, and progressive thinkers. Before long, Emma had begun to give regular evening and Sunday talks, commencing with the opening lecture of the "Winter Soirées" series hosted by Benjamin Coleman, an American-born early champion of Spiritualism in Britain. In November 1865, a crowd of invited men and women, who, as Benjamin put it, were interested "in psychological and kindred subjects," assembled at the Beethoven Rooms at the corner of Harley Street and Cavendish Square. Many in attendance were actively involved, like Benjamin, in spreading Spiritualist beliefs on this side of the Atlantic, and so the group must have come eager to hear what Emma had to say.

They could not have been more different from audiences that had gathered to hear Emma in the burgeoning mining towns of California. Before her entrance that night they sat expectantly, dressed in formal evening attire, and listened politely to Benjamin's few words of introduction. Explaining that her style involved addressing her listeners in a "semi-trance state," "guided and influenced in her speaking by spirits whom she recognizes," he said that she would speak that night without any preparation and on "any subject upon which the company might decide."

One of their members suggested a topic, which the group accepted. Then, to hearty applause, Benjamin escorted Emma onto the platform. Next he revealed the subject for the talk, written on a slip of paper, by placing it into her hands: "In what particulars are the teachings of Christianity and the facts recorded in the gospels elucidated and confirmed by Spiritualism?"

A broad and thorny question, perhaps, but one that Emma must have become used to answering, in one form or another, many times in the United States over the past few years. As such, and given her great skill as an orator, she seems to have had no difficulty in delivering a speech—without notes. Transcribed and published later in a booklet, it ran to almost eight pages.

"Your question answers itself," Emma began in an appealing, confident voice, putting those seated before her at ease. "For Christianity is Christ, the Spirit, the Divine Spirit; the Spirit of our Father, made most manifest through his Best Beloved." Thus, Emma, who—like the Fox Sisters before her—was no stranger to the criticism that she was acting against religion—argued that, rather than being a modern and dangerous thing, Spiritualism had in fact "overlaid the ages." She continued by saying that "the Spiritualism at which you marvel, and the Christianity before which you bow, are but parts of the same divine law and alternating life of order."

Before the distinguished crowd—which, as she would later write, included "persons of the highest rank or eminence in literature and science"—Emma would go on to cast Modern Spiritualism in both a rational and more explicitly religious light than she had in earlier speeches. "It is still yet in its hour of dawning," she said; "glorious revelations are only waiting for the fulness of time, to bring in their grand unfoldments; but even now it shadows forth the promise of a science which unlocks the mysteries of creation, and by the study of magnetic matter and spiritual phenomena, the wondrous problem of life and human organization will some day be solved."

At the close of her address, Emma invited further questions. A few audience members—notably all men—put forward inquiries. These ranged from the Pontius Pilate–inspired "What is truth?," to a question about the work of a medium, to this little conundrum: "Can Miss Hardinge throw any light on the mystery of mysteries, the connexion and relation between the nervous matter, called brain, and mind?" To each of these, Emma gave substantial answers that drew awe from those present, including the writer of a subsequent piece in *The Spiritual Magazine*, which lauded her as "a woman who has these highest, manliest gifts." "Who is it in our British Houses of Parliament," the article asked, "dare come forward and be compared with her, under the same conditions?"

In the new year of 1866, Emma followed up these private sessions for invited guests with larger public talks at the St. James's Hall on Regent Street. Now speaking to an audience that would have included many non-Spiritualists, she lectured on the subject of the country where she'd been living and working for the past decade. On the first of these occasions, talking of "America—its social, religious, and political condition," she held her audience in thrall as she spoke with barely an interruption for two consecutive hours.

The Morning Post marveled at her stamina and, despite some quibbles about her mispronunciation of certain words, noted—in a tone reminiscent of that taken in *The Spiritual Magazine*—that "the lady has the faculty to achieve in this not very feminine accomplishment." The London paper also noted, as other publications had already, that this was the same Emma Harding who'd appeared before

London theater audiences back in the 1840s and 1850s. Knowing nothing of her visionary childhood or her early connections with the city's shadowy occult world—not to mention her future claims of once having secretly written political speeches for British members of Parliament—it mused that, during her time as a thespian, she did not "betray any particular evidence of the extraordinary mental powers which she has since manifested in a very different capacity."

Other publications were less kind. *The Illustrated London News* characterized her as having "the verbiage of an American reporter and the accuracy of a cheap cyclopaedia." And the London correspondent for *The Edinburgh Evening Courant* seemed preoccupied with notions of both the United States and manliness, writing that Emma was "a big, rather masculine, not bad-looking dame in blue silk, with a great deal of action, much volubility, and not much of anything better." "Her theme is the eternal Yankee one," it said, colorfully dismissing this as "a glorification of universally diffused pork and peas-pudding and cheap illiterate newspapers." Without a trace of irony, the *Courant* added that "plenty of prosperous snobs" were ready to eat this up "and beget more snobs."

Despite the hostility she experienced from some quarters, Emma could justifiably consider her stay in London a success. Before returning to the United States, about twelve months later, she attended a grand farewell party held in her honor at the St. George's Hall, a newly built theater on Langham Place. The next few years would see her moving back and forth across the Atlantic, spending significant time in both Britain and the United States. This period can be regarded as the start of the lengthy consolidation of a career, and her ultimate self-investiture as chief historian of the movement ignited by Kate, Maggie, and Leah Fox in 1848. Emma published the first of her major literary works, *Modern American Spiritualism*, in 1870—also the year when she married fellow Spiritualist

William Britten and, after decades of changing her name, finally settled on Emma Hardinge Britten, which she would use for the rest of her life.

Modern American Spiritualism was followed by several other books, including *Nineteenth Century Miracles* in 1884 and finally her *Autobiography*, published posthumously at the dawn of the twentieth century. In addition to securing her own position at the heart of this radical Victorian movement, Emma's writing and lecturing over the next thirty years would do much to champion the work of many other notable spirit mediums. One outspoken woman, however—fifteen years her junior and fêted, like her, as a childhood clairvoyant—would find herself an object of Emma's scorn.

The Little Queen

Over the course of her extraordinary life, Victoria Woodhull would present two very different portrayals of her childhood. Certain details remained the same: the hamlet of Homer where she was born in rural Ohio; her date of birth, September 23, 1838; and, as in the case of the young Emma Floyd, Victoria's girlish propensity to see visions. Other elements diverged almost completely in the separate versions.

In the happier story—supported by Victoria's unpublished memoirs, written when she was in her fifties—her childhood home is a place of ordered serenity. Her father, the one-eyed Reuben Buckman Claflin, nicknamed Buck, has a deep regard for learning and enjoys nothing more than discussing "complex law matters" with his bright young daughter. Buck's wife, Roxanna Hummel Claflin, or Annie, comes across as similarly loving—a gentle mother who watches prayerfully over the lives of her brood of children.

But in the alternative tale—the one Victoria told to her first biographer, over two decades earlier—these same devout qualities in

Annie are presented in quite another light. The chief impression is of a mentally unstable, fanatically religious woman prone to erupting into bouts of ecstasy when moved by the Holy Spirit; of cursing and damning with the same ferocity on other occasions, a spray of white foam frothing at her lips. Although this Annie can be tender and caring, she torments her children just as easily, her behavior instilling such alarm in her little ones that they are "thrown into spasms." At this Annie laughs and claps hysterically, looking "as fiercely delighted as a cat in playing with a mouse." Buck, too, in this account is a terrifying authority figure, "impartial in his cruelty to all his children"—a man who takes sadistic pleasure in whipping them with plaited strands of green willow, which he keeps supple in a barrel of rainwater to increase their sting. He is also a man who exploits his offspring for profit, especially Victoria's beloved younger sister Tennessee, sending her out to work in dubious occupations to support the family.

As to which of these stories is the more reliable, the answer is probably neither and both. Too many unconnected reports exist of Victoria's mother's unbalanced temperament to dismiss the worst of these descriptions. And yet, despite her often tumultuous relationship with her children, Annie inspired a protectiveness in Victoria that lasted to the end of her life. Likewise, the image of Buck as upright and legal-minded sits uncomfortably with the criminal scams he is known to have pulled. The local shopkeeper used to say that "he could see more deviltry to do" in his one good eye "than any two men in their four eyes."

Be that as it may, in addition to being a troublesome neighbor and carrying on various unscrupulous moneymaking schemes, Buck did in fact earn his living for a time as a lawyer. As to Victoria's allegations of paternal cruelty—which, even given the era's harsher methods of punishment, feel extreme in their brutality—some of those acquainted with Buck in later years simply couldn't reconcile his daughter's accusations with their own observations of the man they felt they knew. It is worth remembering, however, that those viewing a family from the outside can rarely conceive of its inner workings. It's also the case that a relationship between two people who sustain a lifelong bond does not necessarily preclude a past period of abuse.

When considering the conflicting tales about Victoria's childhood, one has to be prepared to read between the lines of established histories, even if it means disregarding accepted truths passed down by earlier chroniclers.

Something on which all major past narratives seem to agree, and which feels hard to dispute, is that, from a young age, Victoria showed a keen resourcefulness and blazing ambition that distinguished her from her peers. Like the young Emma Floyd—who'd rise to fame as Emma Hardinge—and the three Fox sisters, Victoria received little formal education. She attended school intermittently, probably for only a year in total. Nonetheless, she is said to have impressed her teachers with her quick wit and intelligence, qualities that may have contributed to the incongruously regal manner she adopted even as a child. Fellow pupils called her the Little Queen, after her namesake, Queen Victoria.

On the late September Sunday in 1838 when Victoria Claflin was born, the nineteen-year-old British monarch had been queen for just fifteen months. Her diary entry for the day paints a picture of meandering hours within the turreted stone walls of Windsor Castle, punctuated by leisurely walks and churchgoing. It feels worlds away from the small village among the corn and wheat fields of Ohio in which the American Annie Claflin gave birth.

As an adult, Annie's daughter would record her memories of the events of the date—of which she claimed to have actual personal recollection. She had slid into this life feeling "as if I had been rudely awakened from a death-like sleep." In Victoria's telling of these events, her baby-blue eyes, a much-admired feature throughout her life, moved eagerly about the shabby room. The infant took everything in: her father in conversation with the doctor, the "pain and anguish" on her exhausted mother's face, the cradling arms of the nurse. Even in these first moments, so Victoria said, the newborn "seemed to know all the future without being able to give any expression in words."

Difficult as it may be for many readers to trust the accuracy of this account, Annie herself seems to have felt that her daughter should be believed. Annie would establish a strong bond with this seventh child—of a final count of ten—perhaps founded on their shared proclivity to experience visions. The series of spirits who Victoria would later claim visited her as a child included a solemn old man, dressed in an ancient Greek tunic, who told her that she would one day leave her humble beginnings behind and live in a grand home, that she would make her fortune in a city "crowded with ships" and "publish and conduct a journal." Most significantly and most far-fetched of all—at a time when, exceptions such as Queen Victoria aside, women wielded virtually no political clout—this mysterious visitor claimed that the little country girl would "become the ruler of her people."

When Victoria went public with these revelations, she had reason to suppose that significant numbers of people would accept them as true. By the early 1870s, the majority of her prophecies had come to pass. A cynical audience might give a wry smile and conclude that she simply fit the facts to the words of the Greek spirit guide. But this does not diminish the magnitude of her achievements. Neither should it detract from the fact that it was her seeming ability to commune with the spirit world that would be her ticket to the fame, riches, and cultural influence she would eventually acquire.

In the early 1850s, the Claflins left Homer for Mount Gilead—a small town some thirty miles away, where one of Victoria's older sisters lived with her husband and children. The family left a lurid legacy. Although some claims about their time in the hamlet are wildly exaggerated—such stories gaining traction in later years when Victoria's notoriety had made her a local embarrassment—it's difficult to imagine that many of their neighbors were sorry to see the family go. Documents recently unearthed in the archives of the Licking County Courthouse challenge a well-worn story about Buck committing insurance fraud by torching an unprofitable grist mill he'd owned in Homer for the promised payout. Instead, these papers show that he put the mill up for sale before the family moved. Nonetheless, if viewed as part of the whole of Buck's life, it's understandable how such a rumor could have caught on. Scandal had a way of sticking to the Claflins, a pattern repeated in coming years when they made hurried exits from several future locations.

In Mount Gilead, the family became acquainted in 1853 with another newcomer, Canning Woodhull, whose life and livelihood became inextricably linked with theirs. Canning hailed from the outskirts of Rochester, New York, the city where the Fox sisters had first made their name as spirit mediums. Born and raised in Webster, he must have been at least in his early twenties when the Claflins met him—conservative estimates making him about a decade older than Victoria, then not quite fifteen. It seems that he appeared the very epitome of cosmopolitan refinement to the girl. Canning claimed to be the nephew of Caleb S. Woodhull, a former mayor of New York City, and called himself a medical doctor—a loosely defined profession in those days, perfect for a man with no particular qualifications.

If later newspaper advertisements recommending his services are anything to go by, the kind of medicine he practiced involved placing his patients in healing trances and prescribing his personally concocted salves made of "none but vegetable substances." Questionable as these cures may seem, when he visited Victoria at her home to treat her for the frequent fevers and aches that had been plaguing her for the past two years, she apparently responded well to them. But the doctor's interest was not purely professional. Once Victoria's health had improved, Canning began to keep an eye out for her around Mount Gilead.

One day, he caught up with her in the street to invite her to Mount Gilead's upcoming Fourth of July picnic. As in villages and towns all over Ohio, this would be an occasion when the locals could look forward to a merry afternoon sampling the best of the season's produce, great hunks of cooked meat, and sweet-smelling pies and cakes. There would be flying of flags, singing of patriotic songs, and speeches and toasts aplenty.

Victoria, flattered by the attention of this older man, promised to ask her mother's permission. Annie appears to have offered little objection, but Victoria would later recall that Buck had demanded that his daughter buy herself a new pair of shoes before he would give his assent. This stipulation suggests that he wanted his daughter to look her best, thereby giving her—and by extension her family— the strongest opportunity for benefiting from a potentially lucrative match.

Victoria set herself to work selling apples to make the money. Demonstrating the enterprising flair she had inherited from her father, and which would serve her so well throughout her life, she quickly got the funds together. And so, on the day of the picnic she put on her new shoes and waited eagerly for the arrival of the doctor. Setting off on his arm, she probably felt unusually sophisticated and excited about what lay ahead. The lazy summer day was set to a joyful accompaniment of laughter, chatter, and rousing music, but the mood took a sudden turn when the two got back to Victoria's house. Standing at her door, the doctor turned to look down at her. "My little puss," he said, "tell your father and mother that I want you for a wife."

She had known him for such a short time that his request may have come as a shock. Her parents, though, encouraged the match, and so, sooner or later, Victoria accepted Canning's proposal. Man and girl were married on November 23, 1853, two months past her fifteenth birthday, in Cleveland, on the shores of Lake Erie, about a hundred miles from the Claflins' home.

Cleveland, where the doctor had been living prior to moving to Mount Gilead, was experiencing a population explosion. The recent arrival of the Cleveland, Columbus, and Cincinnati Railroad, along with the opening of the Erie and Ohio Canal two decades earlier, attracted industry and workers to the area. It must have seemed a far cry from the sleepy countryside where Victoria had grown up and could have proved exhilarating for an ambitious girl like her. But whatever hopes had accompanied the young bride on her journey were soon dashed. Canning, it would turn out, was inclined to embellishment of the truth. His talk of Mayor Caleb Woodhull had been exaggerated—the two were not closely related. More seriously, rather than the secure life of a doctor's wife that Victoria might have expected, she found that—unlike in those most rural parts of the state crying out for physicians—far fewer prospects existed for Canning in Cleveland. Worse still, she discovered that her husband had hidden a secret side of himself. He was an alcoholic.

Three days after their wedding, Victoria discovered the truth when Canning stayed out all night at a "house of ill-repute" and came home stinking of drink. Far from her family and now under the authority of an unpredictable man, she must have felt desperately trapped. She later described the feeling of growing older in a single day. Evenings were soon reduced to a pattern of weighing up which painful course of action to take: braving the rough dark to track down her husband in one of his favored haunts or keeping watch at home at the window, listening for the stagger of his drunken footsteps approaching in the early hours.

Fifteen months on, by which time the unhappy pair had relocated to a small wood-frame house in Chicago, Victoria suffered the agonizing birth of her first child in a room so cold that icicles clung to the posts of the bed. Canning, apparently half-drunk throughout the labor, was the only one in attendance on that harsh winter's day. One can imagine how much additional pain—both physical and mental—Victoria must have suffered as a result.

She did experience some much-needed kindness when the concerned woman next door arrived after the birth bearing a plate of good food. This neighbor continued to visit. As evidence of the extent of Victoria's miserable predicament accumulated, one day the neighbor wrapped the baby boy in a blanket and carried him over to the home of another local woman who'd also recently given birth.

With her son now in capable hands, Victoria began to recover some strength. The boy, Byron, too, seemed all right, but what no one knew was that—in the language of the day—he had been born an "imbecile." Although the cause of Byron's condition would never be detected, Victoria laid the blame squarely on Canning's reckless behavior. She and her son went on to develop a warm relationship, but the resentment she felt toward her husband would, one day far into the future, set Victoria on her own shameful course—promoting the repugnant philosophy of eugenics.

Back in the 1850s, however, her attention was fully occupied with the task of simply surviving. Another girl in her position might have crumbled, or turned to drink, or placed her faith in God, as her own mother had done. But with the help of the woman next door and other kind acquaintances, Victoria somehow found the strength to carry on. Records of her daily existence during this period are scant. An 1855 New York State census record locates the couple and their baby in Webster, suggesting that the doctor had moved them back to his family home. The next moment that makes it into Victoria's self-sanctioned biography sees her, her husband, and their small son in San Francisco, where just a few years later Emma Hardinge would make a name for herself as a trance lecturer and political campaigner. For Victoria, San Francisco proved an unwelcoming place, and the change of scene achieved by an arduous land and sea journey did nothing to improve her living situation.

No record has come to light showing that Canning worked as a doctor in San Francisco, and certainly Victoria's account gives the impression of the family surviving initially on desperately little money. Spotting a "cigar girl wanted" advertisement in a city newspaper, she presented herself to the proprietor of one of San Francisco's tobacco stores. Cigar girls were ostensibly employed to stand behind the counter and serve, but also to endure the lewd comments and unwanted advances of the male customers their presence was designed to attract. Victoria later wrote that she lasted only a day in the job, the owner deeming her "too fine" and explaining that he needed a woman who could "rough it." She next worked as a seamstress, a job that would lead to a chance that changed her life's miserable course.

When an actress named Anna Cogswell engaged Victoria to make a set of costumes, the two became friendly and Victoria sought Anna's advice about her own financial troubles.

"I am running behind," Victoria confessed. "I must do something better."

Taking in the blue eyes that looked straight at her, the appealing dark curls, the pretty face and surprisingly regal carriage, Anna did not hesitate. "Then," she advised at once, "you too must be an actress."

And so Victoria began acting in supporting roles in productions with Anna, such as *New York by Gas-light*, based on George G. Foster's notorious book of 1850. Foster, a journalist for Horace Greeley's *New-York Daily Tribune*, had compiled a sensational collection of observations taken from his nocturnal wanderings around the East Coast metropolis. Individuals he encountered on these rambles included gaudily attired prostitutes flashing expensive jewelry and shimmering satin shawls; caddish young men propping up the doorway to an oyster house; adulterers hurrying to a cheap room for an illicit encounter; gamblers spending the night away. One can imagine the kind of wardrobe that Anna and Victoria would have been required to don for their roles. Although Victoria seems to have found acting preferable to the lot of a cigar girl, theatrical work—in an era when the job of an actress was often regarded as similar to that of a prostitute—was not without its own pressures.

Soon, though, she was earning the tidy sum of fifty-two dollars per week, roughly seven times more than she could have hoped to make as a seamstress—and necessary if she was the only breadwinner. She was getting along all right as an actress, but the situation was hardly satisfactory. While out in the evening at the theater, she presumably had the constant worry of how her boy Byron would fare. When he was sober, Canning could be a caring father, but his struggles with alcoholism would continue throughout this period—and, indeed, for the rest of his life.

How Victoria must have longed for someone in whom she could confide all her troubles. Her fellow performer, Anna, had proved a friend, but their closeness could not compare with the relationships she'd once shared with her siblings. In particular, she missed her younger sister, a child of about eight when Victoria left Mount Gilead. Tennessee Claflin had since matured into a pretty adolescent girl, and the family's main source of income.

In Victoria's absence—and influenced presumably by the earlier successes of the Fox sisters and the many young mediums who'd followed in their wake—Buck had begun to present Tennessee as a clairvoyant healer, someone able to cure "old sores, fever-sores, cancers" and all manner of other afflictions. An advertisement placed by Buck in a local newspaper in 1859 billed Tennessee as *"A WONDERFUL CHILD!* . . . endowed from her birth with a supernatural gift." For those prepared to pay a dollar, she would "go into an unconscious state and travel to any part of the world" to track down the absent friends of sitters at her séances and divulge information about their "situation and whereabouts, with all the events of life since they last met." Drawing perhaps, too, from his son-in-law's miracle salves, Buck also mixed up a concoction of his own, which he marketed as Miss Tennessee's Magnetic Life Elixir. The young woman's profile adorned the bottle along with the promise that, if taken three times per day, its "perfectly harmless and purely vegetable" contents could beautify the complexion and cleanse the blood. In years to come, Tennessee would look back on this early graft as a "hard life," which her parents had forced upon her. Victoria, too, would say that she had been appalled to learn of the lucrative "humbug" thrust upon her sister, but her own future involvement in similar practices challenges this notion—especially since she'd claim to share the same clairvoyant abilities on which Tennessee's career was founded.

One strange anecdote from Victoria's time in San Francisco illustrates not just the sisters' supposed psychic powers but also their closeness, which would be so apparent to future commentators once the pair had become famous. While appearing in *The Corsican*

Brothers—the popular Alexandre Dumas story of conjoined twins, separated at birth, who experience each other's pain—Victoria apparently heard a spirit voice calling her to come home.

In the middle of a ballroom scene in which she swayed and turned, clad in dancing slippers and a pink gown of silk, Victoria shivered in awe and excitement as a vision of Tennessee dressed in a striped French calico frock emerged before her eyes. With her attention on the script and players wavering, Victoria watched as Tennessee beckoned with her forefinger and repeated her entreaty that her sister should come home.

When the evening's performance had ended, seemingly now in the grip of a mania, Victoria hurried away from the theater, having not even bothered to change out of her stage costume. She ran, dodging puddles and passersby, through the rain and the fog. Once back at her lodgings, or so the story goes, she bundled her belongings together, along with Byron's and Canning's, her husband being surprisingly willing to immediately accompany her on her voyage. It's possible that he had become so reliant on his wife's earnings by now that he could see no way to make it on his own. Whatever the case, the three soon departed by a New York–bound steamer.

As at the time of Emma Hardinge's first tours across the United States, this trip would have taken several weeks. From New York, they continued on to Indianapolis, where Tennessee had been working. At least according to Victoria's account, when she was reunited with her sister, now in her mid-teens, Tennessee happened to be wearing the same French calico frock she'd had on in Victoria's vision at that San Francisco theater.

Not long afterward, Victoria herself began to ply a lucrative trade as a spiritual healer. For a time, she rented rooms at the Bates House Hotel in Indianapolis. At this upmarket establishment—where, in February 1861, months away from the start of the Civil

War, President-elect Lincoln would give a speech from the balcony to a crowd of forty-five thousand—Victoria predicted people's futures and laid healing hands on the sick. Eventually, she, Canning, and Byron moved again, this time to New York City.

By now, Victoria, in her midtwenties, was pregnant once more. When she went into labor, in April 1861, her husband was once again the sole person present for the birth. If Victoria's memories of Byron's birth were painful, what her mind would preserve of this second labor would be even worse.

Entirely drunk this time, Canning made an even worse job of the delivery of the couple's daughter than he had with their son. In the dead of night, and with the all-consuming focus that childbirth bestows on a woman, Victoria watched in horror as her husband stumbled around their rented room at 53 Bond Street, between Broadway and the Bowery. As the baby arrived at about four in the morning, he grasped for its body with shaking hands. In his intoxicated state, Canning managed to cut the umbilical cord too close to the tiny girl's body and then tie the string with fumbling fingers. Worse still, so overcome by the ordeal was he that, within an hour of his wife giving birth, he abandoned her and the newborn in bed and staggered out into the street while a shattered Victoria succumbed to slumber.

On waking, the realization came to her that she was all alone. And then a further shock. Blood drenched her head, clotting her hair and dampening the pillow. Canning had tied the baby's umbilical cord so inexpertly that the string had slipped away, exposing the girl's innards, from where blood had been weeping while her mother slept.

Mustering all the strength she possessed, Victoria began to pound on the wall, hoping to attract someone's notice. Nobody responded, so she tried again, and again. She was rescued, finally, as after her previous birth, by a female neighbor who heard the commotion. Unable to gain access via the front entrance, the woman tore away the grate of the basement and made her way up to the bedroom—an act that probably saved the baby's life.

When Canning returned three days later, Victoria happened to be looking out of the window. She was greeted by the sight of her husband staggering up the steps of a house nearby, having mistaken it for his own. Watching this episode played out through the glass, something shifted within her. It was now, she would later write, that the question formed in her mind: Why should she "live with this man" any longer?

Victoria would call her baby Zulu—a name seemingly inspired by romanticized images of colonial Africa and a proud warrior kingdom. For Victoria, it perhaps struck a note of defiance in a marriage that often seemed without hope. She would eventually separate from her husband, but, as the events of the next decade would show, theirs would never be a decisive break.

While Victoria struggled to raise her two children with only the partial support of her husband, her younger sister—as an unmarried woman—remained under the control of her father. Tennessee did briefly marry. The man's name was John Bortel. From the scant details that emerged many years later, it seems the couple divorced only a few weeks later. Tennessee was, in any case, soon back within the family fold and in a position to resume her travels, offering paying customers an opportunity to hear her messages from the beyond and peddling her father's dubious wares.

With Civil War raging across the country, grieving families kindled the hope that Modern Spiritualism might offer them a chance to retain a link with lost loved ones. Buck saw business opportunities aplenty in their torment. He was billing himself now as "Dr. R. B. Claflin," the "King of Cancers," able to cure all manner of chronic conditions from bone diseases and consumption to "Female Weakness," "Salt Rheum," and hemorrhoids. He presented Tennessee as a "magnetic doctress" who could "see and point out the medicine to cure the most obstinate diseases" and who had, he boasted, been consulted by "Lawyers, Doctors, Ministers, and many other scientific men."

In Ottawa, Indiana, Buck established a so-called infirmary at the Fox River House hotel. Before long, glowing testimonials, placed by him, began to appear in the press. These accounts claimed that Miss Tennessee Claflin was responsible for healing kidney disease, dysentery, bronchitis, and, of course, cancerous tumors. A scandal erupted when one supposedly satisfied patient, Rebecca Howe, wrote to *The Ottawa Republican* to complain that she had never given such a statement. According to Buck, she had been seen by Tennessee, who had prescribed a salve for the cancer in her breast, and the tumor had disappeared. Not so, the angry woman said. Quite the contrary, in fact: the salve had done no good at all. Instead, she had suffered "extreme pain and aggravation of all the symptoms." Her one wish now was to "prevent, as far as I am able, the injury which might otherwise be inflicted on innocent sufferers." Miss Claflin, the letter writer intoned, was "an imposter" and "wholly unfit for the confidence of the community."

The woman died not long afterward, and Tennessee—though not Buck—was charged in the death. According to the Circuit Court of La Salle County, Tennessee had administered "deleterious and caustic drugs" that had "wholly eaten away, consumed and destroyed" a large portion of flesh. But the verdict was cast in Tennessee's absence: the Claflins had packed up and left. However, as with her brief marriage to John Bortel, Tennessee's involvement in the affair would later return to haunt her.

Did Tennessee feel responsible for what had happened to Rebecca Howe and others who placed their trust in her? Difficult to resist Buck's authority it might have been, but she surely deserves at least some blame for continuing with the charade in other cities. By the mid-1860s, with the Civil War grinding toward its conclusion, there was no end of desperate men and women seeking the soothing balm of spirit mediums and healers. It was a need that Tennessee and Victoria were ready to meet. If extravagant claims had been made about Tennessee's abilities, the same could be said of her sister. In the words of Victoria's first biographer, "she straightened the feet of the lame; she opened the ears of the deaf; she detected the robbers of a bank," and "money flowed in a stream toward her."

While working in St. Louis in about 1864, these talents would bring a new man into Victoria's life. Colonel James Harvey Blood was a married Union officer, five years older than her. He had recently returned from the battlefront, bearing the scars of significant active service, including a partially paralyzed arm, debilitating insomnia, and more intimate issues brought on by a serious stumble with his horse, during which he had injured his perineum. These included "seminal weakness," or involuntary ejaculation—a condition particularly taboo in the nineteenth century, when the release of semen outside of marital intercourse was widely believed to be damaging to the male body.

A committed Spiritualist already, the Colonel—known familiarly by that name—had previously organized talks in the city by well-known mediums including Emma Hardinge. Conflicting accounts exist about how this dashing, dark-haired, and bearded man got to know Victoria. Some said that he sought her out on Washington Avenue when he took his sickly wife to her office for a consultation. Another story, endorsed by Victoria, suggests that, as an injured war hero, he sought treatment for himself—for which of his ailments it isn't clear.

In that version of events, soon after greeting this handsome man, Victoria slipped into a trance and began to speak of deeply personal matters. The Colonel's destiny, she said, apparently unconsciously, was "to be linked with hers in marriage." Such sentiments, coming out of the blue, might have sent some men hurrying away— especially those already wed, or suffering from the kind of potentially embarrassing condition brought on by the wartime injury to his perineum. Future official statements by the Colonel describing his state of health reveal that, over time, his condition would worsen to such an extent that sexual intercourse became impossible. But Victoria's recollections of their first meeting, at least, suggest a fusing of bodies and souls. In the ornate and highly euphemistic language adopted by Victoria's early biographer, any inhibitions seem to have vanished in an instant. In their minds at least, they "were betrothed on the spot 'by the powers of the air.'"

A Valuable Asset

In early April 1865, four years of devastating civil war were finally coming to a close. On the ninth of that month, the last major Confederate army surrendered and a crowd began to gather outside the White House calling for Abraham Lincoln to give an address. One month into his second term, on the evening of April 11, the sixteenth president appeared at an open window of his official residence. Reading his notes by the light of a single glowing flame, he reminded the sea of several thousand onlookers—just blurry shapes among the burning lamps below—that the road ahead was "fraught with great difficulty." Many challenging decisions would have to be made, he said, in order to achieve the successful reconstruction of the battle-scarred nation. For the first time, too, he pledged his support for granting limited voting rights to African Americans—words that had a chilling effect on at least one man in the audience.

Three nights later, that same individual, the well-known stage actor and Confederate sympathizer John Wilkes Booth, slipped into the box at Ford's Theatre where Lincoln had gone to see the popular farce *Our American Cousin*. The shot Booth aimed at close range at the president's head hit its target, plunging the auditorium into chaos. As news of Lincoln's subsequent death spread far and wide—early enough to make the morning editions of the Southern newspapers—fearful disbelief and sorrow flowed through the nation. "The Rebel Fiends at Work," thundered the headline of the sympathetic *Nashville Union*; the *Evening Star*, a Washington, D.C., paper, devoted roughly half of its columns to the developing story and reported flags flying at half-mast, houses "draped in mourning," and bells "tolling mournfully." A hurriedly rewritten late edition of *The New York Herald* featured a notice for the $10,000 reward being offered for the capture of Lincoln's assassins. And in that same city the following afternoon, the forty-one-year-old Briton Emma Hardinge delivered her *Great Funeral Oration* before a crowd of three thousand people. Typeset and bound into a booklet, Emma's commemoration of the president was soon selling at a brisk pace for twenty-five cents. In contrast, the feelings of twenty-six-year-old Victoria Woodhull went unrecorded. A decade into the future, however, she would attempt to write herself and her family into this national story by publicly claiming that her younger sister had once shared with her a premonition of Lincoln's untimely death.

According to Victoria, back in 1861, the adolescent Tennessee Claflin and their parents had been staying at a hotel in Pittsburgh when the president-elect passed through the city on his inaugural journey to Washington. The family waited patiently at the window for a glimpse of Lincoln's carriage. The moment it moved out of sight, Tennessee apparently sank into a chair and exclaimed, "He will never leave the White House alive. I heard a pistol shot and saw the blood running from his head, and his coffin in the carriage with him."

In the same month as Lincoln's assassination, Victoria's new beau, Colonel James Harvey Blood, was elected to the office of auditor of St. Louis—a job that paid $2,500, one of the highest annual salaries in the city. He was also president of the St. Louis Railroad, which operated a system of horse-drawn trams rather than trains. The Colonel was said to have received $3,000 per annum for the job. Although he had also accumulated some heavy debts, he was regarded as a well-off man. It might, therefore, have surprised many local citizens to know that, in addition to these lucrative appointments, he was running a side business. Under the alias J. A. Harvey, he was a "Magnetic and Clairvoyant Physician." Perhaps he sensed that the surname Blood would be anything but reassuring in a so-called doctor.

The Colonel advertised this other mysterious line of work in several out-of-state newspapers, letting readers know that, if they were unable to attend his "crowded" clinic, he could examine and prescribe for their condition by post. Like Victoria's first husband, Canning Woodhull, the Colonel did not have any particular medical qualifications, but as the president of St. Louis's Society of Spiritualists—and as the romantic partner of a woman who had several years' experience of spiritual healing herself—he must have felt up to the job. A February 1865 advertisement in an Iowa paper called *The Weekly Ottumwa Courier* claimed that he could cure asthma, epilepsy, heart disease, and tuberculosis with "his MAGIC TOUCH," and that "All cases of Cancer, no matter how long standing," could be painlessly removed within twenty-four hours by "the Doctor while in the Clairvoyant state."

When rumors spread about the relationship between this elected official and the "Witch of Washington-avenue," as the St. Louis newspaper the *Daily Missouri Democrat* called Victoria, scandal erupted in the city, ultimately leading the Colonel to lose his presidency of the St. Louis Railroad. He was also forced out of his job as auditor. He had by then abandoned the home he shared with his wife and daughter, and on July 10, 1865, sealed himself in marriage to Victoria—notably, not in the place they both lived but in Hamilton County, Ohio. Although some today will regard the Colonel's treatment of his family as callous, many of his friends and acquaintances at the time placed the blame for his behavior firmly on his Spiritualist beliefs and his new love interest. In the words of the *Democrat*, nothing but his desire to "look into the secrets of nature could have so weakened his intellect as to make him fall prey to the machinations of designing and unprincipled women."

Victoria's new bond with the Colonel contrasted greatly with her earlier marriage to Canning Woodhull. Whatever the true state of intimate relations between the Colonel and Victoria at this stage, their partnership was founded on more than physical attraction; the two shared common interests. The Colonel, as a Spiritualist himself, wholly endorsed Victoria's work as a medium. He was also a supporter of women's rights and backed the free love movement, whose reputation had so shocked Emma Hardinge. Victoria's second union differed from her first in another way too: it wasn't legal. If indeed Victoria had dissolved her marriage with her previous husband by then, as she claimed, the Colonel had certainly not divorced his abandoned wife, Mary Anna C. Blood. Owing to the poor administrative networks of the time, the two would probably have got away with these irregularities if not for the fact that Mary petitioned him for divorce. The marriage was not officially dissolved till 1866. The Colonel and Victoria remarried that same year, in Dayton, Ohio, and then—for reasons that remain open to debate—went through a legal separation of their own in 1868. Despite this, they would continue to live together as husband and wife for many years more.

The couple's early life together brought with it both the familiar and the new. They are said to have traveled around Victoria's home state in a covered wagon, giving spirit readings and continuing to dispense dubious medical treatment. They also ventured farther afield. By the winter of 1866–67, a string of advertisements in *The New-Orleans Times* and *The Daily Memphis Avalanche* locate the pair in the American South. The Colonel—or as he introduces himself in these notices, the "Prof."—continued to use the name J. A. Harvey, while Victoria called herself Madame Harvey. This was a rarity for her; for most of her life, she went by Woodhull, the name of her first husband. Perhaps she felt that she had already established something of a minor reputation as Woodhull, or she wanted to signal that—although remarried—she wished, this time, to retain her independence of spirit. Whatever the case, highly unusually for the era, she rarely used her second husband's surname, Blood.

The question of where the Woodhull children were while Victoria embarked on these new adventures is an interesting one, glossed over by early biographies. Often she seems to have left them with members of her extended family, in one case a cousin, Thankful Claflin. Many decades into the future, Thankful would write to Victoria's daughter Zulu Woodhull—by then known as Zula—reminiscing about the days when she had cared for Byron while their mother was working away from home.

It's also plausible that their father lent a hand. Despite the breakdown of the marriage, his life remained intertwined with Victoria's and indeed with the wider Claflin family's. Tennessee continued to work as a spiritual healer, and Canning, still presenting himself as a doctor, sometimes assisted her. Far from the inept, fumbling quack portrayed by Victoria to her first biographer, he is described in press notices as a medical genius. Echoing some of the bold claims made about Buck and Tennessee in the past—and about the Colonel and Victoria—one report from January 1868 suggested that, over the course of fifteen days, Canning had removed a "huge cancer" from the breast of a female patient "without the use of instruments, and without the least pain or the loss of any blood." He even treated Victoria's new love, the Colonel, for various conditions related to his war service.

Even though Victoria and those closest to her were apparently making a good living from this line of work, she had begun to tire of her itinerant lifestyle and was looking for new opportunities. Several years later, she and her sister would recall that they had also wanted to get Tennessee away from the controlling influence of Buck and Annie Claflin. As luck would have it, at least as Victoria would tell the tale, she soon received a sign of hope.

During a stay in Pittsburgh in early 1868, she was sitting alone when a figure in white robes—the spirit guide of her childhood—appeared and wrote on the marble surface of the table before her. The letters that appeared, curiously English characters rather than ancient Greek, spelled out the name "Demosthenes." Victoria, almost thirty years of age at the time, trembled in awe as the writing, faint in appearance at first, grew brighter and brighter until its light filled the room.

She should go to New York City, the figure commanded, even giving a specific address. At 17 Great Jones Street, in Lower Manhattan, she would find a house readied for her arrival.

As with her sudden departure from San Francisco with Canning a decade earlier, Victoria seemingly had no difficulty in convincing her new partner to follow the spirit messenger's words. Not long afterward, and with Tennessee in tow, she, the Colonel, Byron, and Zula—aged about thirteen and seven, respectively—decamped to that very address. According to Victoria's version of events, when she entered the house she found it just as she had envisioned it. The entrance hall and the staircases, the rooms and objects within, were exactly the same. In the library, she took up a book: *The Orations of Demosthenes.* A chill passed through her. In years to come, she'd often talk of this Greek statesman and celebrated speaker from the fourth century B.C., and of how on numerous other occasions he had mapped out the course of her life.

Even without the career advice from her spirit guide Demosthenes, it is easy to understand why Victoria—like Emma Hardinge and the Fox sisters before her—would have been drawn to New York City. Over the past six years, its population had steadily increased, now totaling over nine hundred thousand. New York remained a place where fortunes could be swiftly made and lost. With her considerable charms, ability to capitalize on her talents, and tremendous sense of her own destiny, Victoria must have felt that her chance to succeed was as good as anyone's. On the other hand, as a woman, she had very few legal or political rights. And the New York of 1868, like the world at large, remained a city dominated by men of means.

Big business had enjoyed steadily rising profits since the opening of the Erie Canal in the 1820s, built to establish a connection of waterways between the metropolis, the Atlantic Ocean, and the Great Lakes. Now, in the aftermath of the Civil War—as desperately poor former soldiers arrived in New York City in droves—its wealthiest citizens could revel in a postwar boom period of rapidly escalating wealth. But while those with riches had a fair shot at achieving their dreams, many of the less privileged had to eke out a squalid living within filthy, polluted slums. Conditions were especially precarious for women, and opportunities relatively few. Throughout the city, from smoke-choked narrow streets in the shadow of factories to tree-lined avenues filled with elegant new brownstones, prostitution was a constant presence.

In the words of George Ellington, one disapproving commentator of the day—who nonetheless devoted dozens of pages of his book *The Women of New York* to breathless descriptions of the lives of such "harlots"—there was "no street so fashionable, no neighborhood so respectable, no avenue so aristocratic" that it did not contain a number of houses of ill-repute. Ellington despaired of what New York would become "in point of morals fifty or even twenty years hence" and fretted that "unless a mighty change takes place, it will out-Sodom Sodom." To an observer such as Victoria, however, the widespread condemnation of women who engaged in prostitution—but not the men who indulged in it—represented an inexcusable double standard. And it was one that she would stow in her memory and force before the eyes of the public in the years to come.

In 1868, however, she focused her attentions on making a mark of her own on her new home city. To do this she would turn to two individuals in particular—Cornelius Vanderbilt, the richest man in the United States, and Tennessee.

One of the sisters' aims in traveling east may have been to distance themselves from the other Claflins. Shortly after their arrival in New York, however, Victoria and Tennessee were joined by their parents and an array of other Claflin relatives. Another person to join the swelling numbers was someone who remained very much a part of the extended family business—Victoria's first husband, Canning Woodhull. With this troublesome cast of characters surrounding them once more, Tennessee and Victoria might feasibly have slipped back into their familiar roles as clairvoyant-healers, and this was, indeed, how they first established themselves in the city. By the autumn of that year, advertisements for a Magnetic Healing Institute and Conservatory of Spiritual Science, based at 17 Great Jones Street and staffed by Victoria, Tennessee, and Canning, began appearing in East Coast newspapers. Even in her earliest months in the city, though, Victoria had far grander plans.

Gaining an audience with the shipping and railway tycoon Cornelius Vanderbilt could be accomplished surprisingly easily. The formidable Commodore—whose nickname stemmed from his adolescent days ferrying passengers back and forth between Staten Island and Manhattan—kept his door open to unknown callers. Holding his attention was a greater challenge. Now in his seventies, he placed little value on social niceties and had a reputation for impatience and brusqueness. His usual greeting to those who mustered the courage to approach his bare one-room office on West Fourth Street, standing in the shadow of his mansion on Washington Place, is said to have been "Come! speak quick and be off!" But Victoria and Tennessee had prepared themselves well. Armed with knowledge of the Commodore's keen interest in Spiritualism—not to mention his well-publicized taste for attractive younger women—they had good reason to hope that he would not give them so quick a brush-off.

Their instincts proved right. According to Victoria's public recollections, when they arrived at his door, the Commodore liked what he saw. In Victoria's words, he immediately extended his hand "to aid two struggling women to battle with the world."

What conversation passed between the trio during this first meeting? Perhaps Victoria told him of the encounter with Demosthenes that had supposedly brought her and her family to New York City. Seventeen Great Jones Street stood only a short walk from the Commodore's residence, but although Victoria preferred to insist that the family's new home was a place she had known nothing of before their arrival in the city, this seems unlikely. It was in fact close to the miserable room in which her daughter, Zula, had been born just a few years before. One can well imagine the white-haired tycoon, unaware of this prior history, his eyes moving eagerly over these two beguiling women from rural Ohio. His interest, at least in terms of what Victoria would say in print, was one of "fatherly care and kindness," but this was far from the whole story. And while it is true that the Commodore had a prior interest in Spiritualism—motivated in large part by a wish to establish contact with his late mother and an adult son, George, who had died of tuberculosis—the sisters also held his attention for other reasons.

The Commodore's tough, entrepreneurial father had instilled in him a belief in the value of hard graft, and his son may have seen something of his own work ethic in the enterprising Victoria and Tennessee. What's more, the pair managed to combine their undisguised ambition and flair for business—traits more commonly associated with Victorian men than women—with pretty faces, a flirtatious manner, and considerable feminine allure. To New Yorkers acquainted with the Commodore, the sisters seemed to have come out of nowhere. But soon they could be found regularly dining with him and even advising him—with the aid of the spirits, naturally—on how he should invest his money.

"Why don't you do as I always do, and consult the spirits?" the Commodore was known to ask potential investors. To a woman of means who he hoped would put money into his own New York Central common stock, he offered the reassurance that Mrs. Woodhull had conveyed to him while "in a clairvoyant state" that it would "go up 22 percent within three months." Clearly it suited him to take Victoria at her word on this occasion, but he does seem to have placed genuine confidence in her advice more generally—much to the bemusement of the city's journalists. The fact that he was more willing to attribute her financial savvy to spirit guidance than business acumen speaks volumes about the extent to which female intellect was devalued. As in the case of Emma Hardinge's trance lecturing, it also demonstrates how relatively easy it was to gain audiences with powerful men by supposedly channeling the thoughts of masculine dead spirits. Without Spiritualism, such men would otherwise have been likely to ignore Victoria.

Whether due to spirits or not, the fact remains that, over the period of their collaboration, both the Commodore and Victoria would see their wealth increase. "It would seem that the mantle of the genial old Commodore has descended on their shoulders," a reporter remarked in 1870, looking back at how closely entwined the fortunes of the sisters and the famous industrialist had become. The Commodore still had ten surviving adult children, including two sons. The interest he took in these female protégées over four decades his junior alarmed the Vanderbilt clan. And although Victoria may have tried to claim that the attention he paid them was of a strictly paternal nature, rumors abounded that quite the opposite was true—particularly in the case of her younger sister.

Tennessee was then in her midtwenties. Despite the vast gulf in years between her and the septuagenarian Commodore, the pair began to spend evenings alone, giving rise to a belief that they were lovers. Tennessee is said to have used her magnetic healing hands on the Commodore to return him to a state of vitality and health. Years later, a family member described the Commodore bouncing Tennessee up and down on his lap as he went through the business of the day. She would apparently pull at his long white whiskers and tease him by calling him "old boy." His pet name for her was "little sparrow." A modern audience might feel that their sympathies ought to lie with Tennessee here—a young woman from a relatively poor background trying to make the best of her position within a patriarchal system. Others, and especially contemporary observers close to the Commodore, felt that he was the one being exploited.

The relationship filled the Vanderbilt children with displeasure, if not disgust. Their father had always been an exceptionally inattentive husband to his late wife, Sophia, a first cousin whom he had married when they were both in their early twenties. A serial philanderer, he'd once packed her off to Canada to get her out of the way so that he could pursue his children's governess away from Sophia's prying eyes. On another occasion, when Sophia refused to move from their old home in Staten Island to Manhattan, he'd had her committed to a lunatic asylum until she gave in to his demand. His offspring fared little better. Although he grieved the loss of his youngest son, George, who'd sustained the lung injury that would kill him during the Civil War, the Commodore regarded his surviving children with oft-expressed contempt. Sophia, despite the desolate state of the couple's marriage, may once have provided a safety net around their father's wealth. Following her death in August 1868, the children's concern grew more urgent.

While Tennessee concentrated her attentions on leveraging a power of sorts through her relationship with the Commodore, her older sister nurtured ever greater ambitions for the future. The dawn of 1869 brought with it the twelfth regular National Convention of Women's Rights, a successor to the Seneca Falls gathering of 1848. Victoria made the cold winter's journey from New York City to Washington, D.C., to attend the two-day event at that year's venue, Carroll Hall. As she would recall years later in a fragment of unpublished memoir, the convention, which drew representatives from some twenty states, took place in a highly charged period. The complex business of Reconstruction, spoken of so gravely by the late Lincoln during his fateful last speech, was now well under way, and the Fourteenth Amendment, which enshrined the civil rights of African Americans in law—though far less in practice—had been ratified. With a Fifteenth Amendment supporting the idea of a black male vote now being debated, the demands of female suffrage campaigners had also increased exponentially.

On the morning of January 19, Victoria walked into the crowded anteroom of Carroll Hall and took her place among the audience. Despite the distraction of a malfunctioning furnace, which sent noxious plumes of smoke curling around the room, she listened in rapt attention, feeling a sense of achievement to be seated with such distinguished company. Lucretia Mott—who at seventy-six was characterized by her supporters as "calm, dignified, clear and forcible as ever"—was duly elected president. Elizabeth Cady Stanton, Susan B. Anthony, and Frederick Douglass were among the luminaries who presided over the days' events. Among those who sent letters of regret that they could not attend were Caroline Healey Dall, Emma Hardinge's fellow campaigner for the rights of "fallen women," and Harriet Beecher Stowe, the celebrity author of the antislavery novel *Uncle Tom's Cabin*, the publishing sensation of the century.

Buoyed up by excitement, Victoria felt that female enfranchisement suddenly had become a real and imminent possibility. It had been "the dream of my life" to cast a marked paper in the ballot box, she mused, and now it seemed as if "Woman's day, was soon to materialize." Sitting there inhaling both the irritating smoke and radical ideas, Victoria listened to Senator Samuel C. Pomeroy from Kansas make an "able speech" in favor of suffrage for all American citizens, "black and white, male and female." As he talked, Victoria's private daydreams soared to new heights. It wasn't just the vote that she wanted: "visions of the offices I would hold" under this new system "danced" gaily through her mind.

Victoria's account of the day strikes an upbeat note, but the Washington convention would see its fair share of friction. Ever since suffrage for all American males, regardless of race, had begun to be discussed more widely, a split had developed between groups within the reform movement who had previously worked together in harmony. Campaigners such as Elizabeth Cady Stanton, now in her midfifties, felt adamant that the majority of African American men, whom she categorized as having little education or refinement, ought not to be granted the vote before women of a higher social class had achieved this right. Calling urgently for female enfranchisement, she lamented the folly of American statesmen, "claiming to be liberal," who were, she said, so willing to "amend their constitutions as to make their wives and mothers the political inferiors of unlettered and unwashed ditch-diggers, boot-blacks, butchers, and barbers, fresh from the slave plantations of the South, and the effete civilizations of the Old World." Singling out not just African American males but also poor immigrant men who had come to the United States to seek a better life, she continued: "On all the blackest pages of history there is no record of an act like this, in any nation, where native born citizens . . . have been politically ostracised by their own countrymen, outlawed with savages, and subjected to the government of outside barbarians."

Frederick Douglass and his supporters, both male and female, abhorred this view. As Victoria noted in her written record of the convention, he took an active part in the subsequent debate. About fifty years old at the time, he and the similarly aged Stanton had known each other for many years, but this was the first time that they had clashed in public. Employing the captivating rhetoric for which he'd become so well known, Douglass laid out his opposing argument. In a letter the previous autumn, he had written that a woman's right to vote was "as sacred in my judgment as that of a man." However, at a time when "the Negro" was being "mobbed, beaten, shot, stabbed, hanged, burnt and is the target of all that is malignant in the North and all that is murderous in the South," he felt bound to devote himself foremost to the campaign for black male suffrage—a cause if not "more sacred" then "certainly more urgent." The atmosphere at Carroll Hall must have been electric as other delegates—some sympathizing with Stanton, some with Douglass—weighed in with their own thoughts.

There is no record of Victoria, a minor entity within these circles, voicing her support for one side or the other, at least not to her fellow delegates. But as an increasingly well-known personality within New York City, her presence at the convention was noted by the press—and here a picture of a woman with strong opinions emerges.

On January 28, the New York City paper *The World* remarked on a complimentary piece that had appeared in *The Evening Star*, a publication based in Washington, D.C., which had predicted that Victoria "was destined to act no inferior part in coming conflicts and reforms in the country." *The World's* columnist, barely able to contain his excitement, it seems, assumed his readers would welcome more personal details about "this interesting woman," whom he had interviewed on several previous occasions. Adopting a tone not unlike that of early journalists who visited the Fox sisters at Barnum's Hotel, this reporter made much of Victoria's looks: her "face and form present a spectacle of bewildering loveliness."

"Mrs. Woodhull," he continued, "takes the most lively interest in all the genuine reforms of the day and entertains her own distinctive views ... She believes in woman most completely, but she also believes in man just as thoroughly. She has just been attending the National Female Suffrage Convention, but only partially agrees with the doings of that body." On this point *The World* deemed her particularly sound, and—in language reminiscent of that once used to fête the ascending Lincoln—it hailed her as the "Coming Woman."

Victoria returned to New York City much invigorated. Over the next months she kept a relatively low public profile, while behind the scenes she plotted what she would do next. It's likely that the presence of her parents continued to cause some concern. The journalist for *The World* had mentioned that not only had he interviewed Victoria on previous occasions, but he had also spoken with Buck and Annie Claflin—an illustration of the extent to which, even here in this East Coast metropolis, the couple remained involved in their daughters' lives. An uneasy truce appeared to exist between Victoria and Tennessee and the other Claflin family members who had followed them to New York City, but it would come undone some years later in a spectacularly public forum.

In the early months of 1869, though, the sisters largely focused on building their financial independence. While Tennessee continued her unusual relationship with Cornelius Vanderbilt, Victoria went on using her reputation as a spirit medium to enhance his business prospects. Taking advantage of her close proximity to the Commodore, the increasingly galvanized Victoria worked on absorbing all she could of his financial shrewdness in order to increase her own knowledge of his world of shares and stocks. That summer, however, brought with it an unforeseen event that might easily have thrown both sisters' plans into jeopardy.

Tennessee was not the only young woman who'd been on the Commodore's mind of late. He had begun a relationship with thirty-year-old Frank Armstrong Crawford, a distant female relative from Alabama. Despite the huge age gap between these two as well, the Vanderbilt children evidently felt that a family member who had been brought up in the society to which they themselves were accustomed was a much more suitable choice than the scandalous Tennessee. Though they couldn't have known much about her past life, the Vanderbilts could at least be certain that Tennessee's background was questionable. And so they encouraged the match between Frank and the Commodore, and in August of that year the couple married in a simple ceremony, across the border in Canada.

Although this could have spelled the end of relations between the sisters and the multimillionaire, both sides seem to have been keen to retain a bond. Perhaps the Commodore, usually so callous in his dealings with women, felt guilty for having slipped away to marry Frank in secret. But it is more likely that his next move was motivated by characteristic self-interest.

About a month after the marriage, panic fell upon the financial heart of New York City. Since the mid-nineteenth century, America's largely unregulated financial center had seen its might increasing. In the 1850s, the buildings on Wall Street had still comprised both business premises and domestic dwellings, but by now most families had relocated, leaving the heaving thoroughfare almost entirely to those who formed part of the rough-and-tumble world of the markets. In September 1869, Jay Gould, James Fisk, and Daniel Drew—all aggressive rail investors and Wall Street speculators with whom Cornelius Vanderbilt had longstanding rivalries—made an attempt to corner the gold market. Their strategy, which resulted in a huge hike followed by a sharp fall in the price of gold, led to mass panic among investors.

According to one of the city's papers, *The Sun*, September 22, 1869, saw an atmosphere of "wildest confusion and excitement" overtake the Gold Room of the New York Stock Exchange. By the next day, the drama heightened still further as, according to *The New York Herald*, "a shouting mass of brokers" watched in awe and horror as this supposedly safe commodity fluctuated wildly hour by hour. On September 24—to be memorialized in the history books as Black Friday—there was, in the words of the *Herald*, "Bedlam in the Gold Room" as the price of gold collapsed. "From some," said the paper, there "issued the wild cry of despair, others rushed from the room and sped through the streets like raving maniacs, while a number still clung to the ground refusing to believe the information." The *Herald* had little sympathy for these ruined investors, characterizing them as "thieves, caged in their own trap," but, as the paper was quick to note, from a day littered with heartbreaking losses for many, there had also emerged a number of victors.

Victoria would later recall coolly waiting out the days of the panic in a carriage parked up on the corner of Broad Street and Wall Street—a barely visible female presence, "operating heavily." Sitting there from morning until evening, this spot provided her with the perfect vantage point from which to take in the carnage. Messenger boys sprinted in and out of the secret cut-throughs that served as entry and exit points for the various company houses. Hordes of extra reporters jostled amid the sea of excited speculators, clad in thigh-length coats and top hats, who already crowded the streets. As time went on, the desperation increased: men who'd lost everything stumbling away from the scene of their financial collapse. A different kind of observer might have wrung her hands or shed a tear at their plight, but Victoria had not come here merely to spectate. Presumably using a male go-between to carry out her instructions, her purpose was to make money.

The key to success in an arena in which men all around her were sinking was timing, steel composure, and insider knowledge. Just as Victoria had previously furnished the Commodore with spirit-guided financial advice, now she was able to benefit from his own tips on when to buy gold and when to sell it. The Commodore would emerge triumphant from the wreckage of Black Friday, having reportedly made a killing due to wily maneuvering. Gould, one of the initiators of the disaster, used his own privileged sources of information to allow him to dispense with much of his gold while its value was still soaring high. His partners Fisk and Drew fared less well. Not privy to the same data as Gould, who saw no need to help his associates, they did not profit from the enterprise.

Exactly how much money Victoria made over the period surrounding Black Friday is unclear, but it was certainly substantial. Her claim to have amassed a staggering $700,000 during her time in New York City is probably exaggerated. Nonetheless, it is hard to disagree with her later self-judgment that, while others had seen their prospects crumble, she had emerged a "winner."

Interested parties wouldn't have long to wait to see just what she would do with her winnings. Four months later, this once-poor mother of two from rural Ohio would take those spoils and use them to leverage both herself and her sister into positions of previously unthinkable influence.

The Devil's Wife

On January 19, 1870, just four months after the tumultuous events of Black Friday, two fashionable yet simply dressed women appeared amid the sea of men that flowed across New York's financial district. The visible entrance of two female figures on Wall Street quickly attracted the attention of a hovering journalist from *The New York Herald*, who deemed their presence such a novelty that he alluded to this incredible materialization in his write-up of the day's financial business.

Given their taste for publicity, thirty-one-year-old Victoria Woodhull and her younger sister Tennessee Claflin surely enjoyed the lingering glances and hushed conversations that trailed in their wake. Few of the city's traders seemed to realize that they were Cornelius Vanderbilt's protégées, or that they now headed a brokerage firm called Woodhull, Claflin & Co., due to launch in a couple of weeks. Even the *Herald*'s reporter, who asked around among the crowd, could only glean that they came from the Hoffman House—a grand hotel on Madison Square, noted for its lavish decoration and the scent of scandal that pervaded its corridors. Over the weeks leading up to January 19, 1870, Victoria and Tennessee had leased hotel parlors Nos. 25 and 26 as a base from which to carry out their new enterprise.

Although the article in the *Herald* did not refer to them by name, the sisters recognized themselves at once. And, showing their typical flair for public relations, they dispatched two business cards to the newspaper's editor, each exquisitely engraved and printed on the finest-quality cardstock. They also enclosed a note stating that they "should be glad to make your personal acquaintance when convenient and agreeable."

The *Herald*, sensing a good story, sent one of their reporters to the Hoffman House, located on Broadway between Twenty-Fourth and Twenty-Fifth Streets. On being shown into parlor No. 25, the man found himself within a comfortable space that put him in mind of a "ladies' drawing room." Since neither sister had come in yet, he took the opportunity to scrutinize his surroundings, noting the imposing photograph of Commodore Vanderbilt staring down from the wall and a small picture frame containing the hymnal lyric "Simply to Thy Cross I Cling." The reporter mused on the notion that women, whom he characterized as naturally "cautious and calculating speculators," could take comfort in the fact that, even in such a merciless environment as Wall Street, they could at least "cling with a death grip to the cross."

Just then Tennessee entered the room. Coming in with a light step, this young woman in her midtwenties made an impression at once with her smile and businesslike manner, so very different from the cultivated meekness of many a Victorian lady.

Her visitor sounded a note of caution: "many persons of great experience and with large capital at their backs have been swamped" in the world of stock speculations.

Tennessee responded breezily, indicating that she and her older sister had more experience than he might assume. They had, she said by way of an example, "studied law" for several years in their father's office and now had the support of one of "the best backers in the city."

Taking the hint, the *Herald*'s man remarked, "I have been told that Commodore Vanderbilt is working in the interest of your firm. It is stated that you frequently call at his office in Fourth Street about business. Is this true?"

He must have found Tennessee's guarded answers frustratingly evasive, but before he could have another go, Victoria came in. She, like Tennessee, had dressed plainly again that day, although a single rose made an impact fastened into her dark hair. The reporter felt that Victoria had a more "sanguine, nervous temperament" than her sister, which he predicted—incongruously, given her recent history—might not stand up to a "serious financial shock." On the other hand, his subsequent article would remark on her "air of perfect nonchalance" when she talked of her present situation, her Black Friday successes, and future plans.

The *Herald*'s piece on this encounter with Tennessee and Victoria would make no mention of either sister's past as a clairvoyant healer or spirit medium. At least at this stage, and like Emma Hardinge a few years before, Victoria preferred not to linger on this side of herself when she talked to mainstream journalists. On the other hand, having regularly advertised her services as a medium in the pages of the Spiritualist press until the previous year, she continued to attract the interest of publications such as the highly influential *Banner of Light*, which had been running for thirteen years. But she had begun looking for other ways of getting her views across to a world that was increasingly ready to listen.

Newspaper coverage that followed the opening of the sisters' brokerage firm, on February 5, 1870, often adopted a patronizing or alarmist tone. Journalists labeled Victoria and Tennessee "The Bewitching Brokers" and "The Petticoat Financiers," while cartoonists produced images that reinforced the negative message that they were usurping the natural order. One caricature, from *Harper's Weekly*, depicted the two in an act of unfeminine strength, tugging insistently at the hat and jacket of a man who squirms to escape their clutches. Another parody, from *The Evening Telegram*, went a step further. Here, the women appeared in command of a carriage drawn by the "bears and bulls" of Wall Street, each animal wearing the male face of one of the city's best-known financial speculators. In this flurry of press interest, and despite their best efforts, Tennessee's past work as a clairvoyant physician came back to haunt her—something that she tried to play down. Rather than acknowledging the criminal charge that still hung over her from her days in Illinois, she insisted that she had been "a very good doctor," and that she had healed "a much larger percentage of my patients than the regular M.D.s."

Despite such adversity, Woodhull, Claflin & Co. proved popular, especially with well-heeled female clients. The firm's new permanent headquarters, at 44 Broad Street, around the corner from Wall Street, was kitted out with the latest office equipment, including a telegraphic stock ticker that indicated the price of commodities. Female investors particularly appreciated the private room at the rear of the building, where they could discuss money matters away from the attentions of men. Unsurprisingly, Victoria and Tennessee also had their fair share of male visitors. Some men called out of sheer curiosity, others to offer friendly advice or to cast a grim, silent stare over a scene previously unimaginable to them.

The politician Richard Schell warned the sisters that they stood to lose more money than they made, and well-known banker and broker W. R. Travers echoed these sentiments in his distinctive lisping tone. But Victoria firmly retorted that she and Tennessee "did not come to Wall street to lose money but to make money," and that, should everything go according to plan, it would be Travers who would lose money due to the sisters' competition. The Commodore's longtime rival Daniel Drew, in contrast, had more faith in the women and left their offices impressed.

Unsurprisingly, news of the emergence of Woodhull, Claflin & Co. interested stalwarts of the women's movement. In March, Susan B. Anthony came to visit the new company, seeking an interview with its owners for an article to be published in *The Revolution*, the weekly paper she ran with Elizabeth Cady Stanton. Making her way along Wall Street, passing eye-catching stalls selling "great red apples, pears, bananas, oranges, figs, and the earliest and sweetest maple sugar," the fifty-year-old Susan, her center-parted hair pulled back from her face in a bun, wryly observed that men really did get "the best of everything." She also noted that women were such a rarity in these parts that passersby seemed unable to resist the temptation to stare at any woman who was not one of the stallholders.

When Susan arrived at 44 Broad Street, Victoria appears to have been unavailable. Tennessee, however—dressed that day in plain blue set off with black wool and black feathers—made her visitor welcome. Asked what had brought the sisters into such a masculine world, she explained that it was "the necessity for earning a livelihood," and also her and Victoria's "unfitness for the slow, dreary methods by which women usually earn a living." Most Wall Street figures, Tennessee claimed, had been kind and welcoming, although "there are a few of the 'small potatoes' sort of men, who never mention the name of any woman, even their own mother, with respect; who sneer, and try to get off their poor jokes upon us, but that doesn't hurt us, and it will only last a little while." In keeping with her sister's earlier show of confidence, Tennessee predicted that the pair would soon be just part of the ordinary world of Wall Street, and, therefore, no longer worthy of special attention. Susan, turning to the recent press coverage, suggested that the two had "got off very easy" so far, since the papers had "had nothing very dreadful to say against you."

A modern reader might beg to differ, but when one thinks of contemporary levels of sexism, this judgment was perhaps not so unreasonable. Either way, journalists certainly could not get enough of the exploits of Tennessee and Victoria.

Susan left 44 Broad Street "feeling a great throb of pleasure" and brimming with hope for "better times to come for women—times when they shall vote the right to put food into their mouths, and money in their pockets, without asking men's leave."

Not for another half century would all women in the United States be granted the vote—yet, just two months after the opening of the sisters' brokerage firm, Victoria made a startling announcement that filled the city's pressmen with astonishment, mirth, and horror.

On the morning of April 2, two months after the opening of Woodhull, Claflin & Co., readers of *The New York Herald* woke to the news that the "lady broker of Broad street" currently disrupting the world of high finance was planning to run for the highest office in the land. The next presidential election lay two and a half years away, ample time for Victoria to make serious headway with the electorate, the *Herald* opined, *if*—and this was a huge if—the female vote had been granted by then. But the bold tone of Victoria's message did little to endear her to many women—particularly prominent feminist campaigners who might otherwise have thrown their weight behind her.

Casting herself as "the most prominent representative of the only unrepresented class in the republic," Victoria immediately set up a distinction between herself and others also pushing for greater equality. While they "devoted themselves to a crusade against the laws that shackle the women of the country," she said, she had instead asserted her "individual Independence; while others prayed for the good time coming, I worked for it." She had, she continued, proved herself in business, and now that she had entered the world of politics, she would prove herself there as well. Well aware that her announcement would "evoke more ridicule than enthusiasm at the outset," she said that times were changing and that the "rising tide of reform" could not be rolled back.

In addition to highlighting the pressing need to enfranchise women, this, Victoria's first campaign statement, laid out other concerns. These included the need for penal reform, particularly in terms of the welfare of families of criminals, and a more aggressive foreign policy, especially regarding the Spanish government, which controlled neighboring Cuba. Arguing that the United States did too much bowing to foreign powers, Victoria sought to stir up populist anger by suggesting that American citizens were regularly being murdered abroad by "Spanish cutthroats." She was equally adamant—conveniently, for a newly wealthy woman like herself— that "No special interest ... should be singled out to sustain an extra proportion of taxation" needed to settle the country's public debt.

By this stage, two other candidates, neither associated with major political parties, had thrown their hats into the ring. These were the eccentric Daniel Pratt Jr., characterized by the *Herald* as the "Bohemian candidate," and entrepreneur and traveler George Francis Train, whose adventures were said later to have inspired Jules Verne's as yet unpublished *Around the World in Eighty Days*. Train had defended Irish independence, and the *Herald* classified him as the "Fenian candidate." The paper wondered whether they should next have an "African candidate," such as Frederick Douglass, or even a "Chinese labor candidate." Still, despite such sarcasm, the *Herald* seemed predisposed to support Victoria's candidacy, saying that she had "all the advantages that point to success."

It would go on to publish several more laudatory pieces about Victoria's presidential ambitions, but the response of most of the city's newspapers, as well as those around the country, ranged from bewildered surprise to outright derision. *The Maryland Union* called Victoria's announcement "a curiosity," while Virginia's *Alexandria Gazette* lampooned her writing style. An article in *The Providence Evening Press* of Rhode Island also played the news for laughs, stating that "without sufficient intellect to lecture or write in her own cause," Victoria was relying "upon money to carry her along successfully."

Money was certainly in plentiful supply. Having taken on the lease of a brownstone mansion at 15 East Thirty-Eighth Street in upscale Murray Hill, Victoria had also committed to spending a fortune on her political campaign. Still, even with such wealth at her disposal, she must have felt it abundantly clear that, to counteract the swell of more negative press coverage, she'd have to find a mouthpiece of her own.

To that end, on May 14, 1870, Victoria and her sister launched *Woodhull & Claflin's Weekly*. *The New York Herald* called it "excellent," while the Spiritualist *Banner of Light* described it as "a well-edited, well-printed sixteen page paper, which completely demonstrates what women of *vim* can accomplish when they assume an independent position." In the first issue, Victoria and Tennessee committed themselves to working in "the vital interests of the people" and to treating "all matters freely without reservation." The paper would support Victoria's bid for the presidency "with its whole strength" but would otherwise be "untrammelled by party or personal considerations." Never ones to shy away from controversy, a year and a half later they'd publish *The Communist Manifesto* for the first time in English in the United States.

As with their banking and brokerage firm, the sisters were the public faces of *Woodhull & Claflin's Weekly*, but several other individuals—such as the anarchist Stephen Pearl Andrews and the man known as Victoria's husband, Colonel Blood—did much of the day-to-day legwork. The extent to which the couple focused their energies on building Victoria's public reputation meant that she was often away from her children. Zulu was under ten years old, and Byron's disability meant that, although he'd now reached his late teens, he still needed constant support. Enthusiastic though he was to express himself with mutterings and moans, he would never acquire sufficient language skills to communicate effectively. Victoria's first biographer would paint a picture of him wandering aimlessly from room to room, while charming all who encountered him with the "uncommon sweetness of his temper." As in the past, Victoria's extended family may have helped care for the children. Thanks to her considerable fortune, she could also presumably call on an army of household staff. Additionally, she was still able to lean on Canning, who remained in New York City, and who, when he was not too much the worse for wear from drink, continued to share responsibility for the two children. Although Victoria had long presented herself as divorced from her first husband—whether legally or not is uncertain—his involvement in her life remained such that he had ended up ensconced with her, their children, and the Colonel at their grand new residence on Murray Hill.

Fifteen East Thirty-Eighth Street was a far cry indeed from the squalid conditions in which Victoria, assisted so ineptly by Canning, had brought Byron and Zulu into the world. The house—home also to Tennessee, Buck and Annie, and various Claflin hangers-on— functioned both as a private residence and a public-facing "ladies' clubhouse." It was a place where Victoria could socialize with her brokerage firm's wealthy clientele and strengthen her connections with the kind of individuals who might help her in her bid for the presidency.

A visiting journalist from *The World* granted a tour of the building in September 1870 left in a state of ecstasy. On passing through the huge black walnut front door, he encountered a grand eighty-foot room in the basement adorned with crystal chandeliers and a paneled ceiling "frescoed with Cupids and Psyches in blue, white, and gold." The kitchen boasted all manner of modern conveniences, including four large ovens and—decades before they became a common domestic feature—an enormous refrigerator. Up a sweeping mahogany staircase, he found parlors furnished with carved marble mantelpieces, Etruscan vases, an inch-thick Brussels carpet, and a seven-and-a-half-octave grand piano. White chairs edged in gold and antique blue moiré made sumptuous seating spots. There was an indoor garden replete with hothouse flowers, fish swimming in tanks, an aviary, and a fountain. "The green leaves, the glowing colors, and the fragrance-burdened air" made one "imagine that some marvellous magician had transported the singing birds, spice smells, and laughing water of the Orient" to this palatial home.

Allowing Canning—not to mention the various Claflin relatives—into this self-created Eden could be interpreted as an act of charity. Victoria would call her generosity to her first husband "one of the most virtuous acts of my life." Others would come to regard it instead as a case of an already disconcertingly unconventional woman daring to outrage accepted standards of decency by living with two spouses under one roof.

For the time being, while Victoria's unusual domestic setup remained a largely private matter, she continued to concentrate on bolstering her public persona. On December 21, 1870, the official record of the proceedings of Congress notes the submission of a petition in her name. Known as a "memorial," the document stated that she was "praying for the passage of such laws as may be necessary" to allow all citizens to vote "without regard to sex." January 1871 saw her in Washington, D.C., in person, accompanied by Tennessee, to appear before the House Judiciary Committee. In the days leading up to this historic appearance, the pair had put in considerable time ingratiating themselves with male politicians sympathetic to their cause—and, as the papers strongly hinted, susceptible to their charms. Despite the severe misgivings of many within the women's rights movement, some of its most prominent campaigners were at her side when she made her address to Congress.

The *New-York Tribune* remarked that, as Victoria talked, Susan B. Anthony, seated behind her and wearing a black velvet gown, kept "smiling graciously, and marking off elocutionary pauses with a benign finger." Elizabeth Cady Stanton was also in attendance, as was suffragist Isabella Beecher Hooker, the younger sister of *Uncle Tom's Cabin* author Harriet Beecher Stowe. Isabella, initially distrustful of Victoria's reputation and motives, had ultimately decided that working with her would be better than pitting herself against her.

Speeches by women before Congress were not unheard-of in the 1870s, but they remained rare enough to generate a great deal of press interest. Coverage, however, tended to focus more on the colorful spectacle than on the arguments put forward. *The Press* of Philadelphia lingered on Isabella's "soft, fleecy curls tied down with orthodox precision; the curling feathers of blue harmonizing with her peachy complexion" and on Susan B. Anthony's "smart new dress of black silk, with velveteen overskirt and fancy basque." The unconventional fashions favored by Tennessee and Victoria seemed daring in the extreme. *The Press* commented on the "masculine" coattails of the sisters' jackets and their hair, which they wore clipped short beneath their "brigandish" sugarloaf hats.

According to *The Evening Telegraph*, also of Philadelphia, "The committee was very favorably impressed" with the arguments made by Victoria and some of the other women—although not impressed enough to take any real action to address their grievances. Still, in terms of firming up her political standing, this had been a fruitful trip for Victoria. Back at home, invitations to make further speeches at prestigious New York City venues came thick and fast. Her star appeared to be ascending ever higher.

In early May 1871, the Labor Reform League asked her to speak at the Cooper Union, where Emma Hardinge had given her *Great Funeral Oration on Abraham Lincoln* six years before. A few days later, Victoria appeared at the opening day of the National Woman Suffrage Association (NWSA) convention, an article in *The New York Times* giving her headline billing alongside Elizabeth Cady Stanton and Isabella Beecher Hooker.

However, some within the NWSA, formed two years before, still had their doubts about Victoria. And even before her keynote speech to the audience, the press had begun to associate her political platform with sensation and scandal. Horace Greeley's *New-York Tribune* had reprinted alarming passages from *Woodhull & Claflin's Weekly*, which endorsed the notion of so-called free love by comparing the position of wives in loveless marriages to that of prostitutes, suggesting that *"all love to be holy must be free."* Wary delegates must have hoped that, at the convention, Victoria would tread a more cautious path. Instead, her words from the podium built on these controversial ideas by calling for women to fiercely resist the control of men—a daring opinion that further excited the press. The rival American Woman Suffrage Association, also formed in 1869, rushed to judgment, and some members of the NWSA also voiced their disagreement with Victoria's views. Newspaper readers wrote letters expressing their disgust, one woman demanding to know how "any pure wife and mother [can] read the infamous extracts published in yesterday's paper and not enter their protest. I blush to think I am a woman."

Although celebrated by some within the suffrage movement, for others, Victoria's presence at the convention had ended up as an unwelcome distraction. Problematically for the NWSA, which had closely aligned itself with her, there was no option for Victoria to slink temporarily away to the shadows. And as this drama reached its peak, another even more damaging storm was brewing.

A week and a half before the convention, Essex Market Police Court had issued a warrant for the arrest of James Harvey Blood. Victoria's mother, Annie Claflin, alleged that the Colonel had attacked and threatened to kill her—a claim that her famous daughters disputed. They had appeared at the courthouse the following day to state that the Colonel, who continued to suffer with multiple war-induced health issues, was the victim of a blackmailing scam by Annie and that he would appear the following day to post bail.

On May 15, with Victoria's speech at the suffrage convention still fresh in people's minds, her mother and Colonel Blood made their way to court. The possibility of catching a glimpse of the well-known banking sisters ensured an unusually large crowd, but on this first day neither Tennessee nor Victoria showed up. Nonetheless, those at the hearing listened eagerly to the opening arguments.

Annie, now in her sixties, alleged that, in addition to the attempt on her life, the Colonel had kept up a sustained campaign against her, using various "wicked and magic arts and devices" to alienate her from her daughters.

"Judge," said Annie, "my daughters were good daughters and affectionate children till they got in with this man"—here she paused to give particular emphasis to his name—"Blood." The Colonel, she continued, had threatened her with violence on several occasions, once coming at night into the mansion they all lived in and telling her that he would not go to bed until he had "washed his hands in my blood."

Lines such as these must have seemed a gift to reporters. Fearing that proceedings could become a circus, lawyers for both sides attempted to persuade Annie to tone down her florid language, to no avail. "S'help me God, Judge, I say here and I call Heaven to witness," she declared, "there was the worst gang of free lovers in that house in Thirty-eighth Street that ever lived."

As she began to reel off names, her counsel cut her off unceremoniously: "Keep quiet, old lady." Reluctantly, Annie agreed to hold her tongue, while bitterly complaining that she wanted "to tell the Judge what these people are."

Mary Sparr, a married older sister of Victoria's who'd also been living at the house, gave evidence next. Mary backed up her mother, adding that the Colonel had once been so violent with Annie that Victoria had "tried to take him away by the neck."

The Colonel denied all the allegations, although he did admit to finding Annie "very annoying at times." On one occasion "when she was very troublesome," he acknowledged that he had said that, were she not his mother-in-law, he would "turn her over my knee and spank her," a remark that, though it may have been meant flippantly, is unsettling to modern ears, and raises more questions than it answers.

"Would you really do that?" Annie's lawyer asked. The Colonel declined to respond.

He again kept his silence when Annie's lawyer, inquiring about the unusual living arrangements at 15 East Thirty-Eighth Street, asked, "Do you and Mrs. Woodhull and Dr. Woodhull occupy the same room?" The Colonel's counsel jumped in and encouraged him to tell the court why Canning lived there. To this, the Colonel alluded to Byron's disability and explained that the young man's father helped out with his care.

The following morning, extensive reports of the afternoon's proceedings appeared in *The New York Herald*, along with the thrilling news that Victoria and Tennessee would appear to give evidence that day. Long before their arrival, crowds made up of all strata of society began to fill the courthouse. Those gathered "seemed to feel as though their own importance in the community was enhanced by any connection with the leading actors," a reporter noted. They "thronged the passage ways, pressed against the railings and stood on the benches in their eager avidity to see and hear the heroines of the hour."

At last, Victoria and Tennessee turned up, dressed in black silk suits and with the hats that covered their short curls arranged at jaunty angles. Colonel Blood accompanied them, plus Canning, four servants, and legal counsel.

The court called Victoria first. She said that she'd never felt that her husband posed any kind of danger to Annie. In words that bring to mind Victoria's characterization of past terrors of her childhood, she claimed that, on the contrary, Annie would sometimes abuse the Colonel "frightfully, as if she were possessed by some fiend." Having lived with the couple for the past three years, Victoria said, Annie had left the house on April 1. She'd been staying at the Washington Hotel since, with Woodhull, Claflin & Co. settling all her bills. Victoria went on to suggest that Annie's erratic behavior marked her as insane. "Sometimes she would come down to the table and sit on Mr. Blood's lap and say he was the best son-in-law she had. Then again she would abuse him like a thief, calling him all the names she could lay her tongue to, and otherwise venting her spleen—all without any cause whatsoever." Her mother's real motive, Victoria said, was to release Tennessee from the protection of her older sister, so that the former childhood clairvoyant could go back to "going around the country telling fortunes."

Throughout her testimony, Victoria remained reserved. In contrast, when Tennessee took the witness stand she smiled and gave some appealing glances to the gathered reporters. She agreed with Victoria that the Colonel had shown no violence toward Annie. In fact, Tennessee said, "I don't see how he stood all her abuse." Talking about her own itinerant youth, she recalled that she had been telling fortunes from the age of eleven, but that "Viccy and Colonel Blood got me away from that life, and they are the best friends I ever had." Of the brood of Claflins she and Victoria supported, Tennessee said, "Since I was fourteen years old I have kept thirty or thirty-five deadheads. I am a clairvoyant; I am a Spiritualist; I have power, and I know my power. Many of the best men in the street know my power." Commodore Vanderbilt, she added, knew her power.

Tennessee, it seems, was going off-script here, drawing attention to the sisters' work as clairvoyants and spiritual healers—and, indirectly, the Magnetic Healing Institute that had operated even from their home in New York City. What's more, she was presenting the pair's Spiritualism not as something confined to the past but as an important part of their present and the source of much of their current influence.

Having veered off-course to this extent, Tennessee became more emotional. Even if Annie had tacitly supported Buck's past exploitation of his daughter, she would always hold a special place in Tennessee's affections, and today was no exception. Suddenly, she burst out, "Judge, I want my mother. I am willing to take my mother home with me now, or pay two hundred dollars a month for her in any safe place. I am afraid she will die under this excitement . . ." At this, she rushed to Annie and the two embraced, kissing—an unforeseen act that makes one wonder whether, loyal though she was to her sister, Tennessee may have believed at least some of Annie's accusations.

Several more witnesses were called to the stand. The servants brought to the hearing that day all stuck to the line that Victoria, Tennessee, and the Colonel were "nice, quiet people, and never injured in any way the complainant." The judge closed proceedings, withholding his decision. Victoria, Tennessee, and the Colonel rushed away in a carriage, while Annie left supported by her daughter Mary and Mary's husband, and Canning walked slowly away from the courthouse alone.

Canning was now a part of the public story of his former wife's life, however, and this would continue to chip away at her political image, especially since it seemed to fit so neatly with the scandalous image of Victoria as a free lover. Although the judge ended up dismissing the case brought by Annie, talk about Canning's presence in the house would linger long after her accusations of male violence—and even Tennessee's revelations about her power as a Spiritualist—had disappeared from the minds of many.

Now on the defensive, Victoria decided to retaliate in letters to *The New York Times* and *The World*. She had been vilified, she wrote, "because I am a woman, and because I conscientiously hold opinions somewhat different from the self-elected orthodoxy which men find their profit in supporting." She did not intend to be made a scapegoat, especially since she knew that many of her "self-appointed judges and critics," while hypocritically condemning her in public, were themselves "deeply tainted with the vices they condemn." In fact, she said, she knew of "one man, a public teacher of eminence, who lives in concubinage with the wife of another public teacher of almost equal eminence."

This last statement wasn't so much a private observation as an obvious hint: although most readers would have been unaware of the love triangle Victoria spoke of, the individuals she alluded to were only too familiar to them.

In fact, such was the obviousness of her insult that one of the three recognized himself immediately. On the same day that the letters appeared, Theodore Tilton, the "teacher of almost equal eminence," rushed down to the offices of Woodhull, Claflin & Co. to confront Victoria. According to her later recollections, this strikingly handsome man in his midthirties with flowing auburn hair came storming into 44 Broad Street with a copy of the letter, demanding, "Whom do you mean by that?"

Victoria calmly replied that the men she referred to were himself and the famous preacher Henry Ward Beecher, half-brother of Isabella Beecher Hooker.

Victoria had heard rumors of the affair between the Reverend Beecher and Theodore's wife, Elizabeth, from contacts within women's suffrage circles, including Elizabeth Cady Stanton. Victoria explained that Henry's celebrated status as a moral guardian made her determined to bring his double standards "to the knowledge of the world."

Theodore's rage was quelled when he realized that the focus of Victoria's aims was Henry rather than himself. He invited her to meet Elizabeth—who, like her husband, was a member of Henry's Plymouth Church congregation. For Elizabeth's sake, Theodore said, he had "allowed that rascal to go unscathed. I have curbed my feelings when every impulse urged me to throttle and strangle him."

Victoria let Theodore know how much it angered her that Henry appeared to be living one life in private while preaching the values of quite another from the pulpit. All well and good, perhaps, but she also had a prior grievance with Henry as a member of the

Beecher clan: in the months leading up to Victoria's coded jibe, two of Henry's well-known sisters had gone out of their way to make her life uncomfortable.

In January 1871, the month she'd appeared before Congress, *Woodhull & Claflin's Weekly* had published an article attacking Henry's oldest sister, Catharine, for her opposition to female suffrage. Like Henry, Catharine Beecher was well known throughout the country—in her case chiefly as the founder of the Hartford Female Seminary, which pioneered educational opportunities for young women, and through her wildly popular books on household management, such as *A Treatise on Domestic Economy* and *The American Woman's Home*, the latter written with her even more famous sister, Harriet Beecher Stowe.

The seventy-year-old Catharine would not take Victoria's criticism lying down. She arranged to meet the younger woman for a carriage ride in the mock-pastoral surroundings of New York's newly opened Central Park—a meeting that would do nothing to smooth relations and served only to increase the animosity between them. Catharine's sister Harriet then got involved. The bestselling author of *Uncle Tom's Cabin* had cast Victoria as a character, the morally lacking Audacia Dangyereyes, in her novel *My Wife and I*, then enjoying a serialized run in a periodical, *The Christian Union*, published by Henry.

Taking on the might of a family as famous and respected as the Beechers at a time when she was attempting to build a serious reputation as a presidential candidate speaks volumes about Victoria's unswerving self-confidence. It was also reckless in the extreme—now that she had taken this step, there could be no going back.

Victoria followed up on the hints she'd dropped in *The New York Times* and *The World* by cultivating a strong working relationship, and perhaps something more, with Theodore Tilton. The two

Corinthian Hall, the scene in 1849 of the Fox sisters' first public demonstration of the mysterious knockings. *Photo courtesy of the Collection of the Local History & Genealogy Division, Rochester Public Library (New York)*

Lithograph of the famous Fox sisters, Maggie, Kate, and Leah. *Photo courtesy of the Department of Rare Books, Special Collections, and Preservation, River Campus Libraries, University of Rochester (New York)*

Emma Harding, then in her early twenties, performing as the Queen of the Wilis in *The Phantom Dancers. Photo courtesy of the Victoria and Albert Museum, London*

Emma Hardinge (now with an *e*), photographed by spirit photographer William
H. Mumler. *Photo courtesy of the National Film and Sound Archive of Australia*

Victoria Woodhull, who was noted for her distinctive sense of style. *Photo courtesy of the New York Public Library*

"GET THEE BEHIND ME, (MRS.) SATAN!"—[SEE PAGE 143.]
WIFE (with heavy burden). "I'D RATHER TRAVEL THE HARDEST PATH OF MATRIMONY THAN FOLLOW YOUR FOOTSTEPS."

1872 *Harper's Weekly* cartoon by Thomas Nast, depicting Victoria Woodhull as Mrs. Satan. *Photo courtesy of the Library of Congress*

Georgina Treherne—a double portrait by George Frederic Watts, c. 1856. *Photo courtesy of the Watts Gallery Trust*

Pears advertisement featuring the famous campaigner and Spiritualist Georgina Weldon. *Photo courtesy of Chronicle / Alamy Stock Photo*

were later said to have been lovers. Certainly they spent a great deal of time together, and in 1871, during her presidential campaign, he wrote the commemorative pamphlet *The Biography of Victoria C. Woodhull.* In the florid prose common to many such works of the time, Theodore praised his subject as "one of the sincerest, most reverent, and divinely-gifted of human souls."

In addition to collaborating with Theodore, Victoria pushed her biographer, who maintained an understandably strained relationship with Henry, to arrange a meeting between the three of them. On coming face to face with the famous preacher, Victoria tried to convince him that it would be in his interests, as well as hers, to introduce her at a talk she was due to give on November 20 at New York City's Steinway Hall. Her topic would be "The Principles of Social Freedom," and it would cover some of the same controversial material for which she'd already become well known. Henry reacted to the suggestion with horror. Nonetheless, up until the night of the event, Victoria—standing backstage twisting her rolled-up notes between her hands—held out hope that he might make an appearance to support her. Once it became clear that he would not show up, Theodore agreed to do the honors instead.

Victoria then stepped onto the stage, dressed in black with a watch chain pendant around her neck and a fresh tea rose fastened at her throat. A huge cheer erupted. Tennessee sat in one of the theater's boxes, willing her on. In a separate box sat another of Victoria's younger sisters, Utica Brooker, who—though not present for their mother's legal action against the Colonel that May—had since been supporting Annie Claflin. As such, relations between Utica and Victoria were already strained.

Victoria opened her long speech by giving her general views on the need for individual choice. Initially, the audience reacted with broad enthusiasm, but when she moved to the subject of sexual relations between married couples, many of the young men present fell into raucous applause, causing embarrassment among older members of the crowd. Victoria then went further by proclaiming that since "law cannot compel two to love," if law has "anything to do with marriage" then "love has nothing to do with it." This led to more cheers but also hisses of protest.

Although Victoria hastened to add that relations within "a very large proportion" of marriages were "commendable," she also painted a gruesome picture of the lot of many wives as something akin to that of helpless prostitutes. "All which is good and commendable, now existing, would continue to exist if all marriage laws were repealed to-morrow," she declared. Nearly half of the audience rose to its feet to protest. The rest continued to applaud.

Theodore, fearing that the situation could become desperate, endeavored to instill some calm.

Victoria, too, tried to get a hold of the situation by inviting anyone now loudly voicing their displeasure to join her on the platform to "define their principles fairly."

But this time she was interrupted by her sister Utica, who, to the delight of many, stood up in her box above the stage and shouted, "How could you expect to be recognized in society unless you knew who your mother or father was?"

To this Victoria called back, "I assert that there are as good and noble men and women on top of this earth suffering from the stain of illegitimacy as any man or woman before me."

The noise from the crowd became so deafening that it drowned out the words of both sisters. A police officer entered the box where Utica stood and attempted—unsuccessfully—to drag her away. The house seemed on the verge of a riot. "Yes! I am a free lover!" Victoria suddenly shouted. "I believe I have an inalienable right to change my husband every day if I like. I trust I am understood, for I mean what I say and nothing else. I claim that freedom means to be free."

Somehow, despite the ensuing outrage, she managed to quell the raucous calls. Even Utica, resignedly, sat down. In control of the room again, Victoria brought her speech to a conclusion with what *The New York Herald* would judge as "an eloquent peroration, strongly advocating the cause of free love." Utica, on her feet in an instant to raise further objections, was shouted and laughed down by the audience, which slowly dispersed.

Victoria might have won over a sizable number of attendees that evening, but her wider public reputation suffered significantly as a result of subsequent press reports. Her "Yes! I am a free lover!" ran and ran, and the tone of the coverage became ever more critical. In response, she tried to cement her standing among specific, often radical groups. These included the American Association of Spiritualists, who had elected her as president of their organization in Troy, New York, in late September 1871; those women's rights activists within the NWSA who had not shied away; and Karl Marx's International Workingmen's Association (IWA), which she and Tennessee had joined earlier in the year. In December the sisters, along with Theodore Tilton, Stephen Pearl Andrews, and Colonel Blood, were among the men and women who marched through New York City to honor those massacred in the Paris Commune that May. Many more curious spectators lined the route, the presence of the sisters causing great excitement, especially among the young men present, who attempted to bait them with such lines as "Let me through, I'm a free lover." Their male companions did their best to shield the women from the jeers and laughter, and Victoria and Tennessee are said to have behaved with dignity, not allowing themselves to be riled.

The sisters' credentials as wealthy female pioneers in the world of banking were clearly an uneasy fit with the ideals of communist IWA members whom they marched alongside. At the same time, the women's association with Karl Marx and his supporters was cause for suspicion among their former friends on Wall Street. A speech delivered by Victoria in February 1872 at the Academy of Music in New York City only served to stoke the animosity. Once again, the press painted a picture of a rambunctious full house—so crowded that fashionable ladies lost their bonnets in the scrum and were "forced to stand up packed like herrings in a barrel." Some fainted and had to be carried out of the auditorium. True to form, Victoria made various incendiary proclamations, including describing Christ as a kind of proto-communist and roundly lambasting the country's biggest business tycoons. Even the old Commodore did not escape her blaming finger. "A Vanderbilt," she said, "may sit in his office and manipulate stocks, or make dividends, by which, in a few years, he amasses fifty millions dollars from the industries of the country, and he is one of the remarkable men of the age. But if a poor, half-starved child were to take a loaf of bread from his cupboard, to prevent starvation, she would be sent, first to the Tombs, and thence to Blackwell's Island"— referring to the site of a notorious prison and asylum.

The response from an already hostile press was to accuse Victoria of hypocrisy and attack her character. *The New York Times* called her "an eminently foolish woman." The jibe followed a soon-to-be-infamous cartoon in *Harper's Weekly*: Thomas Nast's celebrated illustration portrays Victoria with horns and wings, and carrying a sign emblazoned BE SAVED BY FREE LOVE. She stands on craggy ground, a few steps ahead of a staggering woman carrying her drunken husband and several children. The accompanying caption reads: "Get thee behind me, (Mrs.) Satan." The downtrodden wife tells Victoria, "I'd rather travel the hardest path of matrimony than follow your footsteps."

The subject of Victoria's own marital past returned to the head-lines again following the death of Canning Woodhull on April 7. De-spite Victoria's past negative depictions of her former husband, the obituary published in *Woodhull & Claflin's Weekly* took a moment to mention his achievements as a physician and speak of the import-ant place he held within her family. Unfortunately for a woman in the middle of a political campaign, the press showed more interest in the way he died, from the pneumonia that had taken hold of a body worn down by alcohol and also opium addiction. Victoria's sister Utica made much in public of the fact that he had been self-medicating with the drug and that his doctors' decision to withhold it had hastened his miserable passing—such details adding a further air of tawdriness to public perceptions of Victoria's homelife.

On the campaign trail, Victoria had the backing, most of the time, of Elizabeth Cady Stanton, with whom she would keep up a friendship for many years to come. Susan B. Anthony, on the other hand, had grown distrustful, opposing all suggestions that the NWSA officially endorse Victoria's presidential candidacy. Victoria launched her election campaign at a convention held in May 1872, as the leader of the Equal Rights Party. By then, journalists had begun casting her supporters and the NWSA as opposing sides. *The New York Herald* noted that "the old faces that are usually atten-dant on women's conventions did not show up" to Victoria's launch event. Instead, "many strange looking people" took their places that morning, clutching "green cotton umbrellas, and satchels containing large and healthy lunches on their knees."

Victoria's radical platform for election included her party's de-mand for a complete overhaul of government institutions, the insis-tence that all important legislation be put to a people's referendum before becoming law, that monopolies be abolished and the govern-ment step in to manage large public enterprises. She also proposed greater regulation to protect workers' rights and an end to capital punishment, and insisted that "minorities, as well as majorities, should have representation in government."

Later that day, however, the question of whom to elect as vice president caused controversy. One delegate's suggestion of Frederick Douglass—neither in attendance at the convention nor a party member—drew shouts of both "Yes, yes" and "No, no." Several people called out alternative suggestions: the famous Spiritualist Robert Dale Owen, Theodore Tilton, and—ironically, given Victoria's private campaign against him—Henry Ward Beecher. These were followed by further endorsements for Douglass. There were also objections, some unmistakably racist, with a few headlines echoing such sentiments the following day: the *Herald* spoke of the prospect of a "Piebald Presidency," and the Oregon paper *The Guard* slammed the putative running mates as "A Shameless Prostitute and a Negro."

Although some of the coverage was positive, Victoria's once unstoppable ascent began not just to drag but to slide irreversibly downhill. Whether or not Frederick Douglass acknowledged his nomination in private, he never appeared by her side in public or tendered an official acceptance. Coupled with these difficulties, Victoria now had money problems. Running a political campaign was expensive, and she was still supporting her extended family. Her once flourishing business, Woodhull, Claflin & Co., had been faring poorly of late; her anticapitalist pronouncements had caused alarm on Wall Street, with Commodore Vanderbilt withdrawing financial support at a time when creditors' notices had begun swirling. Karl Marx and the IWA would also cut links with her.

Victoria's glorious lifestyle at East Thirty-Eighth Street came to an abrupt end, and she and those relatives who still lived with her decamped to more modest dwellings. In June 1872, *Woodhull &*

Claflin's Weekly suspended publication due to her inability to meet its running costs. Even Theodore Tilton deserted her. He'd chosen instead to throw his weight behind *New-York Tribune* editor—and early supporter of the Fox sisters—Horace Greeley, in his own bid for the presidency. But rather than slipping quietly away from the electoral race, Victoria's next move would have such explosive consequences that, for many, it would obliterate all her considerable achievements and fix her in the public mind only as that horned figure, Mrs. Satan.

That September, the American Association of Spiritualists, of which Victoria remained president, held its annual conference in Boston. She went, according to her, "tired, sick and discouraged as to my own future" and ready to surrender her leadership. When the time came for her to address the assembled company, she rose to her feet "to render an account of my stewardship" and then quietly resign her position. Instead, in a version of events that brings to mind Emma Hardinge's trance lectures, Victoria apparently found herself gripped "by one of those overwhelming gusts of inspiration which sometimes come upon me, from I know not where; taken out of myself; hurried away from the immediate question of discussion, and made, by some power stronger than I, to pour out into the ears of that assembly . . . the whole history of the BEECHER and TILTON scandal in Plymouth Church, and to announce in prophetic terms something of the bearing of those events upon the future of Spiritualism." Afterward, and rather conveniently, Victoria would be able to insist that she knew "perhaps less than any of those present, all that I did actually say." Neither could she recall voicing any of the "naughty words" she was said to have used. Her only certainty was that the association, though undoubtedly shaken by what they'd heard, refused to accept her resignation.

Victoria might have impressed a majority of the gathered Spiritualists, but the wider press interpreted her speech less kindly. The *Watchman and Reflector*, a local Christian publication, applauded the fact that most of Boston's newspapers had refrained from printing Victoria's actual words, remarking that this time she had "surpassed even her own indecencies." *The Boston Herald* reported that her address was "never equalled in vulgarity by a speaker before a promiscuous audience in Boston." *The Daily Phoenix*, based in Columbia, South Carolina, described the speech as "most foul and indecent," opining that her accusations against the Reverend Beecher made her "a fit subject for a lunatic asylum." Since few members of the wider public had heard her exact words, only the churning rumors, when an undaunted Victoria relaunched *Woodhull & Claflin's Weekly* in November, she devoted over four large pages of fine print to putting this right, in a piece entitled "The Beecher-Tilton Scandal Case."

The same issue of *Woodhull & Claflin's Weekly* carried an accompanying piece also dealing with the hypocrisy of well-connected men. Here, the sisters accused the prominent Wall Street trader Luther C. Challis and a pseudonymous man—"one of the oldest and *best* in the annals of New York society"—of plying two adolescent girls with alcohol at a masked French ball and then taking the girls to a brothel and raping them. Having satisfied themselves abusing each victim, the paper said, the men brought friends to this house of assignation "to the number of one hundred and over, to debauch these young girls—mere children." For days afterward, "this scoundrel Challis," eager to prove that he had "*seduced a maiden*," exhibited "*in triumph, the red trophy of her virginity*" on his finger.

The initial print run of Victoria and Tennessee's relaunched magazine sold out immediately, "like buttered hot cakes," according to the recollections of one reporter. He had, he said, fought his way "through the army of newsboys and news dealers which actually blocked up Broad Street for hundreds of feet" to obtain a copy.

The sisters claimed that in the period of greatest demand for copies, their paper—usually priced at ten cents—was selling for five times that amount, with five, ten, and twenty dollars not unheard-of; one copy, they said, had gone for the breathtaking sum of forty dollars. In fact, much of the initial demand came from Henry Ward Beecher and his supporters: unaware that another print run had been ordered, they bought dozens of copies of the first in the hope that as few people as possible would read the issue.

For a time it seemed that Victoria had made a smart move—one that could solve many of her financial worries as well as putting her back in charge, to an extent at least, of the news stories about her. This change in fortunes, though, would be short-lived. Mere days before the presidential election on November 5—in a move instigated by Henry's Plymouth Church, which had friends in high places—the sisters found themselves arrested and thrown into New York City's Ludlow Street Jail, charged with circulating obscene material. There they would stay throughout Election Day and beyond, while enfranchised men across the country went to the polls.

Victoria is thought to have received a share of popular votes, but her gender and age—thirty-four—had ultimately prevented her from being listed as an official candidate. Nonetheless, the very fact that, at this point in history, her name had been seriously discussed as a presidential hopeful is a tremendous achievement—but not one that can have given much comfort just then to a woman with the prospect of months of legal wrangling ahead of her.

Luther Challis, no doubt emboldened by the collapse in Victoria's fortunes, would also take action against her. A total of eight charges were eventually issued against the sisters. Several members of the *Weekly*'s staff, including Colonel Blood, would also spend time in jail. But Henry Beecher himself never sued for libel or spoke out publicly to deny Victoria's accusations.

After the sisters' release on bail in early December 1872, a month after their incarceration, Victoria would begin a speaking tour, but her glory days looked to be over. Harriet Beecher Stowe—who'd later write to her literary friend George Eliot to complain of the terrible wrongs done to her "so sweet & perfect" brother—kept up a crusade against the woman who had brought him such unwanted public attention and scrutiny. With Victoria due to give a talk on her prison experiences to an audience in Boston, Harriet appealed to the wife of the governor of Massachusetts, a friend of hers, and Victoria soon found herself unable to get a booking at any hall in the city. Women's rights campaigners and Spiritualists, shocked by her growing notoriety, abandoned Victoria in droves. Emma Hardinge Britten, now back in the United States and married to fellow Spiritualist William Britten, continued to be a vocal critic—something for which Victoria would get her revenge in 1876 by publishing a blisteringly negative review of Emma's book *Art Magic* in *Woodhull & Claflin's Weekly*.

By this time, Henry Beecher had endured his own court battle. In 1875, he'd finally been forced to face Theodore Tilton's accusations of adultery in a six-month hearing billed by the press as the Trial of the Century. The jury had returned an inconclusive verdict, but Henry's supporters spun this as a win for him, and Theodore and Elizabeth, his wife, found themselves socially ostracized. For Victoria, too, the future looked bleak indeed. She had avoided a long stint in prison, but the stresses of the past few years had drained her finances, ground down her health, and ultimately, so it seemed, put pressure on her relationship with the Colonel. The last issue of *Woodhull & Claflin's Weekly*—to which the couple had been so committed—appeared in June 1876. Four months later, on October 6, they divorced again, this time deciding to really go their separate ways.

But anyone who assumed that the fight had gone out of this remarkable woman, who'd already proved herself a mistress of re-invention, seriously underestimated her. In 1877, Victoria, her children, Tennessee, and Annie—with whom she had reconciled—set sail for Britain with the intention of starting afresh. They would eventually be joined by members of the wider Claflin clan, including Buck. Once in Britain, and to the outrage of detractors back in the United States, Victoria would rework her public image once more, this time succeeding in adopting an even less likely new persona—that of a genteel lady of the manor.

Private Frustrations

When Victoria Woodhull arrived in London in 1877, she came to take her chances in the heart of the British Empire, now at the peak of its international powers. And yet this was also a city where old certainties about the existing social order were slowly being eroded. The Second Reform Act (1867) had ushered in widespread change throughout England and Wales and then in Ireland and Scotland. Most significantly, the enfranchisement of male householders in Britain's towns and cities had doubled the size of the electorate from one to two million. The female vote still lay some forty years away, but these reforms had done much to galvanize members of the National Society for Women's Suffrage, which, by the time Victoria began a new existence, in the fashionable district of South Kensington, had been gathering signatures of support for a decade.

Although never as collectively radical as American Spiritualism, with its solid links to the abolitionist and suffrage movements, in Britain, too, the Spiritualist movement overlapped with groups that supported extending the rights of "ordinary" men and women. In 1863, James Burns, future editor of the popular Spiritualist publication *The Medium and Daybreak*, established the Progressive Library and Spiritual Institution on London's Southampton Row. The library offered a wide variety of literature, not just on the activities of Britain's mediums and current Spiritualist culture, but also on social and political reform. Burns's weekly newspaper, established in 1870, would take a similarly radical stance.

A century and a half later, periodicals such as *The Medium and Daybreak*, *The Spiritualist*, and *Human Nature* offer researchers thrilling insights into the mystical world inhabited by believers of the day. In the twelve years since Emma Hardinge Britten first made a name for herself as a trance lecturer in London, many more famous figures had emerged onto the scene. These newcomers did not content themselves with coaxing the dead to communicate via an eerie patter of knocks, or feats of clairvoyant healing, or even channeling the words of the departed in rousing political speeches. Three decades after the mysterious goings-on at Hydesville that had made the Fox sisters' names, people who attended séances often expected more for their money than mere spirit rapping and table turning. And so Britain's best-known mediums now performed amazing theatrical feats: materializing flowers, fruit, and small animals out of thin air; capturing the presence of spirits before the slow-working cameras of photographers, so that these images could be immortalized in grainy black-and-white; and, as in the case of one famed British medium, Agnes Guppy, seemingly transporting herself from one London district to another in a single instant. Guppy and others, including the young and pretty Florence Cook and Mary Rosina Showers, commanded huge fees and attracted extensive coverage in the Spiritualist press. However, it was the thousands of ordinary subscribers to these journals—and believers in the tenets of Spiritualism more generally—who allowed this movement that remained so welcoming to women to retain much of its potency, despite increasing criticism from the male-dominated medical and scientific communities.

Unlike her forebears, Victoria Woodhull, Emma Hardinge Britten, and the three Fox sisters, Georgina Weldon had intended to make neither her name nor her fortune through her involvement with the Victorian séance scene. In 1877, Georgina was not a spirit medium whom people flocked to see, but rather a keen participant. She took part in gatherings in darkened rooms out of an interest in the supernatural and a wish to alleviate the frustrations of a life that had turned out quite differently from the ambitions she'd once harbored for herself.

Born four decades earlier, in South London on May 24, 1837, Georgina shared a birthday with Queen Victoria. Like the American Victoria Woodhull, who emerged into the world a year later, Georgina had believed from a young age that she had a deep connection with the reigning monarch. As a child, she used to tell herself that "if anything should happen" to Britain's ruling household, her family, the Thomases—later renamed the Trehernes—"should become entitled to the throne." Although almost as far-fetched as Victoria Woodhull's girlhood aspirations, Georgina's leisured upbringing did at least offer her the assurance of a future place in aristocratic society. Certainly, her birthplace, at the family home of Tooting Lodge in the suburb of Clapham, then an area favored by London's wealthy, was a far cry from the country village of Homer where Victoria spent her earliest years.

Georgina's father, Morgan Thomas, a minor member of Britain's landed gentry, encouraged his daughter's sense of entitlement by feeding her stories of the family's convoluted royal connections. Four centuries earlier, he insisted, an ancestor of theirs had married

a daughter of Edward IV. Georgina's mother, Louisa Thomas—
formerly Dalrymple—could also claim an impressive lineage: she
was related to the Duke of Wellington, who had triumphed at Wa-
terloo in 1815. As a young woman, Louisa had been regarded as
an unusual beauty. Alfred d'Orsay, the dandyish live-in companion
of Lady Blessington—whose Gore House salons were part of the
crystal-gazing milieu known to the young Emma Floyd—had compared Louisa to "the offspring of Punch and Venus," the former a
reference to her rather florid complexion.

Georgina spent much of her youth in Italy, where her family had
moved when she was small. Educated to the narrow, refined standards of a lady of her day by a steady stream of governesses—seven
coming and going during the course of one year—she still managed
to acquire a fluency in French and Italian and a love of literature.
A favorite novel was Harriet Beecher Stowe's *Uncle Tom's Cabin*,
which the adolescent Georgina described as "the *nicest*, delightful
book I ever read"—a youthfully naïve comment that sits uncomfortably with the sufferings endured by its enslaved central character and described in detail by its author. In her years growing up,
Georgina also cultivated a beautiful singing voice. The latter was
something of which her mother, in particular, approved, knowing
that such a desirable accomplishment would help Georgina to distin-
guish herself at drawing room recitals once she came out in society.
Louisa and her husband had great hopes for their daughter, who, by
the age of sixteen, was attractively plump, with a fine head of dark
hair and captivating blue eyes. Morgan had already effectively set a
bride price on his daughter by refusing to entertain the entreaties of
any future suitors unless they could prove that they had an annual
income of at least £10,000—the hefty sum that had distinguished
Jane Austen's hero Mr. Darcy four decades earlier and which even in
the 1850s still closed the door on most men who were not particu-

larly wealthy landowners. Unfortunately for the ambitious Morgan, Georgina had other plans.

The family returned to Britain in the late 1840s and then again, after a period of more European travel, permanently in the mid-1850s. In 1856, Morgan decided that the Thomases should revert to their historic family name of Treherne—a choice that at first seemed to bode well for the future. Following Georgina's successful entry into society, the young woman's musicality made her much in demand as a participant in amateur theatricals. During one such comedic performance—*Hearts and Tarts, or The Knave Turned Honest* by Augustus Stafford—Georgina found herself sharing the stage with a cast that included a princess, a duke, and three earls. She also began to associate with the Holland House Circle, the crowd of Pre-Raphaelite artists presided over by Sara Prinsep, which, according to a nephew of Georgina's writing over six decades later, revived something of the spirit of Lady Blessington's Gore House salons. The artist George Frederic Watts called Georgina his "little Bambina" and painted a sensual double portrait of her in two distinct poses when she was nineteen. On one side of the picture, in a diaphanous evening dress with a plunging neckline, she assumes the posture of a singer; on the other, she appears as a listener, reclining, eyes closed, on a sumptuous red-covered seat.

Many young women in her position would have been happy to devote themselves to amateur soirées, but, perhaps encouraged by these get-togethers at Little Holland House—attended by the likes of Anthony Trollope, Dante Gabriel Rossetti, and the as-yet-untitled Alfred Tennyson—Georgina began to harbor serious hopes of making a professional career on the stage. Had she attracted the attention of the kind of suitor of huge fortune favored by her father, such a man's standing would presumably have compelled him to declare her aims out of the question. Instead, in January 1858, the twenty-year-old Georgina met William Henry Weldon—known as Harry—a lieutenant in the Eighteenth Hussars.

Harry had nothing like the £10,000 per year demanded by Morgan Treherne. On the contrary, during his army career he had enjoyed himself considerably, living well beyond his means, and was now saddled with heavy debts. What he could offer Georgina were dashing good looks and, perhaps owing to his relatively low financial status, an apparent willingness to encourage her theatrical ambitions. Neither of these qualities endeared him to Georgina's father. On the dark, frozen night of March 10, 1858, Georgina noted in her diary that her furious "Papa and Mama would not hear" of the prospect of an alliance between the two.

Not to be put off so easily, for the next year the couple sustained a clandestine romance via letters that, in Georgina's case, sometimes ran close to thirty pages. Harry did his best to make his missives look similarly lengthy, although their recipient easily saw through the generously spaced lines and large handwriting. Despite the obvious frustrations of having to conduct their relationship in secret, Georgina at times seemed to revel in the level of subterfuge required to evade her controlling father's suspicions. In one letter, she instructed Harry that he must not use an envelope when writing to her but rather "buy a piece of music and roll it as the shop people do." On another occasion, she told him, "I carry my darling's letter over my heart, as my pocket is not safe."

On April 3, 1860, after many months of secrecy, Georgina recorded in her diary her "resolution of marrying Harry, and going on the stage." Thirteen days later, with the help of a sympathetic go-between, the young woman managed to get away to London for what must have sounded to her parents like a harmless week's stay with her godmother—who remained in the dark about what was to come. On the morning of April 21, Georgina and a chaperone, who'd soon make a discreet exit, left the godmother's house at Gloucester Place, one of the more respectable parts of the district of Marylebone. From there, Georgina and Harry departed by train for the army town of Aldershot, some forty miles southwest of London, where Harry's regiment was stationed. Here the couple married in secret, with just three witnesses to watch Harry place a ring on Georgina's finger. Two hours later, she was back on a train to London, without her husband.

Imagination is required to guess at her feelings on the return journey. Exhilaration, perhaps? Fear at her family finding out? Blasé defiance? In the evening, she wrote in her diary, "I am so glad and thankful I am married irrevocably to my heart's first real love, Harry Weldon."

For the moment, their legal union remained private, but it would not stay so for long. Four days later, the newlyweds reunited at a jeweler's on Cockspur Street in London's Westminster district, to buy a decoy ring large enough to cover Georgina's wedding band. While they were still engaged in picking out a suitable item, the door swung open and William Makepeace Thackeray strolled in. The celebrated author of *Vanity Fair* knew Georgina from Sara Prinsep's Little Holland House gatherings. Presumably well aware of the novelist's lack of discretion, Georgina bolted into a side room to take refuge, but unfortunately he had already spotted her and guessed exactly what was going on. That afternoon, he ran into the famed dandy the Honourable Frederick Gerald "Poodle" Byng—by then a septuagenarian and enamored with Georgina's charms. The gleeful writer would waste no time in informing poor Poodle that he had lost his "singing bird," telling him that "Miss Treherne has married some other fellow."

It didn't take long for Georgina's parents to discover the truth. Her father, unsurprisingly, reacted with rage. As his daughter bluntly put it, "The dirty old Guv cut me off within 24 hours." Now she and Harry would have to manage as best they could financially.

Given how stretched their resources suddenly were, Georgina might have assumed that Harry would encourage her stage career, which during their courtship he'd said she could pursue as a married woman. But if he had ever meant what he said, now that the couple had tied the knot Harry went back on his word. In an era that celebrated the sharply defined gender roles of husband and wife as the manly "lofty pine" and feminine "clinging vine," it would have been expected that Georgina, as the supposedly submissive partner in the relationship, would simply accept the decision of the head of the household without question. And initially, outwardly at least, she appeared to do just that, but as the months and years went on, the unjustness of it all would come to fester.

Despite Harry's broken promise and the sadness of a miscarriage, after which Georgina and Harry were never able to have a child, they seem largely to have been content in their early years together. They lived in a modest cottage in the town of Beaumaris, on the Welsh island of Anglesey. Here, Georgina enjoyed doing up the house, tending to its gardens, and collecting shells from the nearby pebbled shore. The couple took extended stays in London and at the country homes of some of the nation's most illustrious families, where Georgina's singing continued to earn admiration. But it is a sign of her stifled creativity, perhaps, that she often found cause to complain about these society engagements. At one charity concert, organized by Catherine Gladstone, wife of the future prime minister William Ewart Gladstone, Georgina shared the bill with opera singer Jenny Lind—who had witnessed the spirit rapping that rang out in young Kate Fox's presence well over a decade earlier. Despite the widespread belief that the Swedish Nightingale, now in her forties, was the greatest of the age, Georgina carped privately that she was "the image of a shrunken crab apple!" She vented her fury that the "horrid old scarecrow and humbug . . . had put herself down for five solos and me for one."

When Georgina's father, Morgan, died in 1867, the two remained unreconciled, but his daughter kept up limited contact with other members of the Treherne clan. Two years later she used her family's connections with the attorney general to the Prince of Wales to find her husband a new job. Harry became Rouge Dragon Pursuivant at the Heralds' College, the British body responsible for the granting of new coats of arms. At about this time, he also came into a considerable inheritance, these changed circumstances allowing him to purchase the lease for Tavistock House, on Tavistock Square, in London's Bloomsbury district. A former home of Charles Dickens set within a quiet, amply shaded garden, the house at first seemed to suit Georgina, reminding her of a country retreat. Dickens had even added a large room designed especially for the purpose of staging private theatricals.

But it was during Georgina and Harry's time at Tavistock House that marital relations between the couple ran into serious trouble. By the early 1870s, Georgina—never, by some margin, the idealized image of a Victorian lady—had begun to exhibit character traits that caused alarm among many of her family and friends, governed as they were by strict codes of conduct. She would come to embrace vegetarianism, then widely regarded as an unfathomable fad; wear her hair short; and don the kind of loose-fitting dress favored by reformers who disapproved of the restrictive, tightly corseted fashions of the age. Worse still—influenced by some earlier success teaching music to poor girls in Wales—she decided to set up a musical academy and residence for impoverished children at her new London home, where she planned to turn these unsophisticated pupils into "*finished*" artists. Harry never much liked the idea of the children lodging at his home, but according to a letter Georgina wrote to a friend, he reluctantly gave his "unwilling consent."

Admitting that the first three pupils to her National Training School of Music were "the most awkward specimens of mankind that ever were beheld," Georgina remained full of enthusiasm for the girls' future. To help with the considerable costs of dressing and feeding them for the five years she planned to look after them, she intended to have them perform in concerts at which she would collect the profits. Then, after she had "done keeping" the girls, they would give up a third of what they had earned from their future careers, and Georgina would plow that money back into her school. Soon, the rooms of Tavistock House became filled with occupants: besides more members of her academy, the majority of them orphans, there were pet dogs, various members of household staff, and the venerated French composer Charles Gounod, then in his fifties and a favorite of Queen Victoria. In 1871 he gave a private drawing room performance for the monarch at Windsor Castle.

This married man had met and befriended Georgina through London's music scene, coming to Tavistock House the year he performed for the queen. Gounod's stay with Georgina was supposed to be for just three weeks, but he would end up remaining for two and a half years. Adopting the role of business manager to the maestro, Georgina organized Gounod's concert bookings, undertook correspondence on his behalf, and made the most of his constant presence by turning her popular Sunday at homes into major society get-togethers.

As in the case of the ménage à trois of Victoria Woodhull, Colonel Blood, and Canning Woodhull, the composer's extended residence under the Weldons' roof raised eyebrows. According to Georgina's later recollections, Gounod's wife, Anna Zimmerman, who lived across the Channel, felt sure that the two were having an affair—something that Georgina claimed "made me almost die of laughing." But it wasn't just Gounod's spouse who believed that Georgina was her husband's lover. Rumors abounded among friends and acquaintances, eventually reaching the ears of Georgina's own family members. Such whisperings would further contribute to the impression of Georgina's many scandalous qualities, which would later be used against her.

Whether or not Georgina was an unfaithful wife, it's certain that her husband had begun looking elsewhere for romance. For some time, he'd been involved in a relationship with another woman, Annie Lowe, who'd been deserted by her husband. By the mid-1870s, Harry had apparently had enough of his unconventional wife and the musical academy that dominated their homelife and remained the source of gossip in the world outside. Among his objections were some of his wife's domestic lapses. Georgina was completely out of step with the times in allowing her pupils to go barefoot. She permitted them to let off steam in an organized quarter hour of shouting each day, and she channeled her charges' supposed natural destructiveness into industry by encouraging them to rip skeins of cloth into tiny strips, later to be used for stuffing pillows. When they had a concert engagement, she ferried her motley crew around in a converted horse-drawn omnibus painted with the words MRS WELDON'S SOCIABLE EVENINGS; the vehicle was widely considered to be "horrible" and "insane looking." Georgina also involved her pupils in domestic experiments with spirit communication, rumors about which compounded impressions of her perceived eccentricities.

In 1875, Georgina's disgruntled husband moved out, leaving her the use of Tavistock House and settling the sum of £1,000 per year on her. This seems to have been a relatively amicable arrangement, and life could have gone on in this manner for some time had Harry not had a change of heart. Three years later, on April 14, 1878, Georgina received a visit at home from two men that would change her life forever.

That Sunday morning, Georgina was dusting some books in the library. It might seem strange that the lady of the house should have been engaged in a task more commonly undertaken by servants, but Georgina had never shied away from getting her hands dirty. In her days back in Beaumaris in Wales, she had scandalized the local gentry by cooking meals, skinning rabbits, and not even bothering to remove her grimy apron when guests came to call. On this particular day, there was a great deal of housework to do, so it was typical that Georgina had decided to pitch in.

She had recently returned from a lengthy stay in France with pupils of her school, a married Frenchwoman, Angèle Ménier, and Angèle's daughter, Bichette. Mother and child had been living among the assembled company at Tavistock House since 1876, during which time Angèle and Georgina had formed an intense and volatile friendship—something that, as in the case of Charles Gounod, Georgina's former lodger, would eventually lead to speculation that the two were sexually involved.

Georgina's stay in France had been interrupted by a troubling letter from a friend suggesting that all was not well at Tavistock House, and so she had left Angèle, Bichette, and the orphans behind and returned to London alone. On arriving back at her Bloomsbury residence, she'd found the once well-kept garden in disarray. Weeds tangled the drive leading up to the entrance, and her first impressions were of depressing decay. Inside, she found things no better. Bugs infested the walls and the cistern overflowed. Worse still, a great number of Georgina's belongings had been packed into trunks, ready to be carted away by Angèle's husband, Anacharsis Ménier, also supposedly a friend of Georgina's, whom she'd left partially in charge of the house. Anacharsis insisted that these items were security for a debt Georgina owed him—a charge she flatly denied. The building's temporary custodian, James Samuel Bell—employed by Harry in his wife's absence—had not put up any sort of a fight, and so Georgina must have felt that she had returned in the nick of time. Once she had recovered her composure, she sent for the police. As things stood on that Sunday in mid-April, Anacharsis had appeared before Bow Street Police Court and, bail having been denied, been remanded to prison.

At about ten that morning, the doorbell rang and Georgina's maid, Elizabeth Villiers, whom she called by her surname, came in to announce two gentlemen, Mr. Shell and Mr. Stewart.

Georgina had not been expecting anyone, but, living in a house formerly owned by Dickens, she was used to strangers turning up in pilgrimage at the property. Eventually she wrote a pamphlet on the subject, entitled *The Ghastly Consequences of Living in Charles Dickens' House*. On this occasion, the fact she already knew a man named Stewart reassured her. She instructed Villiers to let the pair in. Georgina—still up a ladder, feather duster in hand as they entered the room—soon realized that this was not the Mr. Stewart of her acquaintance. Instead, it was a man in his mid-thirties whom she characterized as being "all blinks, winks and grins" and looking "like a . . . Christy minstrel" washed of his blackface makeup. However, the explanation he gave for coming to call gave her no reason for suspicion.

"You do not know us well, but we have often seen you," the men said, explaining that they were Spiritualists; "we have read your works on the education of children in *The Spiritualist*, and are very desirous of placing some children with you."

Georgina informed them that she had left her orphan students in France for the moment, to which the men voiced some disappointment. They went on to question her about her personal beliefs regarding the world beyond the grave. When asked if she considered herself a spirit medium, she said no, but confessed to recently seeing ghostly materializations of showers of falling stars—a lucky sign, she believed. To Georgina, the stars seemed to augur a favorable end to her legal troubles with Anacharsis Ménier, which had already caught the attention of the press. In some as yet unknown way, Georgina predicted, "this Ménier bother" would turn into "a moment of triumph."

The men took their leave soon afterward—their departure along the drive watched by the building's current custodian Bell and Villiers, the maid.

Noticing that the pair seemed in an unusually good humor as they made their way down the drive—and quite possibly displaying an insider's grasp of the situation himself—Bell remarked, "Look how those gentlemen are laughing and hugging each other. Don't they seem to think they've got a fine prize!"

Even Villiers, whose knowledge of what was happening appears to have been as limited as Georgina's, seems to have seen danger ahead. "Oh bother!" she fretted, in reply to Bell. "Missus must have been talking about Spiritualism."

That afternoon, Georgina received another visit, this time from Gen. Sir Henry de Bathe, an old friend whom she hadn't seen for some time. He appeared to have come simply to pay a social call. Oddly, he chose to remain at the house for only ten minutes.

The day would bring another unanticipated ring at the doorbell. At around half past eight in the evening—a most improper time for an unexpected guest to call—Bell came to tell her that the two men from that morning had returned. Before Georgina had even given him permission to show them in, she noticed that, rather than waiting outside, her visitors had followed Bell in. More disconcertingly still, she recognized at once that these were not, as Bell had said, mistakenly or otherwise, "'those gentlemen who came this morning" but two entirely different men.

Confronted by Georgina, the new pair admitted that they were, quite clearly, not Mr. Shell and Mr. Stewart, but that the earlier pair had sent them on this errand, which was why they had given those names. They wished to talk more with Georgina about the orphans Mr. Stewart and Mr. Shell hoped to place with her. And, like the two men from that morning, they wanted to discuss her Spiritualist experiences.

More relaxed in their company now, she told them, among other things, about a white rabbit with black ears, tail, and paws. It had appeared apparently out of thin air at a séance held by the famed medium Agnes Guppy and then been given to Georgina. After "four or five months," it had "disappeared as mysteriously as it had appeared."

Comfortable as she'd felt when the men were there, once they had gone, she felt a wave of anxiety wash over her. She would later recall her words to visiting former maid Elizabeth Jordan, known as Tibby—Villiers having gone out for the evening. "Oh, Tibby, I feel dreadful!" Georgina cried. "Something awful has come over me. I feel as if black clouds were floating down over me one by one, and I can see all black! I feel as if I were in the most dreadful danger! What can those men be? I am in some horrible trap."

Her first thought was that the men had been sent by Anacharsis, the imprisoned husband of Angèle Ménier, who had tried to make off with trunks full of her possessions. Who else, after all, could have been behind the day's unnerving occurrences?

Once Tibby had departed, Georgina bolted and chained the door, even though Villiers had yet to return. Time dragged. At about a quarter to ten, the bell rang again. Although Bell suggested that it was just the maid returning, a certainty that she was in "grave danger" overcame Georgina. Bell opened the door a crack, wide enough to make out a carriage waiting on the drive and yet another man and two women outside. The trio informed him that they wanted to see Mrs. Weldon. He told them that she had retired to bed and shut the door in their faces. This did not stop them from ringing and knocking for several more minutes—insistent sounds that further tested Georgina's nerves.

The mistress of the house was right to be suspicious, for these new three, and indeed the men from earlier that evening, had in fact been sent by the winking, grinning man of that morning. His real name was Lyttleton Stewart Forbes Winslow. He was a medical doctor and the owner of two lunatic asylums.

Dr. Winslow, masquerading as Mr. Stewart, had made the journey to Tavistock House that day accompanied by his father-in-law, James Michell Winn, also a doctor. Dr. Winn had assumed the identity of Mr. Shell. The visits were the culmination of many months of plotting by Georgina's husband. Harry had been secretly in contact with members of her family, asking leading questions about his wife's mental state and suggesting that she ought to be committed to an institution.

Such words would have made an impact since, during the years of her estrangement from Harry, Georgina's father's mind had become increasingly unbalanced. Morgan Treherne had finished his life as a live-in patient at an asylum run by another doctor, George Fielding Blandford. Harry had also consulted Georgina's brother, Col. Dalrymple Treherne. As Georgina would later recall, rather than letting her know what her husband was doing behind her back, Colonel Treherne had privately told Harry that he had the family's "full consent" to lock her up, and that "it should have been done long ago!"

Georgina's second caller of that day, Sir Henry de Bathe, whom she had trustingly assumed had just dropped by out of friendliness, had also been in cahoots with Harry and had recommended Dr. Winslow's services to him. Dr. Winslow subscribed to the belief that there was a proven link between Spiritualism and madness. As such, he had proved a sympathetic listener to Harry's claims.

Whereas the Fox sisters, Emma Hardinge, and Victoria Woodhull had all seen themselves publicly accused of deceiving gullible believers for money, Georgina Weldon—as, apparently, just such a gullible believer—was in a position that could be regarded as both more blameless and more vulnerable. In *Spiritualistic Madness*, Dr. Winslow's pamphlet of the previous year, he had described what he saw as a dangerous American import as "the curse of our age," and "one of the principal causes" of the supposed recent increase in cases of insanity in England. Moreover, he argued: "It is a well-known fact that in America the mediums become haggard idiots, mad, or stupid; this has been frequently stated in the American journals; and not only do the mediums become so, but also their auditors."

He was far from the only member of the British medical establishment to take such a view. Given the female-dominated nature of the world of the séance, several prominent male physicians of the period drew a connection between women who communed with the dead and hysteria allegedly brought on by trouble with their reproductive organs. A woman such as Georgina Weldon, then—who took an interest in Spiritualism, displayed what was deemed decidedly odd behavior, and did not conform to acceptable gender norms—would immediately have piqued the interest of an individual like Dr. Winslow.

Dr. Winslow also had a financial incentive for taking Georgina into his care: the expectation was not that she would come to one of his asylums for a brief stay or to "get better." Rather, Harry hoped to incarcerate her, for a fee, for the foreseeable future. With Georgina out of the way under Dr. Winslow's supervision in the district of Hammersmith, five and a half miles southwest of Tavistock House, she should no longer cause Harry embarrassment. And her absence would leave him free to deepen his relationship with his mistress, Annie Lowe.

Once the visitors' carriage had at last departed, Bell, instructed by Georgina, went out and locked the gate. He also managed to attract the attention of a policeman passing on his nightly beat, allowing Georgina to make the pleading request that an inspector be sent over there the following day. By then it was close to midnight and Villiers had finally arrived home.

Georgina's maid was shocked to see her mistress in such an unusual state of agitation, white-faced and trembling. The effect soon transferred itself to Villiers as well, so that both women suffered a terrible night's sleep. Once Georgina had pulled herself from her bed the next morning, she absorbed herself by writing letters, including to the editors of the magazines *The Spiritualist* and *The Medium and Daybreak*, who she hoped might be able to help her out of her as yet unknowable predicament. In addition, she absorbed herself with her copy of the London paper *The Standard*, which contained a report of Anacharsis Ménier's appearance at Bow Street Police Court.

After speaking with the police, who called as promised and said they would return to the house that evening, all she could do was wait. No one else came to call that morning. Bell and Villiers relaxed, but Georgina continued to fret. Her conversations with the previous day's visitors kept replaying in her mind, as did lines from the article in *The Standard*. According to the report, Anacharsis's defense counsel had argued that he thought "it possible that the lady, who has been carrying on the orphanage in a house well known as the former residence of Charles Dickens, without the co-operation, apparently, of her husband, might be laboring under some delusion as to the doings of my client." Georgina, who had been in court for these proceedings, representing herself for the prosecution, felt certain that Anacharsis's lawyer had said no such thing, and she had written to *The Standard* to inform them so.

Although she knew nothing yet about the plot hatched by her husband to remove her from their marital home, the word "delusion" must have instilled her with fear. Contemporary "sensation novels" such as *The Woman in White*, by Wilkie Collins, and real-life cases covered in the newspapers told of individuals incarcerated in asylums on the flimsiest of medical evidence. Surely they struck terror into the heart of a woman like Georgina, so roundly regarded as different. Her thoughts began to turn toward another woman and fellow Spiritualist who, although personally unknown to her, had made a strong impression on Georgina through the many recent column inches devoted to her.

Louisa Lowe had become something of a celebrity due to the treatment she had suffered at the hands of Britain's medical establishment and her eventual breathtaking escape from its clutches. As the day wore on, Georgina began to ask herself if she dared send word to this well-known woman.

She was still deliberating that evening when Bell came in to announce that Mrs. Lowe herself—summoned by a note from the editor of *The Spiritualist* to whom Georgina had written—had arrived at the door. Overwhelmed by happiness, Georgina at once admitted Louisa, but her joy would be short-lived. She had been with Louisa only ten minutes when a panicked Bell returned to the room.

"Those three have come, have pushed their way in," he exclaimed, referring to the trio who had tried to gain access to the house the night before. He could not get rid of them. Overpowered, he'd had to listen, he said, as they conveyed the message that he now passed on. The three had informed Bell that they were in no hurry and that they would wait to see Georgina.

Their words sounded like a threat and a challenge, but it was one to which Georgina rose. Looking back on these events, she'd come to realize that, unlike the "ashy pale" Bell, she actually "felt quite brave now."

Ghastly Consequences

Without the quick thinking of Louisa Lowe that day, things might have ended very differently for Georgina Weldon. But as both a fellow Spiritualist and someone who'd overcome an unimaginable ordeal inflicted by her own husband, Louisa was in a unique position to offer Georgina support.

A clergyman's wife in her late fifties, Louisa had lived an outwardly comfortable life with her husband and children until around 1870. Behind the scenes, however, her marriage had been miserable. She had fled her home on several occasions—to take the waters in German spa towns or stay with her sister or mother. She had once even attempted suicide by imbibing an overdose of opium, but had vomited up the drug instead and so survived. In 1869, she had discovered Spiritualism at a séance where she saw tables tapping and tilting "in a wonderful way." Not long afterward, she witnessed "passive writing"—the practice by which a departed spirit apparently expresses its thoughts through the pen of a living person.

Although such feats had thoroughly convinced Louisa, they'd

only added to the strength of her husband's long-term complaints that she had a disordered constitution. For most of their married life, the Reverend George Lowe had regarded his wife as hysterical, but these new beliefs of hers must have struck him as a particularly worrying development.

Louisa's Spiritualism can be interpreted as an outlet for her to voice subconscious fears. She began to experiment with spirit writing herself, sitting alone with ink and paper, watching as indecipherable scribblings appeared, followed by letters, then words, then whole sentences. Eventually these included accusations, made by an all-knowing unseen presence, that her husband had committed adultery with several women, and a suggestion that he had abused their seven-year-old daughter. Louisa took to spending days at a time conversing with the spirit world on paper. Then, following what she felt she had learned, she began to make vocal accusations, which she aired beyond the confines of her home. She once rushed to the house of one of the named women to confront her—worsening relations between her and her husband still further.

Sometime after this confrontation, Louisa left home again—this time refusing to return—and Rev. Lowe decided to make good on a prior threat to see his wife incarcerated in an asylum. The success of his plans in this direction were such that Louisa would spend a year and three months locked up in a series of private institutions—her Spiritualism, so tightly interlinked with her accusations against her husband, used as an example of her insanity. Only after months of protests that fell on deaf ears was the lunacy certificate that had condemned her rescinded.

Once she'd regained her freedom, Louisa got herself a Spiritualist lawyer, Henry Diedrich Jencken, who would, incidentally, marry the celebrated former child medium Kate Fox—now living in London—that same year. With Jencken's help, Louisa tried to bring a case against the Commissioners in Lunacy, established in 1845 to oversee asylums in England and Wales. She held this public body responsible for what had happened to her. When this effort failed, she devoted herself to writing articles and pamphlets to raise public awareness of the corrupt state of Britain's lunacy laws, which she argued had condemned "many sane and still more merely eccentric and quite harmless persons" to languish forgotten in institutions. In 1873, she founded the Lunacy Law Reform Association (LLRA), and in February 1877, fourteen months before her arrival at Georgina's door, Louisa appeared before a parliamentary select committee to give evidence both of her own treatment at the hands of the authorities and that of other unfortunate individuals.

All her experience, therefore, allowed Louisa to appreciate her hostess's predicament in a way that even Georgina herself could not. What's more, Louisa's widely publicized tribulations of the past few years had helped her acquire unusually in-depth knowledge of the law in this area, enabling her to counsel her new acquaintance on exactly what she should do to save herself.

To Georgina's utter astonishment, the strange man and two women at the door produced a lunacy order, the document giving them permission to take her into custody. Georgina saw what she took to be the false statement and signature of her husband requesting that his wife be placed in Brandenburgh House, one of Lyttleton Stewart Forbes Winslow's asylums in Hammersmith. A second signature, by her old friend Gen. Sir Henry de Bathe—who had dropped in the day before, apparently on a casual call—only further convinced her that the document must be "an impudent forgery." She resolved to telegraph her husband at once to try to resolve the matter.

Louisa, in contrast, was deeply suspicious of Harry from the outset, warning Georgina that she "did not know how bad" husbands could be. She advised Georgina to lock herself at once into the library while she went to fetch the police.

There was no key to the library, but Georgina did her best to barricade herself, piling large music books on top of each other against the door. At least she could be glad that, by this point in proceedings, James Samuel Bell seemed firmly on her side. He did his best to stall the three intruders, while Georgina waited impatiently inside the library, hoping and praying that the stack of books would hold firm until Louisa returned.

In this anxious state of mind, she penned another letter pleading for help, this time to her "dear old friend" William Ewart Gladstone, as she'd referred to him in a happier missive of some years earlier. At the age of sixty-eight now, Gladstone had enjoyed the first of an eventual four terms as prime minister and was known to take an interest in Spiritualism—something that Georgina must have hoped would make him especially sympathetic to her plight. However, the extraordinary contents of her letter and its fevered tone—understandable though her panic was, under the circumstances—would make confusing reading when taken out of context, and leave her recipient wondering about her state of mind. Still unable to believe that her husband had sent the three intruders to her door, Georgina's missive placed the blame firmly on that "reptile" Anacharsis Ménier.

She accused him of waging a war of attrition against her. His supposed actions included: trying to use violence to damage her throat, attempting to frame her for murder by strewing bottles of poison around her house "in the hope the children would get hold of them and poison themselves," and "insidiously spreading" rumors that Harry was trying to have her committed to an asylum. "But *do* for God's sake, Mr. Gladstone, have this seen to at once," Georgina implored him. "It appears the Law affords me no protection, that any spiteful person who will bribe two blackguard Doctors to swear I am mad may procure a warrant and come in my own house and carry me off." What then, she asked, would become of her "ten dear little children"?

While Georgina had been pouring out her fears on paper to Gladstone, Louisa had set off at a determined pace. She happened to live on Keppel Street, within a ten-minute walk of Tavistock Square, and unfortunately, as Georgina would later discover, she had made her way to the Tottenham Court Road police station that she knew best rather than the nearest one on Hunter Street. Not only was the Hunter Street station closer to Tavistock House, but officers there—unlike those based at Tottenham Court Road—had been the ones to visit the day before and so had already gleaned some sense of Georgina's troubles. This meant that when Louisa returned with two men dressed in the neat dark blue uniforms and tall, rounded helmets that identified British policemen, these constables were extremely slow to grasp the gravity of the situation.

Louisa, however, at first believed that their presence would ensure the safety of her fellow Spiritualist. She persuaded the terrified woman to leave the security of the library so that the matter could be sorted out in the presence of these representatives of the law. Speaking with the knowledgeable confidence of a seasoned campaigner, Louisa demanded that the officers throw out the trio from the asylum. They, in turn, insisted that Georgina should come with them.

"Where to?" asked Georgina.

They did not reply, and Louisa interjected, "Indeed, you must not go!"

The male visitor, whose real name was Wallace A. Jones, was the keeper of Dr. Winslow's asylums. Jones commanded the two women, nurses Sarah Southey and Mary Anne Tomkins, to seize the woman they'd come here to remove. Loudly backed by her new ally Louisa, Georgina protested that they were assaulting her, while the officers, still apparently unable or unwilling to grasp what was going on, observed the scene without taking action.

Georgina, recalling the incident later, would muse that she might as well have been speaking "Hebrew or Chinese" for all the impact her words had on the policemen; "they never moved, and I feel convinced they would have let me be carried off bodily." Thankfully, Louisa took control once more, commanding Georgina to lock herself back into the library while they waited for a second party from the Hunter Street police station, whom Georgina's maid had gone to fetch.

When at last the new police officers entered the house, they asked the trio to produce their warrant. It had been signed not only by Sir Henry and Harry but a third individual, C. E. Armand Semple—a doctor and another of the previous day's mysterious visitors, who had arrived with fellow medical man Dr. John Rudderforth. Everything appeared to be in order, but the police seemed at a loss as to what they ought to do, since there was also the compelling argument that the three were trespassing on Georgina's property. And so, unable to resolve the matter, the police sent the group from the asylum away.

Once they'd departed, Louisa and Villiers convinced Georgina that, for her own safety, she too must leave Tavistock House without delay. And so, having snatched up a cloak and bonnet, her feet still clad in only her indoor slippers, she "stampeded down the square" with Louisa and the two jumped into a hansom cab, which sped off in the direction of Louisa's home on Keppel Street.

Georgina had managed to escape her pursuers for now, but danger remained imminent. The asylum warrant had an expiry date of seven days hence. As Louisa no doubt explained in the gravest terms, until it ran out Georgina still risked being carted off against her will.

That very night, in fact, another party returned to Tavistock House, again just before midnight, to make a fresh attempt at taking Georgina away. These individuals would soon also visit the nearby headquarters of Louisa's LLRA, at 64 Berners Street. It could only be a matter of time before they sought out their prey at Louisa's home address, and so—having had no reassuring word from Harry to put her mind at ease—Georgina went on the run, hiding in the homes of sympathetic confidantes. In a cruel twist of fate, she'd discover that one such house lay only a few hundred yards from Dr. Winslow's asylums in Hammersmith. No doubt unsettled by being in such close proximity to her would-be captors, Georgina disguised herself as a Sister of Mercy and fled once again, this time heading northward to stay with American friends who lived on Porchester Terrace in London's affluent Bayswater district. In this fashion, she managed to keep one step ahead of her pursuers for the duration of the asylum's warrant, after which she made appointments to see two separate doctors who certified her as completely sane.

Armed with this information, Georgina contacted family members and her husband with a view, initially—and despite the great wrongs done to her at their hands—to negotiate some amicable arrangement. She even went so far as to sign a conciliatory document: "On condition of Mr. Weldon giving me the use of Tavistock House and allowing me £1000 per annum as heretofore I promise on these conditions to conduct my affairs in such a way that nobody can object to." She would, she continued, be "perfectly ready to be appealed to by my husband or by my family" were they to decide she was failing to meet these conditions.

Discussions between the two sides broke down, however, after Georgina visited the home of Harry's co-conspirator, his friend Sir

Henry, and confronted him about his part in the plot to have her locked away.

As Georgina would recall in her diary, Sir Henry was out when she arrived, and at first the calm, reassuring manner of his wife almost convinced the visitor that she must be mistaken. Still, Georgina held her ground. When, in time, Sir Henry entered the house, "as jaunty and friendly as ever," she remained on guard, refusing to shake hands with him.

Thrown off balance by the awkwardness between them, Sir Henry began to fidget. When Georgina put her complaints to him, he "tried to laugh it off" and suggested that, if anyone was to blame, that person was her mother.

Georgina continued to press him, as she put it, in "sledgehammer fashion," demanding to know if he had signed the lunacy order.

In the end, her diary records that he admitted, "Well, Madarme, I don't deny I have something to do with it."

She pressed. *"Did you sign that Lunacy Order?"*

"Well, Madarme, yes . . ."

She cut him off before he had the chance to say anything more. "General de Bathe, you will repent this," she informed him, adding, "You will both repent this."

This second threat, meant for the hovering Lady de Bathe, could just as easily have been directed at Harry or indeed any of the doctors who'd colluded with him to have her removed from society, especially the asylum owner—and zealous critic of Spiritualism—Dr. Winslow. Later, pouring out her sense of frustration and betrayal on paper, Georgina would include another unflinching note of warning: "And may God give me the means, give me the allies to ruin them."

No one, least of all Harry, caught up in his plans to rid his life of Georgina, could have guessed how far she'd be prepared to take her desire to expose those who had plotted against her. At this stage, her estranged husband could only go over events in his mind and contemplate how the intended incarceration of Georgina had gone so badly wrong. But rather than censuring his own recent behavior, he directed his frustration at Dr. Winslow, writing to tell him that "the business has been woefully mismanaged."

Georgina's family seemed equally keen to abdicate responsibility. Despite evidence to the contrary, in their sustained correspondence with Harry, her mother and brother now claimed that they had never been fully aware of her husband's intentions and had only wanted to provide her with a temporary spell of care, so that she could get well again. Unknown to Georgina, on receiving the frantic letter she'd written while barricaded in the library, Gladstone had written to one of her sisters, Emily Louisa Williams, enclosing a copy of Georgina's words and inquiring about her mental health. Williams replied that the family had "*always* thought" Georgina "most eccentric" but also asserted that they had known "nothing of this horrible incident till my mother heard from her."

Georgina focused her fury on those she cast as the chief culprits. Presumably she felt that she needed at least a few supporters. But her own account, aired in *The London Figaro* the following year, gives a sense of her inner sadness at her family's betrayal: "What reason can my mother give for never letting me know of the plot thickening against me? That is what puzzles me the most. What could have been her object in not warning me of my danger?"

In October 1878, six months after the procession of mysterious visitors at Tavistock House, Georgina would have the chance to air her complaints before a court of law. Appearing before Frederick Flowers, the magistrate at Bow Street Police Court, she applied for the granting of summonses against those who had signed the order to place her in a lunatic asylum. She would find the magistrate a sympathetic listener but not one who could offer much help. He suggested that, as long as they could be supported by the statements of witnesses, some of her complaints "no doubt" entitled her "to legal redress." The strongest of these, he believed, was the argument that, as she had been forced to barricade herself into a room for some time, this amounted to illegal arrest. Mr. Flowers therefore advised her to consult the Commissioners in Lunacy. To this Georgina replied that she had already done just that and been politely informed that they couldn't take up her case, since she had never actually been committed to an institution. Mr. Flowers felt skeptical that this could be true and attempted to assure Georgina that, even be that as it may, she could still bring an action for false imprisonment.

Now it was Georgina's turn to share her own doubts. Under the law as it stood regarding the rights of married women, how could she bring an action against anyone without the approval of her husband? And it was hardly likely, was it, that Harry would give his approval to legal proceedings against himself?

Despite Georgina's failure to obtain lawful summonses, her story earned her considerable sympathy in the court of public opinion. Coverage of her appeal to Flowers appeared in the Spiritualist and mainstream press, helping to raise her profile. She sang in the Promenade Concerts at Covent Garden and was warmly received. In November, she gave a talk on the unjustness of the lunacy laws at the St. James's Hall on Regent Street, where Emma Hardinge had delivered some of her first trance lectures in London about a dozen years before. The London-based *Illustrated Sporting and Dramatic News* noted in a supportive article that "in every phase of her life" thus far—in her abilities as a singer and "daily inexhaustible charity" as the head of a home orphanage—she had displayed "original talent and strong individuality."

Although her speech at the St. James's Hall was not particularly well attended, owing perhaps to the high cost of admittance—with five shillings being charged for the best seats—her winning smile and relaxed stage manner made a strong impression on the two-hundred-strong crowd sparsely distributed in a venue that could have held two thousand. One journalist in the audience, summing up her performance, commented, "That she is no lunatic she satisfactorily established by the simple narration of her wrongs." She endeared herself to all by stating at the outset that, as this was her first time speaking in public, she'd be grateful if, should she fail to raise her voice enough, someone could let her know.

"Can you hear out there?" she called to the back seats.

The response came back: "Very well, indeed."

To this Georgina responded, "Oh, that's all right," before beginning her opening remarks. She doubted that the "mad doctors" would try to take her again, she said, although if they could secretly poison her she believed they would.

The audience, clearly already under her spell, answered with vehement hisses. Throwing caution aside, she freely named Drs. Winslow; his father-in-law, Winn; Rudderforth; and Semple—all of whom had visited her at Tavistock House in disguise, at Harry's behest—as well as his friend Sir Henry de Bathe. She then informed the crowd that she intended to go on holding meetings like these until the lunacy laws were reformed: "It might be vulgar to make a noise, but unless some one denounced the present abominable system of confining sane persons as lunatics the evil would never be remedied." She had been told, she said, that women ought to leave such problems to "masculine minds," but no man had yet "had the courage to come forward" to seek to remedy the system.

Georgina found herself supported in her call for reform by publications as illustrious as the *British Medical Journal*, which was perhaps unusually critical of the actions of Dr. Winslow—whom they could have defended, after all, as one of their own. Although careful not to criticize the judgment of the Bow Street Police Court magistrate, who had ruled that Dr. Winslow's conduct had been "strictly according to the law," the article gave its opinion that what had happened to Georgina illustrated the worrying limits of "the present possibilities of the law of lunacy." Making a marked distinction between others in the medical profession and the likes of Dr. Winslow, the author of the piece suggested that "a private asylum keeper is, commonly, in a certain capacity, a hotel-keeper; in another capacity, the governor of a house of detention; and, in a third capacity, a physician and man of science." Given the current public concern that such a position was open to abuse, the magazine asked whether it was not "time for the profession to consider whether it cannot protect itself against vilifying suspicions of the kind, by abolishing the present private asylum system, and obtaining an amendment of the law."

One might have assumed that all the publicity Georgina had achieved for the cause would have set her and Louisa Lowe—who'd come so valiantly to her rescue back in April—on course for many years of fruitful collaboration. But despite their shared beliefs as Spiritualists and their common social agenda, the two were already at loggerheads, which put a stop to future plans of working together. In truth, neither woman seemed to like sharing the limelight with the other. It hadn't taken Georgina long to became frustrated with what she regarded as Louisa's more reticent approach to campaigning. Louisa had tenacity and a forceful character. But in her published works, at least, she was motivated by an awareness of Victorian sensibilities to present herself as a docile lady forced into a position of note by the cruel actions of others. Her pamphlet series *Quis Custodiet Ipsos Custodes?*—meaning "Who Will Guard the Guards Themselves?"—published in the early 1870s, is written in a noticeably measured style compared with some of Georgina's writings that deal with similar subjects. An appendix that closes the first volume finishes not with Louisa's own words but rather a statement by Dr. William Rhys Williams of Bethlehem Royal Hospital in Surrey, who had examined her. The statement notes that Louisa is "evidently highly intellectual" and unconventional in her views—both qualities more widely tolerated in men than women. It is also quick to note that, each of the three times the doctor visited her, her "behaviour and manners" were "most ladylike; and even when pressed with regard to Spiritualism she betrayed no excitement, but defended her opinions in a calm and ladylike manner."

For her part, Louisa had decided that Georgina could be unnecessarily heavy-handed. One incident in particular illustrates their two very different approaches. With the orphans still in France, Georgina had opened her home to women she saw as kindred spirits: those who had escaped the clutches of their spouses who'd had them institutionalized as lunatics. When one of their number—who had been shut away by the actions of her military husband—began to talk about seeking reconciliation, a flabbergasted Georgina made it clear that she felt badly let down and actually regarded this as a personal betrayal. Louisa, in contrast, took a more nuanced approach. Realizing that this woman pined after her children, now residing thousands of miles away with their father in India, Louisa encouraged her to try to patch things up with her spouse and also allowed the woman to move into her nearby home on Keppel Street, since continuing to live with Georgina had become too difficult. Georgina became so angry that she refused to return the belongings the woman left behind when she fled to Louisa's house. And so Louisa began legal proceedings on behalf of the woman, which would see her and Georgina fighting it out at Bow Street Police Court.

Sadly, the rift between the pair would never fully heal. In years to come—recalling the day Louisa's quick thinking and desire to offer protection had resulted in her outwitting the trio sent by Dr. Winslow—Georgina would go as far as to make the following outrageous statement about the woman whom she should surely have always regarded as her savior: "I had not been with her an hour before I felt I should prefer a lunatic asylum to her company."

Georgina managed to maintain more cordial relationships with other Spiritualists. In fact, she made a real effort to build these bonds, frequently appearing in British Spiritualism's best-known publications and at gatherings attended by some of its most famous figures. Despite the fact that she was not a celebrity spirit medium, the well-publicized persecution she had faced because of her beliefs resulted in her eventually being cast as a prominent member of the movement.

In November 1878, *The Medium and Daybreak* reported on an event at Langham Hall on Great Portland Street, a well-known London concert venue where, in years gone by, Georgina had regularly led her students in musical performance. The occasion this time was a public lecture, held in honor of two celebrity mediums: Daniel Dunglas Home (pronounced Hume), a Scotsman whose skills allegedly included the ability to levitate to heights of several feet, and Kate Fox Jencken, now married to her lawyer husband Henry. Kate was now in her early forties. She and Georgina were the only two women seated on the speakers' platform, accompanied by five men. *The Medium and Daybreak* reported that after the main portion of the talks were over Georgina and Kate left the platform together, "the former lady having to fulfil another engagement of a public character elsewhere."

Georgina certainly kept herself busy, thriving on the kind of packed schedule with which the young Kate, thrust suddenly into the public gaze, had so struggled. Over the months to come, Georgina reinstated a regular program of at homes at Tavistock House. At these gatherings, intended not just for sympathetic Spiritualists but for all "lovers of justice," she combined musical entertainment, in the form of singing from her old friend Charles Gounod's compositions, with readings of her lecture *How I Escaped the Mad Doctors.* "Every class of person is WELCOME," tickets for the event declared.

Georgina later published *How I Escaped the Mad Doctors* as a pamphlet. It told the story of her ordeal in dramatic fashion, recalling the literary style of one of the era's beloved sensation novels. Accompanying text for these performances, which took place in the theatrical space designed by the property's former resident Charles Dickens, reminded audience members that "Mrs. Weldon gives these Lectures on the principle that 'a drop of water will wear away a stone.' Although her room can hold but 250 persons, still she hopes that her limited public may unite with her in doing all they can towards LUNACY LAW REFORM and the showing up of the practices of MAD DOCTORS."

The Medium and Daybreak summed up the atmosphere at Georgina's at homes by noting that "most people who read the papers know something of her and the bitter wrongs endured at the hands of those who ought to have been her best and closest friends; but to feel the hot, indignant blood course swiftly through the veins, and the most generous sympathy evoked, one must go and hear for oneself." The fact that those who'd tried to commit her to an asylum had failed served only to "prove her in possession of those high and lofty faculties with which God has so richly endowed her," the piece declared. Reminding its Spiritualist audience that Georgina's beliefs in this area had been used as an example of her madness, the author closed by telling readers that it was "incumbent upon every man and woman to give their sympathy and help to her, for in helping her, they help and protect themselves."

If Harry hoped that after this initial burst of activity Georgina might eventually grow bored with her campaign against him and let the subject drop, he underestimated his estranged wife. He had banned her in the past from a stage career. Now, not only would she actively pursue one, but she would make his behavior toward her an integral part of her public performances. An added frustration to the man who had sought to shut her quietly out of view was that, thanks to press interest in her case, Georgina continued to hone her public speaking voice and to build an audience eager to hear what she planned to do next.

Harry would have been even more dismayed if he'd had chance to eavesdrop on a conversation between Georgina and Charles Reade, the popular author of *Hard Cash*. Reade's 1863 novel, somewhat overshadowed by the success of Wilkie Collins's *The Woman in White* a few years earlier, had similarly dealt with the subject of vulnerable patients who found themselves at the mercy of those who ran Britain's private asylums. Reade advised Georgina that, since she couldn't pursue those who'd attempted to have her committed in the courts, garnering maximum publicity was the best way to go. To be successful, he said, she should adopt an "almost American" approach.

As Georgina understood only too well, this nineteenth-century Englishman meant that she should attempt to keep her story in the news through the use of bold and unusual methods of self-promotion—even those that risked being seen as embarrassing or vulgar. Unfortunately for Harry and the men who had helped him, Georgina would embrace Reade's words with gusto. Over the next decade, she'd put the strategy into practice in ways that would help to transform Britain's legal landscape while also humiliating her ex-husband and his co-conspirators as much as she possibly could.

Public Triumph

W hen it came to drumming up publicity, Georgina Weldon was certainly inventive in her methods. Over the coming years, she'd employ sandwich-board men bearing accusatory placards to parade outside the offices and asylums of the doctor Lyttleton Stewart Forbes Winslow. She'd arrange for a hot-air balloon piloted by the celebrated aeronaut Captain Joseph Simmons to scatter leaflets highlighting her campaigns across a stretch of Britain's south coast. And she would keep up her program of increasingly popular lectures during which she spoke of the injustices she'd suffered and called for legal reform to help others who had fallen foul of Britain's lunacy laws.

Although deeply irritated by her actions, neither Dr. Winslow nor the other culprits, whom she continued to name in public, initially retaliated with anything like the same force. But in late 1878 to early 1879, Georgina published a serialized account of her life in the weekly political and cultural magazine *The London Figaro*. The piece seemed deliberately inflammatory and designed to provoke a response from her husband Harry Weldon, his friend Sir Henry de Bathe, and the various medical men who had conspired to lock her up. "The Story of Mrs. Weldon. Written by Herself" began with its author expressing the wish that her enemies would write something about her. Whether they opted for "book, pamphlet, or letter" it didn't matter, she said. "But—'Oh! that they would lay hold of the rope I laid out to them, that they might hang themselves!'" The columns that ran over the following weeks included a reproduction of a letter Dr. Winslow had written to the *British Medical Journal*, justifying his actions. In a rebuttal, Georgina picked apart the doctor's various claims about his professional conduct and his conviction that, at least at the time when he intended to admit her to his asylum, he firmly believed her to be insane. Georgina would go on to challenge Dr. Winslow to provide evidence backing up his claims: "Was I melancholy? Was I foaming at the mouth? Was I epileptic?"—this last condition once widely believed to be caused by mental illness, or even possession by spirits. On the contrary, she argued, perhaps bending the truth more than a little, "People have great deal difficulty in believing that it is actually true anyone ever pretended I was insane, because from my youth up I have always been unusually tidy, methodical, even-tempered, useful, business-like." The young Harry, in contrast, she characterized as 'an empty-headed, indolent young man, who had only two ideas—spending money and looking after other women." Sir Henry she also depicted as an untrustworthy "lady-killer."

Dr. Winslow's response to Georgina was to write once again to the *British Medical Journal*, which had recently asked its readers whether "it was right, just, or tolerable that this lady should be seized upon in her own house and immured" in an asylum. Dr. Winslow argued that, since it was Georgina's husband himself who had requested that this medical man assess her mental state, he failed to see what other action he could have taken. "Surely you would not have had me examine her in the street, or in anyone else's house than her husband's." Although the journal printed Dr. Winslow's letter, theirs was, once again, far from a sympathetic response. In a note added to the foot of his missive was the comment: "Stripped of its irrelevant matter, Dr. Winslow's letter appears to confirm our views . . . We do not think it a difficult matter to suggest improvement in private asylums, and believe that at no very distant period they will, in their present form, be improved off the face of the land."

The January 22, 1879, edition of the *Figaro* also included an interview with Victoria Woodhull—now living in London's Kensington and described as "a lady of world-wide celebrity"—and so readers of that week's edition of the paper were treated to insights into the lives of two flamboyant and controversial women associated with the Spiritualist movement. By this stage, Georgina had already aired multiple grievances against Harry. She used the four columns devoted to her story in this issue to outline how he had plotted to have her placed in an asylum, and to suggest that his aim had been to deprive her of her annual £1,000. She also wrote that he hoped to gain a divorce from her so that he might marry one of his friend Sir Henry's daughters, Kate. Especially given that Harry already had a longstanding mistress, this last accusation appears to have been wide of the mark. For his part, Harry insisted that he barely knew the young Kate de Bathe, who he said he had met only a handful of times. Georgina also alleged that Harry's plan had been to bribe a lawyer to help him forge documents and find false witnesses in order to get her out of the way.

On February 14, 1879, about a month after these assertions appeared in the *Figaro*, Georgina recorded in her diary that the day had brought "no Valentine for me, but the very delightful news that Weldon and Sir Henry de Bathe have applied for a criminal information against the *Figaro*." The pair intended to sue the editor, James Mortimer—an act that, handily for Georgina, would not affect her financially. Safe in that sense, she must have hoped that the case would attract extensive press attention, allowing her to highlight the plight of all people caught in her sort of situation, as well as publicly shaming those concerned with what had happened to her.

Once legal proceedings began, the editor of the *Figaro* attempted to offer an apology. It was refused, and the case of *The Queen v. Mortimer* commenced at the end of June. It was followed eagerly, not just by Georgina, but also by the many readers of the country's Spiritualist press who for over a year had been absorbing the twists and turns of the story of this fellow believer. A report in *The Spiritualist*, reprinted from the London evening paper *The Pall Mall Gazette*, paints a vivid picture of proceedings at the court of the Queen's Bench Division at the Guildhall—a center of London's civic life since medieval times.

Harry was the first witness to be called by the prosecution. Now in his early forties like Georgina, he took pains to present himself as an upstanding, fair-minded man who had simply been dealt a bad hand. He had acted purely on the advice of medical professionals, he insisted, who believed that a period of confinement was the only viable course of action to cure the wife he characterized as delusional. He disputed all of the key accusations made by Georgina in print: that he hoped to marry the twenty-year-old Kate de Bathe, had ever attempted to bribe a lawyer, or had tried to divorce his wife or get rid of her in any other "bad sense."

Sir Henry took the stand next. And like his friend before him, he insisted that Georgina's words, made public in James Mortimer's *Figaro*, were entirely false.

The aim of the defense appears to have been to mitigate Mortimer's role. His business manager asserted that Mortimer left the selection of content for the publication solely to the paper's subeditor, who—frustratingly for those on Mortimer's side—had disappeared shortly before the start of the trial. When cross-examined, however, Mortimer was forced to admit that he did indeed take a personal interest in the *Figaro* and that the absent subeditor had, in fact, been his own servant.

Mortimer, addressing members of the jury directly, emphasized that, once he'd realized how upset Harry was by publication of the article, he had "taken every honourable step" to try to appease this man, a stranger to him, to avoid the necessity for this current court action. Summing up Mortimer's argument, *The Pall Mall Gazette* suggested that the *Figaro* editor felt pained that "he should be punished for having shown sympathy to a defenceless woman whom he believed to have been cruelly wronged." What's more, "The truth was that he was being prosecuted by Mr. Weldon for allowing his wife to air her grievances in his paper, and this was a striking illustration of the danger of interfering between husband and wife."

The jury was told that they must first decide whether the article constituted libel. If they should find that it did, then they must also come to a decision as to whether the defendant had shown that the piece had been published without his knowledge or consent, as his business manager had suggested. The jury duly found Mortimer guilty, but sentencing was postponed until November, to allow him the chance to appeal. In the interim Mortimer filed seven affidavits in mitigation of punishment. But unhappily for the worn-down editor, they did little to help his cause. On November 17, he received a three-month sentence and was ordered to pay a £100 fine.

From Georgina's point of view, all of this was very disappointing. In addition to any sympathy she may have felt for Mortimer, her serialized article had not produced the results she'd wanted. Harry and Sir Henry appeared to have been vindicated, and while the case had achieved coverage in a limited number of Spiritualist and mainstream papers, it had hardly been one of 1879's news sensations. Taking precedence were the Anglo-Zulu War and the grisly "Barnes Mystery" murder of Julia Martha Thomas by her maid Kate Webster. Georgina could not have known that another battle before the courts lay just around the corner—one that would at last deliver the kind of outcome for which she had hoped.

Georgina's Promenade Concerts the previous autumn had come about thanks to an arrangement between her and the French composer and musical promoter Jules Rivière. In October 1879, while James Mortimer was still preparing for his sentencing before the Queen's Bench Division, another series of Rivière's Promenade Concerts opened at the Theatre Royal in Covent Garden. These performances featured several named vocalists, including Georgina herself, a choir she had coached, and one hundred musicians.

Rehearsals leading up to the grand opening had been more than typically fraught. Georgina and Jules both had strong opinions on the artistic direction their concerts ought to take and how they should be promoted. Georgina, seeing herself as one of the big draws of the evening, joked that she would "do my best to get accused of murder," explaining to the seasoned impresario, "What brings money and crowds are people accused of crime." Initially, Jules seems to have gone along with several of her ideas for increasing publicity, believing that, though she threw herself into things "at the devil's own pace," he could act as a moderating influence. As time went on, however, he began to worry that the scandal surrounding Georgina might have a negative impact on his artistic reputation. The pair also clashed over the size of the choir, with Georgina envisioning an enormous company of voices of the kind she'd known when working with her former houseguest, the composer Charles Gounod. Jules, on the other hand, who controlled the purse strings for these shows at the Theatre Royal, felt that Georgina's ambitions ought to be more modest.

For him, the chief focus was the visual appeal of the female—though not the male—members of the choir. He felt that they should be "pretty or at least passable," since "the fellows who pay their shillings like to see fine girls." Showing an extraordinary lack of delicacy, he also advised Georgina, "You must be the eldest and least pretty." The women's cosmetics, "excepting yours," he felt, "should be uniform. You in the midst of them—superb!"

As the date of the concerts drew nearer, disagreements between the pair became magnified, and their relationship failed to improve even once the season was in full swing. Things came to a head on October 25, when the theater mandated that they abandon their usual program to make way for a patriotic benefit on the twenty-fifth anniversary of the Battle of Balaclava, a bloody clash midway through the Crimean War. Space was found for seven military bands and the tragic actor T. Swinbourne's recitation of Alfred Tennyson's celebrated poem "The Charge of the Light Brigade," which memorialized the most famous incident of the battle.

All this left no room for Georgina and her choir. Determined not to be left out of the evening entirely, she and some of her allies took seats in a theatrical box. From here she must have anticipated, correctly, that she could draw the audience's attention, thereby disrupting the spectacle onstage. Some would claim that she went further than this: handing out copies of the supportive Spiritualist magazine *The Medium and Daybreak* and tossing down publicity circulars about herself to an applauding public. Such was the resulting fury of Jules and the Theatre Royal's management that after the weekend Georgina discovered that her contract had been terminated.

On Monday evening, however, she returned to take her place in the audience once more, having purchased a ticket in the name of a member of her choir. She did the same the following night—occasions when either she or one of her party distributed more leaflets featuring her portrait and biography. By the third night, the theater seems to have had enough. When she and her steadfast companion Angèle Ménier—now back from France with Georgina's school of orphans—tried to enter the premises on Wednesday evening, they found the way barred.

The two sides could never agree on who started the violence that followed. Georgina would suggest that that "old pig" the acting manager Samuel Hayes was responsible. She accused him of pushing her on the stairs. James Sidney, private secretary to the tenants of the building, claimed that Georgina knocked off his hat and injured his eye. Both sides served summonses on the other and met in court in early November.

About a week before the editor of *The London Figaro* was sentenced as a result of the articles he'd published about her, Georgina arrived at Bow Street Police Court. Outside, a throng of people who'd been unable to gain entry jostled to catch a glimpse of the woman whom the weekly newspaper *The Graphic* depicted as "the irrepressible lady who has set her mind on bring[ing] about a reform of the Lunacy Laws."

For those lucky few who managed to get a seat, Georgina's testimony did not disappoint. She gave a colorful account of what had happened at the theater, eliciting laughter around the courtroom when she mimicked James Sidney exclaiming, "By jove, she has given me a black eye." After this, Georgina said, he held her arm and forcibly walked her down the stairs, depositing her with a police officer who took her name and address. When, under cross-examination, she was asked about knocking off Sidney's hat, she retorted, "And I would have knocked him down if I could."

With all the accusations flying back and forth, Sir James Ingham, presiding magistrate at Bow Street, dismissed the summons against Samuel Hayes, saying that even Georgina's own witnesses had failed to show that he had committed any "unnecessary violence." Sir James ordered Sidney and Georgina to be "bound over in their own recognisances in £50 to keep the peace for three months—a period which would cover the festive season."

That might have been the end of the matter had Georgina, who still held much ill will against Jules Rivière, not written to four different friends of his, accusing him of being a crook and a bigamist. Unsurprisingly, word soon made its way back to Jules and, on December 9, 1879, he served her with a writ for criminal libel. Two days later she was back in the dock, this time at Clerkenwell Police Court. Once he had heard extracts from the letters sent by Georgina, the magistrate committed her for trial at the Central Criminal Court. As *The Globe* noted, Georgina "did not attempt to deny the allegations at all." In fact, rather than quailing at the prospect of this forthcoming day of judgment, it seemed that she positively welcomed it.

On March 3, 1880, *The Pall Mall Gazette* reported that Georgina had appeared in court and entered a plea "five yards in length justifying the libel on the ground that it was true and that it was published for the public benefit." The prosecution, describing Georgina as "a lady . . . of considerable musical attractions," briefly outlined the professional relationship she'd had with Jules Rivière before reading out some of the most incendiary passages from the letters she had written. She had called him "a fraudulent bankrupt" and accused him of marrying a Frenchwoman while his English wife was still alive. In one missive, she had written that "Rivière must be done for; he is one of the biggest scoundrels unhanged."

Jules's legal counsel did not deny the bankruptcy, but it was not true, they said, that he'd been condemned as a felon. In any case, the lawyer stated, his client had since repaid all his creditors, and the sorry episode to which Georgina's letters alluded had taken place twenty-three years ago. As for the allegation of bigamy, they would concede only that Jules had married his second wife fourteen years after he'd last seen his first spouse and in the genuine belief that this first woman was dead. Therefore, they felt that there was "no real foundation for the charges made by the defendant."

Over the next three days, the trial played out before an enthralled company of members of the public and the press. On March 5, the jury returned a verdict of guilty against Georgina. Summing up the case, the recorder characterized her behavior as "the raking up of a man's past life in order to bring him into contempt, because you have a quarrel with him." This sentiment moved *The Daily Telegraph* to muse that it seemed "ladies, as well as gentlemen, suffering from a real or imaginary grievance, are apt to say in their haste that the persons against whom they have a grudge are but slightly endowed with the cardinal virtues of veracity and integrity. In other words, they lose their tempers and forget themselves."

Whether Georgina had really lost her temper and forgotten herself is far less certain than the *Telegraph* believed. When sentencing took place two months later, on May 24, her forty-third birthday—she was ordered to serve four months in prison. This, however, would not be the public relations disaster that many must have expected.

It did provide an opportunity, though, for Harry, her estranged husband, to accomplish at least part of the plan that he'd tried to put into action the previous year. The day after Georgina was remanded into custody, he arrived to evict Angèle Ménier and the orphans, who had been living again at Tavistock House since their return from France. From Newgate Prison, Georgina could only try to keep up with developments from afar. She wrote letters to the home secretary and the speaker of the House of Commons, pleading with them to reduce her sentence. In sadder moments, she wondered to herself how women could "endure men." But looking back on the experience of her captivity, she would recall occupying herself by singing and learning poetry by heart as well as keeping busy with the prison-assigned task of mending linen. "I did not mind the smallness of my cell," she wrote, "nor my bed being hard. Lovely thoughts came to me. I owed no one anything, no kindness, no help."

In the end, Georgina's incarceration was cut short after just five weeks. At half past nine on the morning of June 30, 1880, she emerged in sprightly form through the heavy doors of Newgate to greet well-wishers who showered her with flowers. Once inside a waiting carriage, she departed with the echo of cheers ringing in her ears like a victory call. It seemed that with every attempt made to silence her, her public following grew stronger.

From this point onward there would be no stopping her. Within days of her release, she'd secured a spot at a benefit concert at the Royal Grecian Theatre in London's Shoreditch, booked to give a talk on her experience of prison life. The bill advertising her appearance displayed an attractive photograph of her alongside the tantalizing promise that she would be "dancing on the platform." Wrote one gossip columnist: "If I can get a chance of putting my arm round Georgina's waist and of tripping with her on the light fantastic, I shall be a happy man."

On July 13, Georgina took to the stage at the packed Great Central Hall on Bishopsgate to speak not just of her time behind bars but of her personal history. This allowed her to conflate her recent imprisonment for libel with the wider cause of lunacy reform for which she much preferred to be known. Addressing the clamoring audience, she said that she realized it was "not considered respectable" for a woman to speak in public. But since she was "speaking in the cause of liberty and justice," she "did not care a button" what anyone thought.

The progressive crowd could not get enough of her. She left the stage during a piano interlude, reappearing, to everyone's delight, in replica prison garb: checked gown, cap, and apron, with an enormous brown spotted handkerchief gripped in her hand.

Above the wild cheering, a female voice was heard to call, "What a shame to put so lovely a woman in so vile a dress!"

"She'd look bonny in anything," a man answered.

There followed shouts of "So she would" and more rapturous applause.

Paying audiences might have loved her, but to her aristocratic family Georgina's public speaking remained a source of considerable embarrassment. In a scolding letter, her brother all but equated her outspokenness with madness. "All you have done since the infamous attempt to confine you in an asylum morally justifies the action of your husband," Dalrymple Treherne wrote. "All respectable persons would say with me, 'Now is the moment to compromise.' If you persist in your foolish endeavours, ruin awaits you—material, physical, and moral ruin."

But Georgina was not in a compromising mood. Legal options for getting even with Harry and seeking an overhaul of the lunacy laws that had almost taken her freedom remained limited. Over the next couple of years, however, she kept herself in the public eye by publishing further pamphlets about her life and the urgent need for legal reform, while continuing with her prison stage act and her public lectures and songs. Then, in 1882, she at last found a way to force her estranged husband to face her in court. Still legally married, though separated from Harry and barred from their former home of Tavistock House, Georgina decided to sue him for the restitution of her conjugal rights—a profound embarrassment to him.

The offense of "subtraction"—that is, the absenting of a husband or wife from the marital home and bed—carried a prison sentence of up to six months.

The press would have a field day picking over the case of *Weldon v. Weldon* that July. Harry had originally answered Georgina's petition with accusations of adultery on her part, but before the jury was sworn in, his legal counsel advised the judge, Sir James Hannen, that, although his client had "been desirous of defending himself," after consulting with his advisers he "was not in a position to support his defence" and had decided to withdraw the accusations. It had probably occurred to Harry that, in comparison to his own position as an officer of arms, his wife—an ex-convict, albeit a popular one—had far less to lose in terms of social standing than he did himself. If he were to have pursued his claims of Georgina's adultery, his own continuing relationship with Annie Lowe might well have been dragged into the open.

Although Harry's withdrawal of accusations against his wife may have been welcome, Georgina's lawyer argued that, now that Harry had made the charges, Georgina should at least have the chance of denying them, allowing the jury to rule on the matter. The judge agreed that this seemed reasonable—a decision that he would find himself regretting almost immediately.

In the witness box, Georgina scoffed at the idea that she had committed adultery, calling Harry's words "an infamous lie." She went on to try the patience of Sir James by naming specific individuals associated with Harry's claims and refusing to quietly accept his admonishment for airing such details in public. Ordered to leave the box, she declared with frustration: "I hate the way in which this case has been hushed up; it's disgraceful." Sir James countered sternly that it was "evident that this case is accompanied by other feelings which I have no wish to encourage."

Nonetheless, as Harry mounted no defense, the judge advised the jury that they should find Georgina not guilty of adultery. This left Sir James only the task of granting Georgina her request for restitution of conjugal rights, with costs.

Regardless of what the court had ordered, Georgina's husband felt no inclination to take her back into his life. One might have thought that this would have been far from what Georgina really wanted, either. But, at least temporarily in the aftermath of the verdict, she seems to have been determined that the pair should pursue just this course. In a lengthy letter to her estranged husband, she insisted that Harry should "bow to the inevitable; you married me— and I want a home and I am determined to have one. The law gives it me; the only reparation it *can* give a married woman." Perhaps unsurprisingly, Harry still could not be persuaded.

Within a matter of months, though, the passing of the Married Women's Property Act of 1882 would make Georgina's statement about the limitations of the law a thing of the past. The centuries-old requirement that a married woman could bring a case to court only with the support of her husband disappeared, and this suddenly opened the possibility of Georgina's mounting civil actions against Drs. Winslow and Semple, Sir Henry de Bathe, and, of course, Harry himself.

In 1883, Georgina began litigation against all four of these individuals and many more besides, including men she felt had wronged her over the course of her musical career. By now she was renting an office at Red Lion Court, where she sat, according to Francis Charles Philips, a prolific author of the day, "amid a chaos of ink-bottles, stumps of pens, papers and memoranda, legal and otherwise." According to Philips, in a description that bears similarities to contemporary assessments of Victoria Woodhull's appearance, Georgina's "dress was plain and with a certain picturesque primness about it, but was in perfect taste. Her hair was cut short; her features, which were public property, were extremely vivacious, and her eyes strangely brilliant and piercing." Her mannerisms, Philips felt, embraced both feminine and masculine qualities. He marveled that "dates, figures, facts were ready with her for anything; she could tell you with the lucidity of a practised counsel what her case was, what she considered her due, and what she believed to be her chance of getting it."

In March 1884 Georgina's lawsuit against asylum owner Dr. Winslow came to trial—a case that involved the subpoenaing of almost every single player in the April 1878 plot against her. *Weldon v. Winslow* was heard at the Queen's Bench Division by Sir John Walter Huddleston, baron of the exchequer. Georgina, representing herself—as she would for the majority of her future court actions—appeared on March 13 in the black gown and elaborately draped cap that would soon become very much part of her public image. Her opening speech was lengthy. By the time the gathered company rose that day, she still had not finished. On the second day, much to the relief of the restless judge, proceedings at last moved on to cross-examination.

On the subject of her behavior over the past few years, Dr. Winslow's defense counsel, Edward Clarke, asked whether she "thought the only course was to libel people all round."

"Yes," she replied.

Asked whether she employed sandwich-board men to harass the doctor, she said, "Yes, I will show you the bills if you like."

When Mr. Clarke's brief questioning was finished, Georgina turned to Baron Huddleston and, betraying her lack of legal experience, exclaimed that Dr. Winslow's lawyer had not really asked her anything. Despite Georgina's admirable ability to acquaint herself quickly with many aspects of the law, she nevertheless clearly did not realize that she had just made the tactical error of admitting on record that she had invited libels.

Louisa Lowe was called as a witness next to tell the story of her involvement in Georgina's escape. She described how her former friend had asked her to help remove the man and two women from the asylum.

"You did not use any personal violence, I presume?" the judge asked.

To this, Louisa conceded, "Well, a moderate amount of shoving."

This was met by gales of laughter all round. There would, in fact, be much laughter over the four days of the trial—an unusual legal spectacle that distinguished many of Georgina's courtroom performances.

James Samuel Bell, the man employed by Harry to look after Tavistock House, also gave evidence, as did Dr. James Edmunds, one of the two doctors who had examined Georgina after she emerged from her seven days in hiding and declared her sane. His testimony introduced even more merriment into the proceedings.

Baron Huddleston asked him about persons suffering from mental illness: "Is it not a fact that, besides the raving lunatic asylums, the great preponderance of the patients are only mad on one subject, and perfectly sane on all others? For instance, a man may imagine himself to be a teapot?"

Without skipping a beat, the doctor volunteered that "Sir Isaac Newton fancied he was a teapot."

"Really, Dr. Edmunds," Clarke countered, "you will imperil the sanity of all the great men who ever lived." At this, the room descended into mirth once more.

On the question of whether it was a sign of madness to hear voices, Georgina asked the doctor, "St. Paul heard a voice, was he crazy? Was Balaam crazy when he heard his ass speak? . . . Joan of

Arc heard voices, was she crazy?—You see, I don't believe in mad doctors, but I do believe in spirits—which is the most dangerous?"

By the time a police sergeant and inspector had also given evidence, and Georgina had announced that she "may as well now put Dr. Winslow into the box," she was laughing as much as anyone.

Unfortunately for her, calling the doctor as one of her own witnesses turned out to be another mistake on her part. Her questioning over that day and the next was often so harsh that, as the judge wryly observed, she risked "discrediting your own witness."

Georgina took every opportunity to openly insult Dr. Winslow. "You are what is called a specialist in lunacy, are you?"

"Yes."

"I suppose it is a kind of breed?"

To this, Dr. Winslow gave no answer, but the crowd once again rewarded her with guffaws of laughter.

"We can't have that, Mrs. Weldon," the judge said.

Georgina protested, "It is quite right, my lord, it is a breed."

But the judge reiterated his message that they couldn't have that.

Despite his expressed disapproval at times, Baron Huddleston appeared to enjoy the novelty of seeing a woman—especially one as entertaining as Georgina—speak for herself in court. Under different circumstances, he said, he "might have taken time to consider my judgement, but the facts are fully before my mind, and I am bound to state the conclusion to which I have arrived." He felt personal sympathy for Georgina and great concern about the law as it stood—which made it so easy to admit a sane person to an asylum—but the judge conceded that it was the law, nonetheless, and that he was still "bound to obey" it. By that law, Dr. Winslow had done nothing wrong, which left the judge with no option other than to dismiss the suit and order Georgina to pay costs.

It was a bitter pill to swallow, only slightly tempered by the support she received from the many people waiting outside to cheer her departure. But with her usual characteristic defiance, she returned to court the following day to ask for a new trial—a request that would be granted two weeks later. The trial would take place that November. In the meantime, Georgina and Dr. Winslow would clash in court again during the July 1884 action *Weldon v. Semple.*

This time Dr. Winslow attempted to do a better job of shoring up his diagnosis of Georgina in the mind of the court. He spoke of a letter passed on from her mother to Harry during the period when the family was secretly in conversation with him. It was an emotional missive in which Georgina vented her frustration at persecutions she felt she'd suffered; and in Dr. Winslow's eyes, the sentiments expressed provided sufficient evidence of her insanity. The doctor also alluded to erratic behavior on her part that he said had driven Georgina's husband away.

Georgina demanded to know exactly what she had done to banish Harry from Tavistock House.

"He said you picked up a lot of children in the streets and they upset water in the room over his head," Winslow replied, "and it ran through and he was driven from room to room."

Under cross-examination by Georgina, the doctor was asked, "And did it never occur to you that he was out of his mind talking such stuff?" The question made the courthouse laugh as much as usual, and the affronted doctor retorted that certainly it had not.

From here, things went from bad to worse for Dr. Winslow, not to mention the defendant Dr. Semple—who had signed the asylum's warrant to have Georgina put away. Although some of Georgina's activities may have sounded infuriating, they were hardly convincing enough to persuade a jury that lunacy lay at the heart of her actions. In his summing up of the case, the judge Sir Henry Hawkins spoke of its great significance not only to the parties present "but to the public generally." He went on to add that, having listened to all the evidence, the current state of the law filled him with "terror and alarm." Singling out Dr. Winslow for particularly stern words, he said that he believed that "nothing could . . . be more improper" than this man being the same one to choose the doctors who would certify the admission of Georgina to his asylum. The judge noted further that Dr. Winslow had prepared these doctors—including his father-in-law, James Michell Winn—with a statement beforehand "as to the condition of the woman they were going to see"—a course of action bound to "warp the judgment of those who were about to make the examination." He concluded by putting three questions to the twelve jurors before they retired.

After just an hour and a quarter, the twelve—all men—returned to give their verdict. In answer to the question "Was the Plaintiff, Georgina Weldon, in fact a person of unsound mind when she was seen by the Defendant, Dr. Semple, and when he signed the certificate on the 14th April, 1878?," the foreman answered, "No."

"Was the Plaintiff a proper person to be taken charge of and detained under care and treatment, either to prevent her doing harm to herself or others, or her property, or for any other cause or reason?"

"No."

"Did the Defendant *bona fide* and honestly . . . personally examine the Plaintiff?"

"No."

The judge asked several more questions, including whether Dr. Semple had "maliciously" signed the certificate "for a sinister motive, such as malice, or to secure a patient for Dr. Winslow."

The jury said that, yes, Dr. Semple had acted from "some sinister motive."

Georgina was awarded the sum of £1,000 in damages plus £20

for the charge of trespass, and applauded again by a large crowd as she departed the scene of her triumph.

Formally vindicated, she was now a true celebrity. As such, she would continue to appear, cast in an increasingly heroic guise, in both the Spiritualist and mainstream newspapers over the next few years. In September 1884, fresh from her victory against Dr. Semple, *The Medium and Daybreak* found her in optimistic form: she had, she said, "every reason to hope" that before she was done with the law courts, "a most unusual spirit of common sense may purify and pervade that atmosphere, which legal sophistry has so long choked and poisoned."

She continued her musical performances, speaking frequently at such events about her courtroom appearances. That same month, as reported in the capital's theatrical paper *The Entr'acte*, she trod the boards at the London Pavilion, in a music hall act playing the character of Serjeant Buzfuz, Dickens's comically verbose lawyer in *The Pickwick Papers*. When she met Dr. Winslow in court yet again, that November, for the *Weldon v. Winslow* retrial, things went much better for her. The charges were the same as before (with Georgina accusing the doctor of trespass, assault, wrongful imprisonment, and libel), as was the cast of witnesses, but a new judge and jury interpreted the evidence quite differently, finding in Georgina's favor and awarding her £500. Within three years, her renown was such that she had become the face of the popular Pears soap brand, appearing in advertisements emblazoned with the claim that she was "50 to-day" but, "thanks to 'Pears' Soap,'" her complexion was "only 17."

Still, not everything went Georgina's way. In her starring role in a George Lander play about wrongful incarceration, *Not Alone*, she failed to make the same kind of impact. London's *Islington Gazette* gave her performance the lukewarm assessment that "she passes muster as an actress." *The Era* remarked that although the play "sufficiently serves the purpose for which it is obviously intended," it was not "the kind of drama that can have any enduring success on the stage." In fairness, Georgina had not had a great deal of time to rehearse—the play opened just weeks after her release from a second stint in prison, brought about by a further libel action against her former musical collaborator Jules Rivière.

During this incarceration—a six-month spell in Holloway Gaol— she was said to have been treated as a "first-class misdemeanant." On exiting as a free woman, wearing a white hat and a pink dress, she waved repeatedly to the prison governor, who watched her departure from an overlooking turret. Having negotiated her way through the usual crowd of well-wishers, Georgina stepped into a carriage decorated with bouquets—part of a procession made up of several vehicles, three brass bands, and people waving banners bearing supportive messages. One read: "All honour and long life to Georgina Weldon, the brave exponent of justice, the champion of people's rights, and the heroine of Lunacy Law Reform." Cheers rang out along the four-and-a-half-mile journey from the jail to Hyde Park, where the horses were set free of their harnesses. With Georgina still ensconced in the carriage, a team of men pulled it by hand to the head of the Serpentine. Here, she held forth for an hour in a public meeting attended by as many as seventeen thousand people.

When Harry Weldon read about the day's events in the press, he must surely have wondered, once again, and not without considerable exasperation, at the course his wife's life had taken since the fateful action he'd tried to set in motion in April 1878. The strangest twist of fate, however, was perhaps who lay behind the well-orchestrated program of events on her release day. That would be two men, both by now well known to Harry, who'd recently formed the Mrs. Weldon Relief Committee—the doctors she had dragged through the law courts, Lyttleton Stewart Forbes Winslow and C. E. Armand Semple.

Bizarre as it seems, the two men may have felt that joining forces with Georgina offered them a chance to rebuild their tattered reputations, while Georgina had perhaps decided that accepting their offer of help could only serve to highlight the extent of her moral victory. In an example of the extent to which both sides were prepared to let bygones be bygones, later that year Dr. Semple and his family temporarily moved into the house where Georgina was now living on Gower Street, only a short walk from Tavistock House—the scene of their first encounter.

As for Dr. Winslow, on the evening of Georgina's release from prison, he was voted in as the chair of the organization he had founded to help his old adversary. For some time, the pair would remain on cordial—if decidedly odd—terms, with Dr. Winslow composing comic verse about their past entanglements and jokingly addressing her as "My dear Lunie" in his correspondence to her. In one letter, written five years after they had faced each other in court, he remarked, "Lunacy law is not what it once was, thanks to you and me." Even his longstanding opposition to Spiritualism and Spiritualists mellowed as he grew older. In his memoirs, published in 1910, he admitted that his views had changed considerably. As noted by the Spiritualist magazine *Light*, in his later years he himself experimented with hypnotism and trance phenomena and even delivered lectures to Spiritualist audiences in which, according to the article, he now "marvelled at his former attitude."

Although Georgina's campaigning clearly had a vindictive edge, by keeping the issue of unjust incarceration at the forefront of public debate through the mid-1880s she made an important and much-needed contribution to the eventual reform of the country's laws.

The passing of the Lunacy Act of 1890 ushered in a period of greater regulation: only legal certification signed by a magistrate could be used to commit a patient to a private asylum, with certification lasting just one year before the patient had to be recertified.

After a long run of success, toward the end of the 1880s Georgina began to slip away from the center of the public gaze, as the press moved on to fresh news stories—most significantly, the horrific Jack the Ripper murders of 1888.

In the year when this spate of senseless killings unleashed a wave of panic across the country—and countless spirit mediums claimed to have used their clairvoyant abilities to uncover clues about the Ripper's identity—Maggie and Kate Fox, whose childhood claims had ignited the Spiritualist movement, emerged once again on the world stage.

End of an Era?

O n October 21, 1888, a startling newspaper advertisement
appeared in New York City. Block capitals declared that at
the Academy of Music, that evening, the audience would
witness the "DEATH OF SPIRITUALISM." The performance
would amount to "A THOROUGH AND COMPLETE EXPOSE,"
an onstage battle of "SCIENCE vs. SPIRITUALISM." What's more,
the legendary Fox sister Margaretta Fox Kane would be the star
attraction.

That night, hordes filled the famed theater where Victoria
Woodhull had delivered an address to a boisterous crowd during
her 1872 run for the presidency. In the words of the next day's *New
York Herald*, the place hummed with "the wildest excitement."
Among those present were hundreds of agitated Spiritualists, still
not quite able to believe that one of those who'd initiated their movement forty years ago should now emerge from her relative obscurity
of recent times to try to strike its death blow. Also in attendance,
seated in a prominent theatrical box, sat Maggie's sister, Catherine

Fox Jencken. Although Kate wouldn't be sharing the platform with her sibling, her conspicuous presence gave the impression that she supported Maggie's actions. It would not have escaped the attention of the crowd that the eldest sister, Ann Leah Underhill, was not in attendance.

After some opening discourse from the night's compère, Dr. Cassius M. Richmond, Maggie entered the stage, eliciting cheers and hisses all around the auditorium. Now in her midfifties and clad all in black, she cut a very different figure than that of the lively adolescent who'd first appeared in public in 1849 at Rochester's Corinthian Hall. The unhappiness of her later life, especially the struggles with alcoholism that had plagued both her and her younger sister, showed on Maggie's gaunt face. She drew out a pair of heavy-rimmed glasses strung on black cord, placed them upon her nose, dropped a curtsy to the audience, and, standing, began to read from a prepared confession.

That she had played such a large part in "perpetrating the fraud of Spiritualism upon a too confiding public" had, she said, been "the greatest sorrow of my life." Lifting her hands heavenward, she continued, "It is a late day now, but I am prepared to tell the truth; the whole truth and nothing but the truth, so help me God!"

Further clapping and hissing followed. Once it had died away, Maggie went on with her speech, laying the blame for her part in the decades-long "deception" on her young age at the time of its beginnings. Perhaps wisely, she didn't state how old she had been— about fourteen—since her words probably gave the impression that she was rather younger than this. Instead, Maggie preferred simply to insist that she had been "too young to know right from wrong."

At this point Dr. Richmond brought on three somber-looking male doctors, who knelt on the floor by the now seated Maggie, who removed her shoe. The audience waited.

Then it began, softly at first, the mysterious knocking. Each doctor took his turn to place his hands on Maggie's shoeless foot before announcing to the audience that he could hear the infamous rapping sounds emanating, not from any hidden spirit presence, but from her clicking big toe.

In the stunned silence that followed, Maggie climbed up onto a small wooden table, so that the packed theater could get a good view. Having placed her foot against a wooden board designed to amplify sound, she stood, seemingly unmoving in her stocking feet, while more raps rang out. The knocks came louder now, louder in fact than one might have thought it possible for a toe to make, even with the aid of a sounding board. Indeed, contrary to what the crowd had just been told, the noises appeared to come not just from her foot but also from behind the backdrop of the stage, the rigging above, and the galleries packed with seated onlookers.

Still, apparently now relieved of a long-held secret burden, Maggie became animated: clapping, dancing, and calling out, "Spiritualism is a fraud from beginning to end!"

Climbing down from the stage, into the audience, she daringly placed her toes, clad in nothing but a layer of stocking, against the shoe-clad foot of one man. In an act that harked back to the twin aspects of theater and inquisition of her early Corinthian Hall performances—but that this time seemed to place her in a position of greater control—Maggie asked the man to tell the house what he felt. He was able to confirm that, like the doctors, he could feel vibrations.

At the conclusion of the evening's program, applauded by Kate up in her box, both sisters found themselves surrounded by enthusiastic new supporters. Spiritualists in attendance, the *Herald* said, "almost frothed at the mouth" before departing the theater muttering "furious threats" against the two women now recast as the would-be destroyers of their movement. The newspaper's own opinion of the evening's entertainment was, perhaps not unreasonably, that "one moment it was ludicrous, the next it was weird." Modern Spiritualism could "never recover from this crushing blow," the *Herald* said. On the other hand, another of the city's papers, *The World*, felt that, even in the aftermath of Maggie's pronouncements, "spiritualistic imposters" would continue to "find as many fools as ever and continue to make their cheats profitable."

Although Maggie's decision to speak out had come as a shock to many of those who'd bought tickets for that night's performance, her animosity toward Spiritualism, including her own work as a spirit medium, had in fact been strengthening for the past thirty years and more.

It had its roots in her relationship with the celebrated Arctic explorer Elisha Kent Kane. The two had first met in the 1850s while Maggie was giving spirit readings in Philadelphia, accompanied by her mother, Margaret. An avowed skeptic, Elisha had nonetheless felt a strong compulsion to attend a séance held by the pretty, vivacious Maggie. He'd frequently returned to see the young woman, still not yet twenty years old, and thirteen years his junior. He had taken her out driving in his carriage, and had presented her with a diamond ring set in black enamel.

Maggie's family had quickly become aware of his pursuit of her, but Elisha had insisted that the two keep their courtship secret from the wider world. It would be quite impossible to wed, he had said, until he'd completed his next Arctic voyage—and until Maggie had acquired the kind of accomplishments he felt a wife of his ought to possess. He sent her gifts of books, urged her to commit herself to further studies, and tried to persuade her to abandon the lucrative career that he considered so unseemly.

Elisha's proprietary behavior toward Maggie did nothing to endear him to her older sister. Leah's concerns are likely to have been twofold. Firstly, during an era much concerned with strict codes of conduct, she probably felt genuine concern and displeasure: after all, Elisha risked tarnishing Maggie's reputation beyond repair if word got out that he was courting her in private without making any public commitment. Secondly, having worked hard to establish the standing of all three Foxes as a trio of spirit mediums, Leah cannot have welcomed Elisha's interference in their profitable, though always precarious, methods of earning a living.

Initially, Maggie, too, had pushed back against her suitor's criticisms. In one letter, filled otherwise with innocuous matters—she told him, for instance, that she'd named her new canary Kent in his honor—she declared that "spiritual manifestations are spreading all over the world. Some of the greatest men in the world have become believers in the spirits." In time, however, under ever greater pressure from each opposing side, Maggie would come around to seeing things entirely from Elisha's point of view. By May 1853, when he set out on his lengthy Arctic expedition, Maggie appears to have all but given up her work as a spirit medium.

Elisha and the crew of his ship, the USS *Advance*, had embarked on a long and dangerous mission: to map uncharted areas and search for the missing British explorer Sir John Franklin, who'd vanished during an expedition in the late 1840s. In Elisha's absence, while Leah and Kate were based in New York City—the latter soon to be observed by Emma Hardinge Britten working long and stressful hours at the headquarters of the Society for the Diffusion of Spiritual Knowledge—Maggie agreed to enroll in a school of Elisha's choosing, in Crookville, a small manufacturing village outside Philadelphia. Elisha would pay all of her expenses and had asked his aunt, who lived in Crookville, to keep an eye on the girl. He must have hoped that these measures would prove enough to keep Maggie on his preferred course, and that in his months, and years, of absence she would not fall again under the influence of Leah, whom he had taken to calling "the Tigress."

Eighteen fifty-three turned into 1854; 1854 into 1855. In the autumn, Maggie learned at last that her beau was on board a steamship headed for New York City. This was not the *Advance*, the vessel on which he'd departed two years earlier. During the arduous voyage, which had seen many of his crew lose their lives, the *Advance* got stuck in an ice floe and had to be abandoned. The exhausted men had continued across treacherous Arctic terrain in smaller boats and on sledges before finally being rescued by a passing ship.

Maggie was not the only one enthused by the prospect of seeing Elisha again. The press had at last caught on to rumors about their relationship, and speculation abounded that "the celebrated Dr. Kane would shortly lead to the altar Miss Margaret Fox, of spirit rapping celebrity." But the newspapers' excitement would prove premature. In the face of the resulting public furor, the families of both sides raised loud objections and for a time the couple's future seemed uncertain. In 1856, however, they renewed their commitment to each other when, according to Maggie's later recollections, they became husband and wife, "marrying" in the presence of some of her family members, in a ceremony that had no legal recognition. Shortly after, Elisha left the United States once more, this time bound for Britain, where he would present a copy of his new book about his voyage to Jane, Lady Franklin, the grieving wife of the missing Sir John Franklin.

Once on the other side of the Atlantic, Elisha fell seriously ill, his physical weakness brought on by numerous maladies that he'd contracted during his years of travel. Medical opinion had it that, rather than returning to the eastern United States right away, he ought to divert his homeward journey with a sojourn in a warmer climate. Elisha chose to visit Cuba, but he would not make it home from there alive. Maggie's letters to him, sent care of the American

consul in Havana, remained unanswered. He died, never having for-
malized his union with her, on February 16, 1857.

In the aftermath of his death, Elisha's family denied that there
had been any sort of romantic relationship between him and the
infamous Fox sister, let alone that a marriage had ever taken
place. With Elisha dead, gone too was any realistic prospect for
Maggie to lead the kind of respectable life that her lover had envisioned for her.

Apparently out of respect for his memory, she would continue
to avoid working as a spirit medium and convert to Catholicism—a
step she said Elisha, though not a Catholic himself, had urged her
to take. In 1866, following several years of legal wrangling with
the Kane family, Maggie allowed the correspondence between her
and her lost love to be published in *The Love-Life of Dr. Kane*. The
book presented her in print as the wife she believed she was in spirit,
Mrs. Kane.

The Love-Life of Dr. Kane attempts, not always successfully, to
cast Elisha as a heroic figure—and someone who had done his best
to rescue Maggie from what he regarded as the sordid life of a spirit
medium. Sympathetic references to Maggie's sister Kate appear
many times within these pages. Notably absent are direct references
to Leah. Instead, this older sister, who had shaped the careers of all
three Fox women, is referred to coldly as "a relative" and her actions
interpreted in a negative light.

Unsurprisingly, publication of the book did nothing to repair
the already strained relations between Leah and Maggie. Another
source of tension was the pronounced difference in their economic
circumstances. Since giving up her work as a medium, Maggie had
struggled financially—a major influence on her decision to publish
the letters. Leah, on the other hand, who'd always done very well
out of Spiritualism, had been enjoying a life of even greater lux-

ury since marrying the successful businessman—and Spiritualist—Daniel Underhill in 1858. In the end, out of sheer necessity, Maggie would return to her old practice of giving spirit readings for money. But she harbored bitterness, much of it directed at Leah, ensconced in her elegant home on West Thirty-Seventh Street, with its luxurious décor and indoor aviary.

By the evening in October 1888 when Maggie took to the stage at the Academy of Music, the youngest Fox sibling, Kate, had developed a similarly bitter anger toward Leah. As Emma Hardinge Britten had observed, in the days when they'd both been stationed at the SDSK building on Broadway, Kate had often found herself ground down by the stresses of working such long hours for ever more demanding audiences. As a result of the relentless pressure, she—like Maggie—had increasingly found solace in alcohol. Rumors about Kate's addiction abounded within the Spiritualist world of New York City, especially once she started to drink on the job. In later years, Kate would remember people plying her and Maggie with baskets of champagne when they were mere girls. A close friend lamented that, in her early thirties, Kate had held a private séance for a "very fashionable family on Fifth Avenue" and come home "crazy with brandy." He also wrote of an occasion when, later in life, she'd been discovered sitting alone "in a miserable saloon, drunk."

In October 1871, Kate had set sail for Britain in search of a fresh start. Settling in the nation's capital, she'd been embraced by London's Spiritualist community. A year later, in December 1872, she married Henry Diedrich Jencken—the Spiritualist barrister who'd acted on behalf of Georgina Weldon's rescuer Louisa Lowe during the legal battles following her incarceration in an asylum. The wedding was widely covered by Spiritualist and mainstream publications on both sides of the Atlantic. *The New York Herald* reported that the spirit world displayed its awareness of the nuptials via the chorus of raps that rang out during the ceremony in the neoclassical surrounds of St. Marylebone Parish Church. Following the birth of their first child, Ferdinand Dietrich Lowenstein Jencken—known as Ferdie—rumors began that he, too, had unusual powers. While he was still a baby, it was said, a pencil had been placed between his grappling fingers, which had then written a message in Greek that translated into the biblical line "Who believes in me shall live."

In 1885, Kate's older sister Leah reproduced a lengthy article about Ferdie—originally published in the London Spiritualist magazine *The Medium and Daybreak*—in her book *The Missing Link in Modern Spiritualism*. Leah had high hopes for this part-memoir, part-history of the Modern Spiritualist movement—so much so that she'd had a number of copies specially bound in purple velvet to send to various European luminaries, including Queen Victoria. Sadly, the queen's journals from the period carry no mention that the gift ever made it into her hands, but Leah may have felt reason to hope that it would be gratefully received. In the years following the death of Prince Albert in 1861, there'd been a flurry of rumors about the queen embracing Spiritualism. Optimistic believers suggested that she had tried to contact her late husband with the aid of spirit mediums, including, so it was claimed, her well-known Scottish servant John Brown.

Leah's book, although indisputably fascinating to anyone interested in the nineteenth-century séance scene, needs to be read with care. Her recollection of dates and chronology is often hazy, and she tends to gloss over episodes for which she was met with criticism, including from her own flesh and blood. *The Missing Link* gives virtually no hint of any friction between the sisters. But it is telling that, other than captioning a picture of Maggie with the name she'd adopted, Margaretta Fox Kane, Elisha does not intrude upon these pages.

By the time the book came out, Kate, now the mother of two small sons, had returned to the United States. The boys' father, with whom Kate had enjoyed a happy and relatively stable decade, had passed away in late 1881, having suffered a stroke. With Henry gone, Kate had felt the pull of her homeland, and, on arriving back in New York City, she and her sons had moved into Leah's house. In time the pull of alcohol took hold of Kate once more, leading to tension with Leah and further devastating consequences.

On May 4, 1888, five and a half months before Maggie's dramatic stage appearance, Kate, who'd moved to her own apartment on East Eighty-Fourth Street, was arrested and locked up. Under the wisecracking headline "The Spirits Too Much for Her," the following day's *New York Herald* reported that "one of the notorious Fox sisters" had been charged with "drunkenness and flagrant neglect of her maternal duties." The paper suggested that neighbors had complained of her erratic behavior, but Kate suspected that Leah and other Spiritualists, embarrassed by her conduct, were really the ones to blame for her detention and the fate of her two boys. Ferdie, aged fourteen, and her younger son, Henry, thirteen, had been removed from their mother's care and placed in the city's Juvenile Asylum.

When the news reached Maggie, on an extended stay in London, she fired off a shocked response to the *Herald*, which they would print on the twenty-seventh of that month. Her absence, when Kate must have needed her most, Maggie said, would have added to her "darling sister's depressed state of mind." As for Maggie herself, the news had "nearly killed" her. Her next paragraph, however, turned the attention from Kate to Spiritualism, the movement that had governed the sisters' lives for the past forty years, and which was now intertwined in both of their minds with their hostile feelings toward Leah. "Spiritualism is a curse. God has set His seal against it!" Maggie declared. Spiritualism had always been "a curse and a snare to all who meddle with it. No right minded man or woman can think otherwise."

She would go even further in an interview she granted to the same paper once she'd resumed her life in New York City that September. By this stage, her younger sister had regained custody of her boys and the three had fled to Britain, where Kate would stay until shortly before Maggie's Academy of Music confession. As Maggie would reveal to the *Herald*'s reporter, their concerned aunt had played no small part in the boys' escape. On learning that Ferdie and Henry were being held in the Juvenile Asylum, Maggie had telegraphed the relevant New York authorities, not in her own name but that of Kate's brother-in-law Edward Jencken, the boys' legal guardian. Maggie, in the guise of Edward, demanded that the pair be released immediately into the care of their mother and brought to London. This was duly done. As Maggie would delightedly relate to the astonished journalist, on all four family members being reunited, the boys greeted her with the cry "Hello, Uncle Edward!"

In her conversation with the *Herald* reporter—conducted about a month before she stood up before that theater crowd, working her big toe in her stocking feet—Maggie struggled to hide her emotions. She covered her face with her hands at times and paced the modestly furnished room. She almost broke down at one point, when she recalled memories of Elisha, but managed to hold herself in check. When her thoughts turned to Leah, though, Maggie's anger exploded.

In answer to a question about why she had worked as a medium for so long if she despised everything about Spiritualism, Maggie raged that her older sister had "made me take up with it. She's my damnable enemy. I hate her. My God! I'd poison her. No I wouldn't, but I'll lash her with my tongue." It was the pressure of this existence inflicted upon her by Leah, she said, that had caused her, too, to "drown" her "remorse in wine."

Maggie told her visitor that she intended to expose the fraud of Spiritualism, and that she would start with the mysterious knocking. At this, a series of raps rang out, startling her seated guest, who felt almost sure that they had come from under his chair. He glanced around the room, trying to learn the origin of the sounds. Then the knocks, which Maggie would claim a month later to have been produced by her clicking toe, seemed to travel from under the man's chair to beneath the table on which he leaned. When Maggie stood and led him to the exit, more taps reverberated, apparently from the area outside the door.

Turning to his hostess, the reporter asked, "How do you do it?"

"Well," Maggie replied, "I want to keep my explanation till the night of my lecture."

Once that lecture had taken place a month later, many more reporters would air their views. In terms of the mainstream press, the response to Maggie's onstage confession tended to range from wry amusement to the confident writing-off of Spiritualism. The *New-York Tribune*, so supportive of the sisters during their first appearances in the city, said that members of the academy's audience that night had "got their money's worth in fun." The paper felt that the evening marked the successful beginnings of an "anti-humbug crusade." California's *Sacramento Daily Record-Union* looked forward to the day when "spiritualistic manifestations" would be regarded as "follies and the mere deceits of a half century," while, across the ocean, *Lloyd's Weekly London Newspaper* commented that "if any further proofs were necessary to expose the silly subject of so-called spiritualism, they have been supplied by Mrs. Kane."

The response of Spiritualist publications was, understandably, more heated. In Massachusetts, the Boston-based *Banner of Light* raged at the "ignorance and misconception of the average secular journalist" for giving so much credence to the Fox sisters' importance. The long-running magazine put forward the alternative view that "the Fox girls"—women in their fifties by then—had "wanted both notoriety and money. Among the Spiritualists they could get neither, so they went where they belonged." The British magazine *Light*, printed in London, chose to focus on the Fox sisters' alcoholism: "Painful, therefore, as it may be, we are compelled to say that no credence is to be attached to anything that these ladies may say."

Two hundred miles north of the nation's capital, in Manchester, *The Two Worlds*, edited by the sixty-five-year-old Emma Hardinge Britten, was more measured in its condemnation. Nonetheless, it made similar allusions to the pair's addictions and related indiscretions. Comparing Kate and Maggie unfavorably with Leah, *The Two Worlds* noted that, unlike her younger siblings, this oldest of the famous Foxes had "not only practised professional mediumship in far wider fields of action than either of her sisters, but did so without a slur on her noble character, a stain on her name, or the slightest tarnish to her good true womanly life in public or private." This was, it should be noted, a different judgment from the one put forward in *Modern American Spiritualism*, Emma's written history of the movement published eighteen years before, which praised all three sisters equally.

In the years since Emma's *Great Funeral Oration on Abraham Lincoln*, she had enjoyed a varied and decidedly modern career, bringing out pamphlets and books, and lecturing on social, political, and spiritual issues on both sides of the Atlantic. Although her cultural impact had decreased from the heights of her 1860s successes, she remained a stalwart of the nineteenth-century séance scene and, thanks to her literary output, a revered custodian of Modern Spiritualism's history. In the late 1870s, she'd undertaken a tour of New Zealand and Australia with her husband, fellow Spiritualist William Britten, to spread the word about the movement. The two had been living in the Cheetham Hill area of Manchester since the early 1880s, and Emma had been in charge of *The Two Worlds* since 1887.

From Emma's earliest days as a medium and trance lecturer, Spiritualism had given her not just a voice but an audience eager to listen. For the greatest part of her life, she had been embraced and subsumed by the movement. Her *Autobiography*, published posthumously in 1900, touches on her stage and political careers but concerns itself chiefly with her life as a Spiritualist. The idea of her publicly endorsing Maggie Fox's confession would have been quite unthinkable.

Victoria Woodhull Martin—as she'd been called since marrying the British banker John Biddulph Martin in 1883—felt equally resistant to altering her beliefs. At the time of her departure from the United States, Victoria's politics and free love philosophy had perhaps eclipsed her association with Spiritualism in the minds of many American people. On arriving in Britain in 1877, however, she had renewed her public commitment to the movement. In 1879, in an interview with *The London Figaro*, Victoria declared that what had brought her across the waves was not in fact a wish to escape the bad publicity she'd endured in her homeland following her spat with the Beecher family. Rather, she said, messages she'd received from the spirit world had persuaded her to relocate. As she put it, she and her sister had come "to this country under spiritual guidance, and all our movements since have been under spiritual direction." Scoffing at rumors that she and Tennessee Claflin had received hush money from the family of the late Commodore Vanderbilt, who had died in 1877, Victoria suggested that they had instead regained their prosperity thanks to further helpful intervention from beyond the grave. This had, she said, enabled the two women to recover their riches through their "spiritual power and by speculations in stocks."

By the time of the Fox sisters' stand of 1888, both Tennessee and Victoria had shored up their economic circumstances to an even greater extent—Victoria by marrying into the Martin banking dynasty and Tennessee by wedding the wealthy textiles trader Francis Cook, whom Queen Victoria had made a baronet in 1886. Since then, Tennessee had been able to call herself Lady Cook. Despite the fact that Victoria's past work as a clairvoyant healer had often seemed more cynical than the passionate trance lecturing of the young Emma Hardinge, she had retained her interest in the spirit world well after her wealth had made it financially unnecessary.

In the years to come, in addition to continuing to harbor political ambitions, Victoria would embrace fresh areas of interest. Toward the end of the 1890s, she'd take up motoring—one of the earliest women in Britain to do so. In her midsixties, she would become a founding member of the Ladies' Automobile Club, established in 1904. She combined pastimes like these with decidedly darker ones, such as her strengthening enthusiasm for eugenics. Scholars have sometimes sought to explain Victoria's engagement in this dangerous philosophy by pointing out that its ideas were widely accepted at that time, half a century before Adolf Hitler's Third Reich would take them to their horrifying conclusion. Nonetheless, it is difficult for a modern audience to read Victoria's 1891 pamphlet *The Rapid Multiplication of the Unfit*, which promoted selective breeding, without experiencing feelings of revulsion or regret. At the same time, it should be noted that she cared for her own son, Byron, at home until the end of her life, although his learning disabilities, according to this booklet, made him unfit to be born.

Her magazine *The Humanitarian*, begun in 1892, also promoted eugenics, in addition to exploring wider social issues. When Victoria sent a copy to her former adversary Emma Hardinge Britten in 1897, the socially conscious Emma responded positively, calling it a "noble magazine." Emma's letter of thanks—written in her characteristic almost indecipherable scrawl—throws new light on the relationship between these two pioneering Victorian women. It suggests that in their later years they were able to put "circumstances occurring in America" behind them and focus instead on their shared pasts, and presents, as women whose voices were first heard by the public thanks to their involvement with Modern Spiritualism.

Victoria's continued fascination with this world led her to join Britain's Society for Psychical Research—an organization still in existence today, devoted to scholarly research into the type of unexplained phenomena associated with the Victorian era's Spiritualists. Following her death in 1927, Victoria would leave all her property to Zula. Had her daughter predeceased her, however, the society would have been a chief beneficiary of Victoria's will.

In those last months of 1888, when frustrated Spiritualists were reacting with anger toward the younger Fox sisters, Georgina Weldon, too, had refused to let the unsettling news from across the Atlantic affect her involvement in Britain's Spiritualist scene. Three weeks after the issue of *Light* that had interrogated the reliability of Maggie's declarations, a notice appeared in the same magazine stating that Georgina was due to address the crowd at a forthcoming meeting of the London Spiritualist Federation. The next month, the same magazine reported that, still sticking to the winning combination of séance and song, she would be performing two solos at another meeting of the same organization.

In Georgina's case, her fortunes as a Spiritualist had been mixed. Her beliefs, after all, had almost seen her shut away in an asylum in 1878. On the other hand, it was the actions of a fellow Spiritualist, Louisa Lowe, that had saved her from the clutches of the "mad doctors." In the years since those men had tricked their way into Georgina's home, Britain's Spiritualist community had provided this campaigner for the reform of the country's lunacy laws with consistent support. And so she, too, would remain un-moved by Maggie Fox's revelations. Like Emma Hardinge Britten and Victoria Woodhull, Georgina would maintain her devotion to Spiritualism until the end of her life. After the composer Charles Gounod's death in 1893, she would seek to reestablish the close yet fraught relationship the two had enjoyed when he was alive. In her own mind, at least, the man with whom she had once shared a home began to make his presence known once more, communicating by moving saucers around, and through the familiar activities of rap-ping on tables and writing messages to Georgina through the hand of a helpful medium.

As for Leah Fox Underhill, who bore the brunt of so much of her sisters' criticism, in the immediate aftermath of Maggie's onstage confession she must have been pleased to see *The Missing Link in Modern Spiritualism* frequently cited as a text ideally placed to re-fute the accusations made onstage by Maggie. In the spring of 1889, Leah would make a rare public declaration at an event held in New York City to mark the forty-first anniversary of the birth of Mod-ern Spiritualism. On this occasion, she said that she could not un-derstand why her sisters "should have made such statements." Her hope was that they would "soon be brought back to the truth." But when Maggie read of this, she responded by writing to the main-stream press, proclaiming, "I would rather die of starvation than to be again forced to carry the terrible, loathsome weight of 'spirit medium,' and that is what Mrs. Underhill means by being 'brought back to the truth.'"

By now, the positions of both sides—Leah on one, Maggie and Kate on the other—must have seemed unbridgeable. Maggie had fol-lowed up her public confession in October 1888 with multiple repeat performances. Within a week, she and Dr. Richmond, the evening's compère at the Academy of Music, had returned to the stage, this time appearing across the East River at Brooklyn's Grand Opera House. By November, the two had arrived in Boston, where they gave a similar demonstration at the city's Music Hall, its aim, as *The Boston Herald* put it, to "thoroughly explain the method of doing" behind "the seemingly wonderful feats of the mediums, notably spirit painting, slate writing, manifestations, etc." By December Maggie had reached New Haven, Connecticut, where she and a different man, a Professor Ransom, appeared before yet another excitable crowd.

At one point in the proceedings, when Maggie's new stage partner called for a "committee" of audience members to assist him, a group of male students bolted up onto the platform. In the words of the local *Morning Journal and Courier,* "They made great fun for everybody." The professor asked the young men to tie him into a cabinet in order to illustrate that, even when he was supposedly impeded, he could use the kind of skills employed by escape artists to carry off the feats of ringing bells and playing a tambourine without the assistance of any dead spirits. Therefore, the famed rapping sounds associated with the Fox sisters could easily be accounted for by the surreptitious clicking of a toe. For her part, Maggie took her usual pains to paint an image of her past self as a naïve youngster led astray by her older sister. She and Kate, she told the audience, were "innocent little children" when the first mysterious knockings began. But "I never in all my life received a message from the spirit land," she declared. "No one in the world ever did."

Kate, too, undertook a series of public demonstrations, including in Rochester, New York, where the sisters had first come to public attention following the famous investigations at Corinthian Hall. In an interview promoting her forthcoming tour dates, Kate inferred that she fully supported the stance taken by Maggie and that, like her sister, she wished to renounce Spiritualism as "a humbug from beginning to end."

Those unable to make it to any of their demonstrations in person could read what Kate and Maggie had to say in *The Death-Blow to Spiritualism*—a book whose title appeared to echo the name of an earlier (pro-Spiritualism) pamphlet by Georgina Weldon, *Death-Blow to Spiritualism—Is It?* Maggie and Kate's *Death-Blow*, which appeared on November 17, was authored by a professional writer, Reuben Briggs Davenport, whose journalistic output had nothing to do with Spiritualism. The book's preface sought to excuse its literary style, explaining that it was "written in extreme haste." Given the book's publication date, less than a month after Maggie took the stand at the Academy of Music, no one could call this an exaggeration.

However, the author did have slightly more time than perhaps might have been assumed. A statement accompanying the printed book, signed by Margaret Fox Kane and Kate Fox Jencken, was dated October 15—six days prior to Maggie's public appearance. The pair's endorsement of Davenport's "true account of the origin of Spiritualism" suggests that, even before Maggie took to the stage, they understood how incendiary her words would be. After a lifetime of struggling to make their voices heard above the hubbub generated by the entrepreneurial Leah, the two younger sisters were apparently ready to embark on a sustained campaign given over to setting the record straight.

This could so easily have been the end of the story, and yet there was another twist to come. It would turn out that, even as Kate was asserting her support for Maggie in public, she had been privately articulating quite a different version of events.

In December 1888, Kate wrote a letter to Elizabeth A. Cottell, a Spiritualist friend from her London days, who felt aggrieved enough by its contents that she took the step of passing this private missive to the editor of *Light*. Kate alleged that the organizers of Maggie's appearance at the Academy of Music, although not her sister herself, had made $1,500 from that night alone. Kate, whose subsequent allegations had earned her nothing like that sum, seemed in a despondent mood. She had often wished that she'd remained faithful to the collective of Spiritualists, she said, adding that "if I had the means, I would now return, to get out of all this." More candidly still, looking ahead to the future, she mused that "I think now I could make money in proving that the knockings are *not* made with the toes."

As if Kate's volte-face wasn't enough, by October 1889, almost a year after Maggie's infamous confession, rumors had begun to spread that she, too, would soon go back on her word. *The Boston Herald* reported that, no longer able to make a living from her current occupation as an exposer of Spiritualism, Maggie had decided to resume her career as a medium again. A month later, Maggie talked with Henry J. Newton, president of the First Society of Spiritualists of New York, at his home in the city.

In the presence of several witnesses, the worn-down woman, who trembled as she spoke, informed the gathered company that all she had said of Spiritualism over the past year had been "false in every particular." Once more, she portrayed herself as an innocent victim, this time "of the treacherous horde who held out promises of wealth and happiness in return for an attack on spiritualism, and whose hopeful assurances were so deceitful." Her own spirit guides, she said, had convinced her that the only just way forward was "to refute the foul slanders uttered by me against Spiritualism." She intended to embark on another lecture tour, she said, with this as her aim. Indeed, a month later, on December 20, the *New-York Tribune* carried a small advertisement for Maggie's recantation of her recantation, with this appearance to be held at Adelphi Hall, at the corner of West Fifty-Second Street and Broadway.

But by now both the general public and once-loyal Spiritualists had grown understandably tired of Maggie's ever-changing position. In contrast to the reaction to her previous year's revelations, little was made of her newest stance in the mainstream newspapers in either the United States or Britain. As for the Spiritualist press, it had wholly run out of patience. Quoting the words of one reader, the *Banner of Light* asked, "Who can trust her now?" With more than a nod toward her alcoholism, it remarked that "she expects, like the reformed drunkard, to make the repentant avowals of her own disgrace, the subject of money-making lectures." Who, the writer went on, would pay any attention when, should this new venture also fail, she could easily return to "her old habits or to the enemies of Spiritualism"?

It would be a position taken up by the movement's early historians. Emma Hardinge Britten, by now the author of *Modern American Spiritualism, Nineteenth Century Miracles*, and numerous other works, would use her editorship of *The Two Worlds* to express incredulity that Maggie should now attempt "to unsay all she has said" and have "the audacity to place herself again before the public as a 'spirit medium,' and to demand from spiritualists their confidence for having first declared herself a fraud *as* a spirit medium, and *now* for declaring she was a fraud when she *denied* being a spirit medium!" Comparing both Kate and Maggie unfavorably with their "good and true-hearted" sister Leah, Emma used her furious opinion piece, which ran more than two pages, to put forward the bold suggestion that, in the interests of keeping the pair out of the newspapers, the United States' wealthy Spiritualists should club together to provide "a sufficient subscription to endow these women for life." This money, which would be managed by a group of trustees, would thereby ensure that the two youngest Fox sisters would never again have an excuse to "resort to shameful trickery for the means to live." In 1926, Arthur Conan Doyle, author of *The History of Spiritualism* as well as the Sherlock Holmes books, would quote Emma's early observations of the young Kate Fox at work, "repeating hour after hour the letters of the alphabet." This grinding monotony, Doyle suggested, demonstrated the pressures exerted on both Maggie and Kate. Such exertions, he believed, had driven the sisters first to drink and then to turn their back on the movement.

Now lacking an audience willing to listen, the two younger Fox sisters slid away from public attention, reliant on the kindnesses of the few Spiritualist friends who remained loyal—and who still trusted enough in the powers of the women to continue to use their apparent gifts to try to communicate with dead loved ones.

When Leah, aged in her late seventies, died, in November 1890, devotees on either side of the Atlantic mourned her passing to the spirit world. The *Banner of Light* noted pointedly that "as a Spiritualist, she remained steadfast and firm in her faith to the end." And *Light*, which had not softened its stance against Kate and Maggie in the intervening months, remarked that "she played a more consistent and creditable part than her two younger sisters have chosen." In contrast, when Kate and Maggie died, in 1892 and 1893, respectively, there would be no such wholehearted plaudits. But neither could their former followers forget this pair.

In early March 1893, on learning of the dire state of Maggie's finances at a time when her health was fading fast, the *Banner of Light* had established a fund to help this "pioneer medium" in her hour of greatest need. Before the middle of the month, the same magazine would solemnly mark her "transition" into the world of the spirits. Its obituary prophesied that "future generations" would "rejoice in the results of her grand successes, throw a mantle of charity over and forgive all her failings, and hold in ever grateful remembrance" what she and indeed all three Fox sisters had "accomplished for the people of earth."

In Remembrance

What exactly were the accomplishments of Leah Fox Underhill, Margaretta Fox Kane, and Catherine Fox Jencken? The writer of Maggie's somber obituary in the *Banner of Light* had been referring to the trio's contributions to the growth of Modern Spiritualism. Even by the time of the article's publication, however, in the last decade of Queen Victoria's reign, this once powerful movement had lost much of the impact of its midcentury heyday. And although, 170 years later, devoted believers still mark the anniversary of those first mysterious rappings at Hydesville, the *Banner*'s hopeful predictions of how the sisters would be remembered have not come to pass. But the passage of time offers fresh perspective. Today's readers can indeed marvel at the "grand successes" of Kate, Maggie, and Leah Fox, of Emma Hardinge, Victoria Woodhull, and Georgina Weldon—women who came to wield extraordinary levels of social or political clout in an era when female voices seldom garnered much serious attention.

In 1848, Leah Fish, as she was then known, seized control of the narrative of her younger sisters' stories, shaped until then by the male journalists first on the scene. At a time when most women abandoned by their partners would have felt they had no option but to fall back on the charity of their fathers or brothers, this single mother had already carved out an independent life supporting herself and her daughter by giving piano lessons. When an unlikely new opportunity presented itself, Leah grasped it with an unshakable grip. As the force behind the Fox sisters' public appearances, Leah's apparent authority would eventually isolate the other two, leaving Maggie and Kate so aggrieved that, in 1888, they set out their complaints onstage and on paper in an open act of revenge. Their story does not end happily. But one cannot deny that Leah created opportunities for this younger pair. Her entrepreneurship took Kate and Maggie far from their rural hamlet, rewarded them with otherwise unimaginable levels of fame and influence, and swept aside the usually indestructible barriers that fenced in women of their social background. Thanks to Leah, the three Fox sisters acquired a kind of collective voice within a patriarchal society—severely limited though it was to the invisible knocking sounds that accompanied their presences.

All the great female Spiritualists of the day held similar sway while enduring equivalent limitations. During the late 1850s, British immigrant Emma Hardinge inspired many columns of newsprint in her adopted country thanks to her remarkable "trance lectures." In 1865, her speech commemorating the death of Abraham Lincoln was watched by a New York City crowd of over three thousand and touched countless others on either side of the Atlantic following its publication in pamphlet form. It bears repeating that these were truly extraordinary audiences for any woman of the time, and that—as in the case of the Fox sisters—it was Emma's Spiritualist activities that had delivered these opportunities. When Emma arrived in London some months later, her public talks caused a sensation in the British press. Over the course of her career, her novel status—not just as a spirit medium but also as a rare female orator—earned her unwelcome attention from detractors and even celebrity stalkers, as well as widespread admiration. Emma had found a way for her words to reach enormous numbers of people. Yet many who flocked to hear her sincerely believed that she was merely the earthly mouthpiece for the thoughts of dead men.

In the late 1860s, Ohio-born Victoria Woodhull arrived in New York City, armed with both determination and supposed stock exchange tips from the spirit world. Trading on these desirable assets, she and her sister accumulated vast wealth and established the first female brokerage firm on Wall Street. Not content to stop there, they began the magazine *Woodhull & Claflin's Weekly*, and Victoria further extended her public reach by putting herself forward as the first female presidential candidate. In 1872, with universal female suffrage still almost half a century away, this was an audacious move indeed, and, once again, only made possible by the opportunities afforded by her involvement with Modern Spiritualism. But Victoria's Spiritualist support base would have its limits, too, and some of her more outspoken pronouncements—especially her assertions on the subject of free love—would lead to her being shunned by many within the movement.

Among the Spiritualist community at least, Georgina Weldon's position was less contentious. Having escaped the threat of being committed to a London asylum in the late 1870s, Georgina went on to carve out a trailblazing career as a legal campaigner. Deciding to adopt an "almost American" approach to publicity, she used her popular musical soirées, as well as her widely covered appearances in the law courts, to spread her social message. Stints in prison did nothing to quell her enthusiasm, and in fact seemed to galvanize her in her aim to highlight the injustices of the law as it stood. In Georgina's case, her identity as a persecuted Spiritualist had guaranteed her the immediate support of celebrated figures within that world. Of course, it was this same Spiritualist persona that had been used as a basis for her attempted incarceration. This serves as another stark illustration of how Spiritualism could bring both opportunity and intense restriction.

The sad final years of Kate and Maggie Fox's lives further emphasize how mixed the fortunes of well-known Spiritualists could be, especially those who—unlike Georgina, Victoria, Emma, and Leah—appear to have been swept along by events rather than in control of their destinies. The two youngest Fox sisters' disenchantment seems often to have stemmed from a feeling that other Spiritualists were stifling their opinions and not allowing them to speak their true thoughts. After their death-blow confessions of 1888, many former supporters united against them, isolating the pair further still.

Advances in science mean few readers today will trust in the feats supposedly performed by the famed mediums of the Victorian era. In the years since, Spiritualism has steadily lost its appeal. And this, in turn, has led to its devaluing as a historical movement of significance, since the common belief that its key players engaged in trickery or self-deception—to say nothing of the "channeling" of the wisdom of great men—means that it doesn't fit comfortably into neat narratives about the journey toward female empowerment. But we should neither celebrate only the straightforward heroines nor reject the stages in a story's development that disrupt its regular shape.

The lives of Georgina, Victoria, Emma, Leah, Maggie, and Kate were like those of few other nineteenth-century women. In defiance of social conventions of the age, these six visionaries refused to keep silently to the shadows. Instead, through their involvement in the mysterious world of the séance, each found a way to step decisively into the light, where she could be both seen and heard.

ACKNOWLEDGMENTS

I owe the usual enormous debt of thanks to my friend and frequent collaborator, Emma Claire Sweeney, who was the first person I told about this idea and who saw it through every stage of its development.

Likewise, Michelle Tessler at the Tessler Literary Agency understood what I wanted to achieve from the start. I am so grateful for her tireless energy, encouragement, and commitment to this book.

I'd also like to thank Ariella Feiner at United Agents, and friends Zoe Green and Jonathan Ruppin for their incisive critiques of early drafts. Thanks also to Molly Jamieson at United Agents.

Jennifer Alton, a wonderful editor, made the experience of preparing the book for publication a joy. Thank you also to Jack Shoemaker for seeing the potential in *Out of the Shadows*, and to Katie Boland, Carla Bruce-Eddings, Janet Byrne, Rachel Fershleiser, Megan Fishmann, Laura Gonzalez, Jordan Koluch, Dustin Kurtz, Colin Legerton, Lisa Reardon, Samm Saxby, Yukiko Tominaga, and all at Counterpoint Press for their support.

One of the joys of my research has been the opportunity for rewarding conversations with archivists, librarians, and fellow researchers in many different corners of the globe.

Special thanks must go to Judith Dann and Christina Gray of the Robbins Hunter Museum in Granville, Ohio, and Marc Demarest, author of the *Chasing Down Emma* blog. All three went out of their way to answer my questions and send me materials on Victoria Woodhull and Emma Hardinge Britten respectively. Charles Harrowell of Senate House Library, University of London, also assisted me greatly in tracking down obscure speeches, rare books, and other Spiritualist materials.

Many thanks also to Joanna Martin, biographer and descendent of Georgina Weldon, for sharing some of her findings with me, and to Anne Monroe for allowing me to quote from her father Edward Grierson's book, *Storm Bird: The Strange Life of Georgina Weldon*.

I am grateful for the permission of Her Majesty Queen Elizabeth II for allowing me to quote from Queen Victoria's journals.

My thanks, too, to Morex Arai of the Huntington Library (San Marino, California); Lyndsi Barnes and staff of the Henry W. and Albert A. Berg Collection of English and American Literature, the New York Public Library; Amy Bowles and staff of Special Collections, Senate House Library, University of London; staff at Canadiana; Celia Caust-Ellenbogen of the Friends Historical Library, Swarthmore College; Julie Crocker of the Royal Archives; Les Gray of the University of Manchester Library (UK); Cara Dellatte and staff of the Brooke Russell Astor Reading Room for Rare Books and Manuscripts, the New York Public Library; Joe DiLullo and Charles B. Greifenstein of the American Philosophical Society Library & Museum; Autumn Haag and Melinda Wallington of the Department of Rare Books, Special Collections, and Preservation, River Campus Libraries, University of Rochester; Michael Hunter of English Heritage, Osborne House; Angus Johnstone of the National Film and Sound Archive of Australia; Wallace Kwong of the Rare Books & Music Reading Room, the British Library; Abbie Latham of the Watts Gallery Trust; Freya Levett of the Victoria and Albert Museum; staff of the Massachusetts Historical Society; Anne Mouron and staff of the Bodleian Library, University of Oxford; Helen Nicholson of Manchester Metropolitan University; Walter D. Ray and staff of the Special Collections Research Center, Southern Illinois University Carbondale; Kimberly Reynolds of the Boston Public Library; Christine L. Ridarsky of the Local History & Genealogy Division, Rochester Public Library (NY); Zoe Stansell of the Manuscripts Reference Service, the British Library; Debbie Thompson of Unilever Archives and Records Management; Mark E. Tillson Jr. of the Burke Library, Hamilton College; and Catherine Watts of the Anchor Society.

The online collections of the International Association for the Preservation of Spiritualist and Occult Periodicals were an absolutely invaluable resource.

During the years I spent researching and writing, many family members and friends sustained me with their kindness and good humor, but especially Susan Barker, Lauren Frankel, and Sarah Moore.

I am as appreciative as ever for the practical advice of my sister, Erica Crump, to whom *Out of the Shadows* is dedicated.

Last but not least, I want to thank my husband, Jack Blanchard, without whose love, support, and desire to share the childcare of our baby daughter, Lola, this book could not have been completed.

NOTES

Original spelling and punctuation have been retained in the quotations, even when the authors have made mistakes. I usually refer to the central biographical subjects by their first names. Individuals who do not appear "in scene" with the central biographical subjects are usually referred to by their surnames. Exceptions to these rules include members of the aristocracy and military, as well as clergy, doctors, jurists, and teachers, whom we meet in a professional context. I have referred to these individuals by their honorifics. When more than one individual who appear in scene with the central biographical subjects share a first name, I have referred to each person by their surname.

Abbreviations

~ associated with the Fox sisters

ALU   Ann Leah Underhill

CFJ Catherine Fox Jencken

EKK Elisha Kent Kane

EWC Eliab Wilkinson Capron

Lewis E. E. Lewis

MFK Margaretta Fox Kane

Missing Link A. Leah Underhill, *The Missing Link in Modern Spiritualism* (New York: Thomas R. Knox & Co., 1885).

Modern Spiritualism E. W. Capron, *Modern Spiritualism, Its Facts and Fanaticisms, Its Consistencies and Contradictions. With an Appendix* (Boston: Bela Marsh, 1855).

Pond Mariam Buckner Pond

Report E. E. Lewis, *A Report of the Mysterious Noises Heard in the House of Mr. John D. Fox, in Hydesville, Arcadia, Wayne County, N.Y. Authenticated by the Certificates, and Confirmed by the Statements of the Citizens of That Place and Vicinity* (Shelburne Falls, MA: J. L. Wade & Co., 1887).

Unwilling Martyrs Mariam Buckner Pond, *The Unwilling Martyrs: The Story of the Fox Family* (London: Spiritualist Press, 1947).

~ associated with Emma Hardinge Britten

Autobiography Emma Hardinge Britten, *Autobiography of Emma Hardinge Britten* (London: J. Heywood, 1900).

EHB Emma Hardinge Britten

MAS Emma Hardinge Britten, *Modern Ameri-*

can *Spiritualism: A Twenty Years' Record
of the Communion Between Earth and
the World of the Spirits* (New York: self-
published, 1870).

~ **associated with Victoria Woodhull**

BVCW Theodore Tilton, *Biography of Victoria C.
Woodhull* (New York: The Golden Age,
1871).

Sachs Emanie Sachs

Tilton Theodore Tilton

VCW Victoria Claflin Woodhull

WCW *Woodhull & Claflin's Weekly*

~ **associated with Georgina Weldon**

Grierson Edward Grierson

GW Georgina Weldon

My Orphanage Georgina Weldon, *My Orphanage and
Gounod in England* (London: The Music
& Art Association, 1882).

Plaintiff Philip Treherne, *A Plaintiff in Person (Life
of Mrs Weldon)* (London: William Heine-
mann Ltd., 1923).

Storm Bird Edward Grierson, *Storm Bird: The Strange
Life of Georgina Weldon* (London: Chatto
& Windus, 1959).

Treherne Philip Treherne

Seen and Not Heard

3 *May 18*: Details in this scene, including the quotations, are drawn
from Queen Victoria's journals: RA VIC/MAIN/QVJ (W), May 18,
1853 (Princess Beatrice's copies).

4 *heard a knock*: Details of what happened in Hydesville on March 31, 1848, including the quotations, are drawn from eyewitness accounts collected in the contemporary source Lewis, *Report*, pp. 5–15, 30–31.

5 *aged about sixty*: The 1850 U.S. Census gives John Fox's age as sixty-one.

5 *Kate*: CFJ was most commonly known as Kate, but as a child she was also sometimes called Cathie. The spelling of Catherine/Catharine in contemporary documents is inconsistent. I have chosen to use an *e* because this is how CFJ signs her own name in an accompanying note to Reuben Briggs Davenport's book *The Death-Blow to Spiritualism*.

5 *pretty, dark-haired*: Details of MFK and CFJ's physical appearance are drawn from the *New-York Daily Tribune*, June 5, 1850, p. 1; Harriet Beecher Stowe to George Eliot, February 8, 1872, Harriet Beecher Stowe Collection of Papers, 1847–1895, The Henry W. and Albert A. Berg Collection of English and American Literature, The New York Public Library, Astor, Lenox and Tilden Foundations; W. G. Langworthy Taylor, *Katie Fox: Epochmaking Medium and the Making of the Fox-Taylor Record* (Boston: Bruce Humphries, 1936), p. 99.

5 *fourteen-year-old*: Both sisters' ages are the subject of some controversy. My decision to settle on these ages as the most likely is influenced by the following sources: "Certificate of Margaret Fox," in Lewis, *Report*, p. 6 (in which the girls' mother described CFJ as being "about twelve" and MFK as "in her fifteenth year" on April 11, 1848); *New-York Daily Tribune*, June 5, 1850, p. 1 (which described the sisters as fourteen and eighteen in June 1850, two years and two months after the time of Margaret Fox's statement). Pond, *Unwilling Martyrs* [family tree], states that CFJ was born in 1836 and MFK in 1834, which could have made them eleven and fourteen on the date in question. This book, published in the United States as *Time Is Kind*, was written by a Fox family descendant.

5 *around fifty*: The 1850 U.S. Census gives Margaret Fox's age (in two separate certificates) as fifty-two and fifty-three, respectively.

6 *Three raps*: Margaret Fox's and Mary Redfield's recollections are

slightly different. Fox recalled that she asked the spirit to make two raps. In Redfield's memory, it was three.

8 *no knocking*: Lewis, *Report*, p. 5.

8 *Lucretia recalled*: Details of Lucretia Pulver's memory of the peddler and the Bells, including the quotations, are drawn from her statement in Lewis, *Report*, pp. 37–39.

9 *A couple named Weekman*: Details of the recollections of Hannah and Michael Weekman and Jane Lape, including the quotations, are drawn from Lewis, *Report*, pp. 34–37.

9 *"during that summer . . ."*: Ibid., p. 40.

10 *"foolish and superstitious reports . . ."*: Ibid., p. 41.

11 *in her midthirties*: As with MFK and CFJ, there is some confusion about ALU's age. Pond, *Unwilling Martyrs* [family tree], states that she was born in 1814, which would make her in her midthirties in 1848. A baptismal record thought to be ALU's is dated April 8, 1813: *Kakiat, Book 20*, Holland Society of New York. On the other hand, the 1850 U.S. Census gives ALU's age as twenty-nine, making her twenty-seven in 1848. ALU's (sometimes unreliable) memoirs suggest that she was even younger, in her early twenties in 1848: ALU, *Missing Link*, pp. 30–31. I have chosen to accept the earlier possible dates because the baptismal record is an official document.

11 *found their way*: Articles from *The Western Argus* (April 12, 1848) and *Newark Herald* (May 4, 1848) reproduced in Herbert G. Jackson Jr., *The Spirit Rappers* (New York: Doubleday & Co., 1972), pp. 13–16. Both reports approached the events at Hydesville with humor, *The Newark Herald* presenting the story in the form of mock rhyming verse.

11 *in her late teens*: In her published account of her life, ALU stated that she married her first husband at the age of fourteen and became pregnant shortly after: ALU, *Missing Link*, pp. 30–31. According to Pond, *Unwilling Martyrs* [family tree], ALU married her first husband in 1829, which would suggest that her daughter was in her late teens in 1848.

11 *burst into the room*: Details of what is said to have occurred in the Little household, and of ALU's visit to Hydesville and subsequent

return to Rochester, including the quotations, are drawn from ALU, *Missing Link*, pp. 31–33.

12 *Report of the Mysterious Noises . . .*: The full title is *A Report of the Mysterious Noises Heard in the House of Mr. John D. Fox, in Hydesville, Arcadia, Wayne County, N.Y. Authenticated by the Certificates, and Confirmed by the Statements of the Citizens of That Place and Vicinity.*

14 *reached Rochester*: Details of ALU's return to Rochester, the house move, and the arrival of CFJ and MFK are drawn from ALU, *Missing Link*, pp. 33–38.

14 *11 Mechanics' Square*: ALU, *Missing Link*, p. 34, states that "Our residence then was on Mechanics' Square." The 1847 *Directory of the City of Rochester* records that Ann L. Fish was living at 11 Mechanics' Square at that time.

15 *"he would conquer . . ."*: Details of Calvin Brown's failed attempt to control the spirits are drawn from ALU, *Missing Link*, pp. 38–39.

16 *heavy drinker*: Details of John Fox's drinking and later sobriety are drawn from Pond, *Unwilling Martyrs*, p. 18.

16 *". . . psychological delusion"*: ALU, *Missing Link*, p. 44.

16 *Elisabeth Granger*: Published contemporary accounts do not give the first name of Lyman Granger's wife. However, an Elisabeth Granger living in Rochester and married to a Lyman Granger appears in the 1850 U.S. Census. The names of the youngest occupants of the house further suggest that this is the correct family.

17 *During a session*: Details of this and the following session at ALU's home the next evening, including the quotations, are drawn from Lemuel Clark's letter of November 1848, reproduced in Wheaton Phillips Webb, A. H. Clark, and Lemuel Clark, "Peddler's Protest," *New York History* 24, no. 2 (April 1943): 232–44.

19 *live elsewhere*: Elisabeth Fish's later residence in her father's home is mentioned in "Extract from the deposition of Mrs. Norman Culver, taken at Arcadia, N.Y., April 17, 1851," reproduced in EWC, *Modern Spiritualism*, p. 422. Although this statement was made three years after the incident recorded by Lemuel Clark, the absence of any mention of Elisabeth Fish on the Fox sisters' New York tour suggests that she had been sent away considerably earlier. In Pond, *Unwilling Mar-*

tyrs, p. 51, the author (a Fox family descendant) repeats a family story that she says took place after the incident recorded by Lemuel Clark. Here, ALU says she has "no patience" with her daughter and talks of sending her to live with someone called Emma, presumably a relative.

19 *dig down*: Details about the earlier dig are drawn from Lewis, *Report*, pp. 10, 16, and 30.

19 *Leah doubted*: Details about the July dig and its aftermath, including the quotations, are drawn from ALU, *Missing Link*, pp. 21–27.

23 *the very table*: George Willets to Isaac Post, October 23, 1848, Isaac and Amy Post Family Papers, D.93, Rare Books, Special Collections, and Preservation, River Campus Libraries, University of Rochester.

23 *"Dear friends . . ."*: ALU, *Missing Link*, pp. 48–49.

23 *"a mission to perform . . ."*: ALU, *Missing Link*, p. 58.

24 *stripped her*: EWC, *Modern Spiritualism*, p. 101.

24 *clear directives*: Details about the directions, including the quotations, are drawn from ALU, *Missing Link*, pp. 61–62.

Heard but Not Seen

26 *spirits had named*: Unless otherwise stated, details of the Corinthian Hall performances, including the quotations, are drawn from ALU, *Missing Link*, pp. 62–73.

27 *"WONDERFUL PHENOMENA . . ."*: Notice reproduced in EWC, *Modern Spiritualism*, pp. 384–85.

27 *"a gentleman and two ladies"*: Advertisement reproduced in Herbert G. Jackson Jr., *The Spirit Rappers* (New York: Doubleday & Co., 1972), p. 48.

27 *mock-Grecian*: Descriptions of Corinthian Hall are drawn from George M. Elwood, *Some Earlier Public Amusements of Rochester* (Rochester, NY: Democrat and Chronicle Print, 1894), pp. 45–46.

27 *said to have worn*: Details of what MFK and ALU are believed to have worn that night are drawn from Pond, *Unwilling Martyrs*, p. 57.

28 *incited only boredom*: *Rochester Daily Advertiser* article reproduced in Jackson, *The Spirit Rappers*, pp. 51–52.

29 *strip-searched*: The account of the sisters' ordeal is drawn from EWC, *Modern Spiritualism*, pp. 391–92, and EHB, *MAS*, p. 45.

30 *charging set fees*: ALU, *Missing Link*, p. 103.

30 *Margaret Fox had reacted*: ALU, *Missing Link*, p. 100.

30 *almost twenty-eight thousand*: William Alexander Linn, *Horace Greeley Founder and Editor of The New York Tribune* (New York: D. Appleton and Company, 1903), p. 69. Linn gives the figure as 27,960.

31 *"remarkable phenomena . . ."*: The article published in the *New-York Weekly Tribune* on December 8, 1849, is reprinted in EWC and Henry D. Barron, *Singular Revelations: Explanation and History of the Mysterious Communion with Spirits, Comprehending the Rise and Progress of the Mysterious Noises in Western New-York, Generally Received as Spiritual Communications* (Auburn, NY: Capron and Barron, 1850), p. 52.

31 *"we really cannot see . . ."*: *New-York Semi-Weekly Tribune*, December 8, 1849, p. 1.

31 *The Drapers*: Details of the Drapers' initial experience with Benjamin Franklin and the following gatherings, including the quotations, are drawn from a letter published in *The Daily Magnet* (Rochester, NY) on February 26, 1850, reproduced in EWC, *Modern Spiritualism*, pp. 83–87.

34 *lone doubting voice*: Details of this incident and its aftermath, including the quotations, are drawn from Frederick Douglass to Amy Post, [March?] 1850, Isaac and Amy Post Family Papers, D.93, Rare Books, Special Collections, and Preservation, River Campus Libraries, University of Rochester.

34 *pen a book*: The full title is *Voices from the Spirit World, Being Communications from Many Spirits, by the Hand of Isaac Post, Medium* (Rochester, NY: Charles H. McDonell, 1852).

34 *Mary B. Allen*: Details of this incident, including the quotations, are drawn from Augustus H. Strong's recollections, which appear in Albert Cronise, "The Beginnings of Modern Spiritualism in and Near Rochester," *The Rochester Historical Society, Publication Fund Series*, vol. 5, 1926, pp. 13–14.

35 *married at fourteen*: ALU, *Missing Link*, p. 30.

35 *substantial pamphlet*: EWC and Barron, *Singular Revelations*.

35 *powers of persuasion*: Details of EWC's arguments, including the quotations, are drawn from EWC to Margaret Fox, February 10,

1850, Isaac and Amy Post Family Papers, D.93, Rare Books, Special Collections, and Preservation, River Campus Libraries, University of Rochester.

36 *Leah was still listed*: *Daily American Directory of the City of Rochester, for 1849–50* (Rochester, NY: Jerome & Brother, 1849); *Daily American Directory of the City of Rochester, for 1851–2* (Rochester, NY: Lee Mann & Co., 1851).

36 Singular Revelations: EWC and Barron, *Singular Revelations*.

36 *who had stayed*: EWC, *Modern Spiritualism*, p. 383.

37 *rather than* super*natural*: EWC and Barron, *Singular Revelations*, p. 6.

37 History of the Strange Sounds . . .: D. M. Dewey, *History of the Strange Sounds or Rappings: Heard in Rochester and Western New-York, and Usually Called The Mysterious Noises! Which Are Supposed by Many to Be Communications from the Spirit World, Together with All the Explanation That Can Yet Be Given of the Matter* (Rochester, NY: D. M. Dewey, 1850).

37 *"not undertake to argue . . ."*: Dewey, *History of the Strange Sounds or Rappings*, pp. i, 22, and ii.

37 *". . . to be humbugged . . ."*: Quotation from the *Rochester Daily American*, reproduced in EWC, *Modern Spiritualism*, p. 394.

37 *"not being overstocked . . ."*: Quotation from the *Northern Christian Advocate*, reproduced in EWC, *Modern Spiritualism*, pp. 396–97.

37 *dollar per day*: Edith Abbott, "The Wages of Unskilled Labor in the United States, 1850–1900," *Journal of Political Economy* 13, no. 3 (June 1905): 361.

38 *$50 and $100*: *Commercial Advertiser* (NYC), February 28, 1850, p. 2.

38 *furious response*: Details of the letter, including the quotations, are drawn from its author's recollections in EWC, *Modern Spiritualism*, pp. 395–96.

38 *"directed (by the spirits) . . ."*: ALU, *Missing Link*, p.115.

38 *better course of action*: Details about the group's travel arrangements and preparations for the tour are drawn from ALU, *Missing Link*, pp. 115–16.

39 *"quite pretty young ladies . . ."*: *Weekly Argus* (Albany, NY), Febru-

ary 16, 1850, p. 55. The skepticism of the *Argus* would continue to be expressed in follow-up articles on February 23, 1850, p. 64, and March 2, 1850, p. 71.

39 *strikingly modern women*: Unless otherwise stated, details about reactions to the Foxes in Albany and Troy, including the quotation, are drawn from ALU, *Missing Link*, pp. 116–22.

40 *caused excitement*: *Troy Daily Whig*, June 4, 1850, p. 2. This report, written after the Foxes had departed the city, remarks on their success in Troy.

The Talk of the Town

41 *beginning of June 1850*: ALU, *Missing Link*, p. 128, gives the date of the arrival of ALU, MFK, and CFJ as June 4, 1850. Other sources, including the *New-York Daily Tribune*, June 5, 1850, p. 1, suggest that they arrived slightly earlier.

42 *people had speculated*: *Commercial Advertiser* (NYC) quoted in EWC, *Modern Spiritualism*, p. 396.

42 *cousin of the famous promoter*: In her memoirs, ALU seeks to disassociate the sisters' choice of accommodation from P. T. Barnum (ALU, *Missing Link*, p. 128), but later authors Amy Lehman and Barbara Weisberg point out that the proprietor of the hotel—A. S. Barnum—was the cousin of the famous showman: Amy Lehman, *Victorian Women and the Theatre of Trance: Mediums, Spiritualists and Mesmerists in Performance* (Jefferson, NC: McFarland & Company, 2009), p. 81, and Barbara Weisberg, *Talking to the Dead: Kate and Maggie Fox and the Rise of Spiritualism* (New York: HarperOne, 2005), p. 106.

42 *"determine at a glance . . .":* Horace Greeley, *The Autobiography of Horace Greeley, or Recollections of a Busy Life* (New York: E. B. Treat, 1872), p. 234.

43 *Greeley first called*: Details of Horace Greeley's first visit, including the quotations, are drawn from the *New-York Daily Tribune*, June 5, 1850, p. 1. Additional details about the room are drawn from *The New York Herald*, June 17, 1850, p. 1.

43 *two years his junior*: My reckoning of ALU's age is based on the baptismal record mentioned in the notes to chapter 1.

45 *three sessions daily*: Details about the sisters' schedule and stay at Barnum's Hotel are drawn from ALU, *Missing Link*, pp. 128–29.

45 *fell ill*: Letter from Jacob C. Culyer to ALU, June 9, 1850, reproduced in ALU, *Missing Link*, p. 159.

45 Mysterious Knockings: Details about this and the blackface version of the play, *Rochester Knockings*, are drawn from Vera Brodsky Lawrence, *Strong on Music: The New York Music Scene in the Days of George Templeton Strong, Vol. II, Reverberations 1850–1856* (Chicago: University of Chicago Press, 1995), pp. 122–23.

45 *"The Rochester Knockings . . ."*: ALU, *Missing Link*, p. 128.

46 *Ripley's report*: Details of the evening, including the quotations, are drawn from the *New-York Daily Tribune*, June 8, 1850, p. 4.

48 *"the lions of New York"*: ALU, *Missing Link*, p. 128.

48 *home on Nineteenth Street*: Ibid., p. 142.

49 *the boy's ghost*: Extract from Horace Greeley's notes reproduced in William Harlan Hale, *Horace Greeley: Voice of the People* (New York: Harper & Brothers, 1950), p. 124.

49 *debut performance*: Lind's debut performance at Her Majesty's Theatre took place on May 4, 1847. Details, including the quotations, are drawn from Queen Victoria's journals, RA VIC/MAIN/QVJ (W), May 4, 1847 (Princess Beatrice's copies); *The Sun* (London), May 6, 1847, p. 2; *Athlone Sentinel*, May 21, 1847, p. 4.

49 *called on Jenny*: Details of Horace Greeley's conversation with Jenny Lind and her subsequent visit to his home, including the quotations, are drawn from Greeley, *The Autobiography of Horace Greeley*, p. 237.

50 *"impossable"*: CFJ to John E. Robinson, October 26, 1850, Isaac and Amy Post Family Papers, D.93, Rare Books, Special Collections, and Preservation, River Campus Libraries, University of Rochester.

51 *distressing letter*: Details of this letter and the attacks on MFK and ALU, including the quotations, are drawn from ALU, *Missing Link*, pp. 122–27, and EWC, *Modern Spiritualism*, pp. 270–73. Both sources include reproductions of letters by R. M. Boulton, in whose home MFK was staying.

53 *reach over a million*: As Barbara Weisberg points out in *Talking to the Dead: Kate and Maggie Fox and the Rise of Spiritualism* (New

York: HarperOne, 2005), p. 211, estimates of numbers of American Spiritualists ranged from one million upward. In Frank Podmore, *Modern Spiritualism: A History and Criticism*, vol. 1 (London: Methuen & Co., 1902), p. 303, the author—a questioning observer—makes reference to estimates that placed the number of American Spiritualists at "over a million" and also "two millions" in 1854, "millions" in 1855, and "eleven millions" a few years later. However, as Podmore asserts, "all these statements are mere guesses."

Dim Prophecies

54 *"never young . . ."*: EHB, *Autobiography*, p. 3.

54 *baffling noises*: EHB, *Autobiography*, pp. 4 and 6.

54 *in 1823*: As in the case of the Fox sisters—ALU, MFK, and CFJ—EHB gave conflicting accounts of her age over the years. May 2, 1823, is generally accepted as the date of her birth since it is supported by a baptismal record for Emma Floyd, dated May 28, 1823: London Metropolitan Archives.

55 *death of the family patriarch*: *Bristol Mercury*, May 3, 1834, p. 3.

55 *"with a breaking heart"*: EHB, *Autobiography*, p. 5.

55 *searing memory*: Details in this scene are drawn from EHB, *Autobiography*, pp. 5–6.

56 *At least twelve people*: Susan Thomas, *The Bristol Riots* (Bristol: Historical Association, 1974), p. 1.

56 Bristol Mercury: Details of EHB's performances in Bristol, including the quotations, are drawn from *The Bristol Mercury*, November 17, 1838, p. 3; February 2, 1839, p. 3; May 13, 1843, p. 5.

57 *honing her soprano voice*: EHB, *Autobiography*, pp. 5–6.

57 *Thomas Welsh*: James Robertson, *A Noble Pioneer: The Life Story of Emma Hardinge Britten* (Manchester: Two Worlds' Publishing Co., n.d.), p. 4.

57 *". . . hear the child pianiste"*: Details in this scene at Erard's showroom, including the quotation, are drawn from EHB, *Autobiography*, p. 6.

58 Banner of Light: Private letter quoted in C. Edwards Lester's "Biographical Sketch of Mrs. Emma Hardinge," *Banner of Light* 26, no. 14, December 18, 1869, p. 2.

58 *Adelphi Theatre*: EHB's roles (she appeared under the name "Miss Emma Harding," without the *e*) are listed in Alfred L. Nelson and Gilbert B. Cross, eds., *Sans Pareil/Adelphi Theatres All-Inclusive Index: 1806–1899 Index of Authors, Actors, Plays, Genres, Singers, Musicians, Dancers, Entertainers and Theatre Management*, The Adelphi Calendar Project 1806–1900 (web), 2016, pp. 494–98.

58 The Chimes: Mark Lemon and G. A. A'Beckett, *The Chimes; or, Some Bells That Rang an Old Year Out and a New Year In: A Goblin Drama in Four Quarters, Dramatised by Mark Lemon and G. A. a'Beckett from the Story by Charles Dickens* (London: John Dicks, n.d.).

58 *performed in Bristol in the 1840s and 1850s*: Notices regarding the compositions of an E., Ernest, or Mr. Reinhold appeared in *The Bristol Mercury and Western Counties Advertiser*, October 6, 1849, p. 4; February 2, 1850, p. 8; November 22, 1851, p. 8; October 16, 1852, p. 8.

58 *penned theatricals*: In her letter published in the *Banner of Light* 26, no. 14, December 18, 1869, p. 2, EHB mentions that her best-known dramatic work is *The Tragedy Queen*, "a two act drama." Confusingly, a one-act comedy of the same name by John Oxenford premiered at London's Lyceum Theatre in 1847. EHB appeared in this play on Broadway in 1855, taking the part of Mrs. Bracegirdle.

59 *the Orphic Circle*: In *The Two Worlds* 1, no. 18, November 18, 1887, p. 3, EHB suggests that she was under thirteen when she got involved with the Orphic Circle. However, as she would routinely give her age as a decade younger than she really was, she could just as likely have been in her early twenties—a period when documentary evidence makes it easier to locate her in London. This article is written under the pen name Sirius, but the fact that most of the information is repeated in EHB's *Autobiography* implies that the two authors are one and the same.

59 *"far above her in rank . . ."*: EHB, *Autobiography*, p. 5.

59 *Gore House*: Marc Demarest discusses his hypotheses on the Orphic Circle and its possible links with individuals who met regularly at Gore House on his blog *Chasing Down Emma: Resolving the Contradictions of, and Filling in the Gaps in, the Life, Work and World of Emma Hardinge Britten* (ehbritten.blogspot.com).

59 *to Michael*: Joscelyn Godwin, *The Theosophical Enlightenment* (Albany: State University of New York Press, 1994), p. 180.

59 *"a period of several years . . ."*: *Two Worlds* 1, no. 18, November 18, 1887, p. 3. Written under the pen name Sirius.

60 Ghost Land: EHB, ed., *Ghost Land; or Researches into the Mysteries of Occultism* (Boston: self-published, 1876). The author of this book, edited by EHB, remains anonymous. Over the years, scholars have suggested possible candidates, most convincingly perhaps EHB herself.

60 *". . . mirror and crystal . . ."*: EHB, *Ghost Land*, p. 100.

60 *"rise from her bed . . ."*: EHB, *Autobiography*, p. 5.

60 *marriage to a "gentleman"*: *Banner of Light* 26, no. 14, December 18, 1869, p. 2. In her letter quoted in this article, EHB writes that she was married at "fifteen." Her age is a matter for debate, since at another point in the missive she has clearly shaved a decade off her life, perhaps for reasons of personal vanity or because she felt that reducing her age at the time she was married would cast her in a more innocent light. Despite this discrepancy, other unlikely-sounding claims in the letter have merit, and so dismissing everything she says seems unwise.

60 *"mystic marriage"*: In his introduction to a twentieth-century reprint of EHB's *MAS*, Eric Dingwall discusses this sham marriage: EHB, *Modern American Spiritualism: A Twenty Years' Record of the Communion Between Earth and the World of the Spirits* (New Hyde Park, NY: University Books, 1970), p. ix. See also: Godwin, *The Theosophical Enlightenment*, p. 200; Jeffrey D. Lavoie, *The Theosophical Society: The History of a Spiritualist Movement* (Boca Raton, FL: Brown Walker Press, 2012), p. 295. It is also worth noting that other commentators have variously suggested that EHB took her changed name from a mesmeric "doctor" named Hardinge and from Emma Harding, a character in the story "Sweet Revenge" by Camilla Toulmin.

61 *Miss Floyd*: *Illustrated London News*, November 2, 1844, p. 283, mentions EHB's recent name change from Miss Floyd to Miss Emma Harding.

61 *"sacred cantata"*: *Bristol Mercury and Western Counties Advertiser*, October 6, 1849, p. 4.

61 *"very capital" glee*: *Bristol Mercury and Western Counties Advertiser*, November 22, 1851, p. 8; October 16, 1852, p. 8.

62 *"vicious aristocracy . . ."*: EHB, *Autobiography*, p. 7.

62 *James W. Wallack*: Details about this offer of work, journey to France, and time in Paris, including the quotations, are drawn from EHB, *Autobiography*, pp. 8–10.

63 *arrived in New York City*: Unless otherwise stated, details of EHB's arrival, theatrical career, and early encounters with Spiritualists in New York City, including the quotations, are drawn from EHB, *Autobiography*, pp. 12–18.

64 *noted her arrival*: *New-York Tribune*, September 17, 1855, p. 7.

64 *"actors of repute and popularity"*: *New York Herald*, September 18, 1855, p. 4.

64 *Mrs. Bracegirdle*: *New York Herald*, September 22, 1855, p. 3.

64 *"a good deal of success . . ."*: *New York Herald*, June 6, 1856, p. 4.

66 *"time, money and credulity"*: *Buffalo Commercial Advertiser*, February 18, 1851, reproduced in EWC, *Modern Spiritualism*, p. 310.

66 *usually attributed to*: The earliest example I was able to find of this term appears in Horace Greeley's *New-York Daily Tribune*, May 8, 1852, p. 9, where it is styled "modern 'Spiritualism.'"

66 *"The carpenters and fishermen . . ."*: EWC, *Modern Spiritualism*, p. 375.

66 *Canal Street*: Details of this séance and Emma's reaction, including the quotations, are drawn from EHB, *Autobiography*, pp. 16–18.

The Path of Light

68 *copper-zinc discs*: Barry H. Wiley, *The Thought Reader Craze: Victorian Science at the Enchanted Boundary* (Jefferson, NC: McFarland & Company, 2012), p. 11.

69 *"beautiful manifestations"*: *Morning Post* (London), April 19, 1853, p. 1.

69 *street stallholder*: Henry Mayhew, *London Labour and the London Poor; A Cyclopoedia of the Condition and Earnings of Those That* Will *Work, Those That* Cannot *Work, and Those That* Will

Not *Work*, vol. 1 (London: Griffin, Bone, and Company, 1861), p. 186.

69 *George Henry Lewes*: Details of this séance, including the quotations, are drawn from *The Leader* 4, no. 155, March 12, 1853, pp. 261–63.

70 *"miserable delusion"*: *Household Words* 6, no. 139, November 20, 1852, p. 223.

70 *skilled as a practitioner*: Claire Tomalin, *Charles Dickens: A Life* (London: Penguin Books, 2012), pp. 160–63.

70 *publicly as an "old friend"*: *Two Worlds* 3, no. 133, May 30, 1890, p. 344.

70 *1854 letter*: Charles Dickens to W. H. Wills, January 25, 1854, Huntington Library, San Marino, California; Graham Storey, Kathleen Tillotson, and Angus Easson, eds., *The Letters of Charles Dickens*, vol. 7, 1853–1855 (Oxford: Clarendon Press 1996), p. 258.

70 *"somnambulic condition"*: EHB, *Autobiography*, p. 15.

71 *Augustus Fenno*: Details in this and the following scene, including the quotations, are drawn from EHB, *Autobiography*, pp. 18–24.

71 *Mrs. Ada Foye*: Ada Hoyt became Ada Coan during a brief marriage and later took on the name Ada Foye.

73 *entirely transformed*: Details of EHB's walk home and the following scene at her boardinghouse, including the quotations, are drawn from EHB, *Autobiography*, pp. 24–26.

74 *"path of light"*: EHB, *Autobiography*, p. 11.

74 *seek the advice*: Ibid., p. 28.

74 *set aside time*: Ibid., p. 31.

75 *off the coast of Ireland*: *New York Herald*, February 18, 1856, p. 4.

75 *By February 7*: Ibid., February 7, 1856, p. 4.

75 *"a large quantity of broken ice . . ."*: *Daily Post* (Liverpool), February 29, 1856, p. 3.

75 Spiritual Telegraph: *Spiritual Telegraph* 4, no. 49, April 5, 1856, p. 3, and vol. 4, no. 50, April 12, 1856, p. 2.

75 Christian Spiritualist: *Christian Spiritualist* 2, no. 49, April 12, 1856, p. 2; vol. 2, no. 50, April 19, 1856, p. 2; vol. 2, no. 51, April 26, 1856, p. 2.

75 *recalling in detail*: Details of EHB's recollections of the sinking of the

SS *Pacific*, including the quotations, are drawn from EHB, *Autobiography*, pp. 31–32.

76 *"researches and experiments . . ."*: EHB, *Six Lectures on Theology and Nature*, n.p., 1860, p. 10.

76 *need to keep supporting herself*: Ibid.

76 *Benjamin Franklin*: EHB, *Autobiography*, p. 36.

76 *"all morbid conditions . . ."*: *Christian Spiritualist*, vol. 2, no. 50, 19 April 1856, p. 3.

77 *"a young English lady . . ."*: EHB, *Autobiography*, p. 38.

77 *Horace H. Day*: Details of EHB's experiences with Horace H. Day and the Society for the Diffusion of Christian Knowledge, including the quotations, are drawn from EHB, *Autobiography*, pp. 39–41, and EHB, *MAS*, pp. 133–35 and 140–41.

77 *Society for the Diffusion of Spiritual Knowledge*: EHB, *Autobiography*, p. 39, refers to this organization as the Society for the Diffusion of Christian Spiritualism, but it was generally known as the Society for the Diffusion of Spiritual Knowledge (SDSK), and that is how she refers to it in *MAS*, pp. 133, 141, and 150.

78 *presidential hopeful*: In 1872, Horace H. Day was among those seeking nomination by the National Labor Reform Party. He lost out to Judge David Davis, who ended up withdrawing his candidacy, by which time it was deemed too late to find an alternative candidate: John R. Common et al., *History of Labour in the United States*, vol. 2 (New York: Macmillan Company, 1921), pp. 154–55.

79 *Ludlow Place*: The location of ALU's home is mentioned in the *New-York Tribune*, December 27, 1856, p. 8.

80 *April 24, 1857*: Details of this performance are drawn from EHB, *Autobiography*, pp. 64–68.

80 *fifty singers*: *New York Herald*, April 24, 1857, p. 7.

80 The New York Herald: Extract from article reproduced in EHB, *Autobiography*, p. 67.

81 *spirit of Benjamin Franklin*: Details of E. J. French's suggestion, EHB's lecture in Troy, and her following two-year program of lectures are drawn from EHB, *Autobiography*, pp. 48–52.

81 *Harmony Hall*: EHB's *Autobiography* does not mention the name of the venue, but it appears in *The Troy Daily Times*, July 3, 1857, p. 2.

83 *live in style*: Pond, *Unwilling Martyrs*, pp. 251–52.

83 *had the pleasure*: EHB, *Autobiography*, p. 54.

84 *trip to Canada*: Unless otherwise stated, details of this trip, including the quotations, are drawn from EHB, *Autobiography*, pp. 82–87.

84 *February 1858*: EHB, *Autobiography*, p. 84, gives the date as November 1858. However, this is contradicted by contemporary reports, such as the *Spiritual Telegraph* 6, no. 45, March 6, 1858, p. 367, and *The True Witness and Catholic Chronicle*, February 19, 1858, p. 4. The muddle seems to have arisen because, when compiling her memoirs decades later, EHB confused a subsequent speaking engagement in Montreal in November 1858 with her first appearance there. As recorded in the *Spiritual Age* 1, no. 49, December 4, 1858, p. 2, her November 1858 appearances covered some of the same subject matter as discussed in her lectures that took place earlier that year.

85 *"priests, lawyers, doctors . . ."*: *Spiritual Telegraph* 6, no. 45, March 6, 1858, p. 367.

86 *"very respectable* physique . . .": *True Witness and Catholic Chronicle* 8, no. 28, February 19, 1858, p. 4.

A Blaze of Glory

87 *name babies*: EHB, *Autobiography*, p. 97.

87 *prison cells*: Ibid., pp. 95–96.

87 *"the command of the Spirits"*: Ibid., p. 101.

87 *"In the best interests . . ."*: Extract from *The New York Herald* reproduced in EHB, *Autobiography*, p. 102.

88 *a letter arrived*: Details relating to this episode, including the quotations, are drawn from EHB, *Autobiography*, pp. 161–70, and *The Memphis Daily Appeal*, November 21, 1875, p. 4. EHB thought that the letters from John Gallagher began coming in 1858. *The Memphis Daily Appeal* article (reprinted from the Spiritualist magazine *Banner of Light*) gives the date as "around 1860." Both accounts were written many years after these events are said to have taken place. Although their central story remains the same in essence, the two narratives deviate in various details. I have erred on the side of cau-

tion when considering these accounts and tried to present the most likely version of events.

88 *Great Police Riot*: This was the name by which the clash was known at the time. Today it is more commonly known as the New York City Police Riot.

91 *speak publicly*: The same version of the story that appeared in *The Memphis Daily Appeal*, November 21, 1875, p. 4, also appeared in *Human Nature* 109, April 1876, pp. 149–53.

91 *Emma gave a lecture*: Details and quotations are drawn from Emma Hardinge, *The Place and Mission of Woman: An Inspirational Discourse* (Boston: Hubbard W. Swett, 1859), pp. 4–6.

92 *"the north and south poles . . ."*: EHB's letter to the *Daily Memphis Enquirer* reproduced in the *Banner of Light* 6, no. 12, December 17, 1859, p. 7. The angry subscriber's letter is also reproduced in the same issue.

93 *"judicious husband"*: *Memphis Daily Appeal*, November 20, 1859, p. 2.

93 *lecture in Memphis*: Unless otherwise stated, details of EHB's time in Memphis, including the quotations, are drawn from EHB, *Autobiography*, pp. 142–44, and EHB, *MAS*, pp. 414–16.

94 *additional suspicion*: Lisa Howe discusses this idea in "Spirited Pioneer: The Life of Emma Hardinge Britten" (PhD diss., University of Florida, 2015), p. 121.

94 *arriving in Alabama*: Details of EHB's visit to Alabama, including the quotations, are drawn from EHB, *MAS*, pp. 418–19. EHB's words were apparently taken down at the time by a Mr. Waters, a "phonographic writer," who was still living at the time of *MAS*'s publication and, EHB said, was "willing to testify" to the published version of events. A fuller, probably more exaggerated version of EHB's visit to the State House, which includes markedly different details, appears in EHB, *Autobiography*, pp. 148–49.

95 *lecture series*: All quotations are drawn from Caroline H. Dall, *A Woman's Right to Labor, or, Low Wages and Hard Work* (Boston: Walker, Wise, and Company, 1860), pp. 1–2, 15–16, and 18.

95 *June letter*: EHB to Caroline Healey Dall, June 9, 1860, Collection of the Massachusetts Historical Society.

96 *"the fallen . . ."*: All quotations are drawn from EHB, *Six Lectures on Theology and Nature*, n.p., 1860, pp. 139–40.

96 *". . . already bleeding"*: EHB to Caroline Healey Dall, June 9, 1860, Collection of the Massachusetts Historical Society.

96 *was never realized*: Howe, "Spirited Pioneer: The Life of Emma Hardinge Britten," pp. 144–45.

96 *"the outcast's friend"*: EHB, *Miss Emma Hardinge's Political Campaign in Favour of the Union Party of America, on the Occasion of the Last Presidential Election of 1864* (London: Thomas Scott, n.d.), p. 3.

96 America and Her Destiny: All quotations are drawn from EHB, *America and Her Destiny: Inspirational Discourse Given Extemporaneously at Dodworth's Hall, New York, on Sunday Evening, August 25, 1861, Through Emma Hardinge, by the Spirits*, 2nd ed. (New York: Robert M. De Witt, 1861), p. 12.

97 *"We advise 'Emma' . . ."*: *Ladies' Repository* 22, no. 1, January 1862, p. 62.

97 *public tour*: Unless otherwise stated, details about EHB's fifteen-month tour are drawn from EHB, *Autobiography*, pp. 181–89.

98 *"Spirit postmaster"*: EHB, *Nineteenth Century Miracles; or, Spirits and Their Work in Every Country of the Earth* (New York: Lovell & Co., 1884), pp. 464 and 551.

99 *reelect Abraham Lincoln*: Details of EHB's involvement in the campaign to reelect Lincoln, including the quotations, are drawn from EHB, *Autobiography*, pp. 203–7, and EHB, *Miss Emma Hardinge's Political Campaign in Favour of the Union Party of America, on the Occasion of the Last Presidential Election of 1864* (London: Thomas Scott, n.d.), pp. 7–9.

101 *"Strong, brave and immovable . . ."*: All quotations are drawn from EHB, *The Great Funeral Oration on Abraham Lincoln* (New York: American News Company, n.d.), pp. 7 and 22.

102 *William H. Mumler*: For a fuller account of Mumler's career as a spirit photographer, see Peter Manseau, *The Apparitionists: A Tale of Phantoms, Fraud, Photography, and the Man Who Captured Lincoln's Ghost* (Boston: Houghton Mifflin Harcourt, 2017).

102 *the question "quite unnecessary . . ."*: EHB, *Autobiography*, p. 123.

102 *"Miss Hardinge . . ."*: *New York Herald*, August 7, 1865, p. 8.

103 *Ann Sophia's homesickness*: EHB, *Autobiography*, p. 210.

103 *"retire into private life"*: Ibid.

103 *lodgings in Chelsea*: EHB, *Autobiography*, p. 212.

103 *"Winter Soirées"*: Details of this speech, including the quotations, are drawn from EHB, *Extemporaneous Addresses by Emma Hardinge. Spoken at the Winter Soirées Held at Harley Street, London, 1865* (London: Thomas Scott, 1865), pp. iii, 1–3, and 9–15, and EHB, *Nineteenth Century Miracles; or, Spirits and Their Work in Every Country of the Earth* (New York: Lovell & Co., 1884), p. 172.

105 *a subsequent piece*: Reproduced in the first source mentioned in the previous note.

105 *marveled at her stamina*: *Morning Post* (London), January 15, 1866, p. 3.

105 *". . . cheap cyclopaedia"*: *London News*, February 10, 1866, p. 131.

106 *"a big, rather masculine . . ."*: *Edinburgh Evening Courant*, January 29, 1866, p. 4.

The Little Queen

108 *unpublished memoirs*: Details in the happier version of VCW's life are drawn from VCW, *Autobiography of Victoria Chaflin [sic] Woodhull* (Bredons Norton, U.K.: self-published, 1895), pp. 1–3, Collection of the Robbins Hunter Museum (Granville, OH). This unfinished "autobiography" is a loose collection of writings bound together as a pamphlet.

108 *alternative tale*: Details of this second version of VCW's life are drawn from Tilton, *BVCW*, pp. 4–7.

109 *"thrown into spasms . . ."*: Ibid., pp. 4–5.

109 *". . . more deviltry . . ."*: *Cleveland Plain Dealer*, November 3, 1957, p. 12.

109 *as a lawyer*: VCW would refer to her father's past legal career in grandiose terms in early newspaper interviews. By the 1880s, after immigrating to Britain, Reuben Buckman Claflin was referring to himself in official documents, such as the 1881 England Census, as a retired barrister.

110 *own observations*: Henry J. Woodhouse to Sachs, March 5, 1928,

Emanie (Nahm) Sachs Arling Philips Archive, Western Kentucky University/Robbins Hunter Museum (Granville, OH), copies.

110 *only a year*: *Atlanta Constitution*, February 11, 1876, p. 3.

110 *Her diary entry*: Queen Victoria's Journals, RA VIC/MAIN/QVJ (W), September 23, 1838 (Queen Victoria's handwriting).

110 *personal recollection*: All VCW's apparent memories of her birth, including the quotations, are drawn from VCW, *Autobiography of Victoria Chaflin*.

111 *solemn old man*: Tilton, *BVCW*, pp. 11–12.

112 *recently unearthed*: Henry B. Curtis v. William Smith et al., March term 1857, Complete Record, vol. 6, pp. 92–107, Clerk of Courts box 2013-31-003, Licking County Records & Archives Center (Newark, Ohio). Judith Dann and Christina Gray, of the Robbins Hunter Museum (Granville, OH), and Miranda Shield, of the Licking County Records & Archives Center (Newark, OH), are responsible for uncovering these documents.

112 *at least in his early twenties*: Tilton, *BVCW*, p. 12, states that Canning Woodhull was "in his twenty-eighth" year when he married VCW. Subsequent biographers have tended to accept this statement at face value. However, the New York State census record for 1855 gives Canning Woodhull's age as twenty-six in that year. VCW's age is given as seventeen, which tallies with the known year of her birth, 1838. If one accepts the information given in the state census, Canning Woodhull would have been about twenty-three or twenty-four when he married VCW in 1853. On the other hand, Canning Woodhull's death certificate gives his age as forty-six years and seven days on April 7, 1872. This would make his age when he married Victoria about the same as that given in Tilton's biography, written with the cooperation of VCW.

112 *Canning claimed*: Unless otherwise stated, details of Canning Woodhull's arrival in Mount Gilead, courtship, and marriage to VCW are drawn from Tilton, *BVCW*, pp. 12–16.

113 *"none but vegetable substances"*: *Muscatine Weekly Journal*, December 25, 1863, p. 3.

113 *all over Ohio*: *Ohio Star*, July 6, 1853, p. 3; *Belmont Chronicle*,

and Farmers, Mechanics and Manufacturers Advocate, July 8, 1853, p. 3; *Ohio Organ, of the Temperance Reform*, July 8, 1853, p. 1.

114 *were married*: The marriage certificate for Canning Woodhull and VCW states that, in accordance with the law, VCW was over the age of eighteen. However, this is inconsistent with the birth date associated with her throughout her life: Marriage certificate for Canning Woodhull and VCW, November 19, 1853, Marriage Records, Ohio Marriages.

114 *her fifteenth birthday*: Tilton, BVCW, p. 12, states that VCW was "in her fourteenth year" when she married, but, assuming that her generally accepted date of birth is correct, their courtship began when she was fourteen, and she had turned fifteen by the time she married.

116 *New York State census record*: 1855 New York State census.

116 *in San Francisco*: Unless otherwise stated, details of the family's time in San Francisco are drawn from Tilton, *BVCW*, pp. 16–18.

117 *Individuals he encountered*: George G. Foster, *New York by Gaslight: With Here and There a Streak of Sunshine* (New York: Dewitt & Davenport, 1850), pp. 6, 38–39.

117 *roughly seven times*: According to the following source, a dressmaker in New York City in 1851 would make about $1.33 cents per day. If working a (then standard) six-day week, this would come to roughly $8.00 per week. If one compares this to the 1883 rate for a dressmaker in California, which was about $1.00 per day, one can make the assumption that VCW was making roughly seven times what she would have earned as a seamstress when she was living in San Francisco in the late 1850s/early 1860s: *History of Wages in the United States from Colonial Times to 1928, Revision of Bulletin No. 499, with Supplement, 1929–1933 (Page 523)* (Washington: United States Government Printing Office, 1934), pp. 219–20.

118 *child of about eight*: Tennessee's exact date of birth is unknown, although it is generally thought to have been between 1844 and 1846. The 1850 U.S. Census gives her age as six, suggesting 1844 or earlier as the probable year. However, future official documents give contradictory information.

118 *"old sores . . ."*: *Penny Press* (OH), October 3, 1859, p. 3.

118 "A WONDERFUL CHILD! . . .": *Penny Press* (OH), October 3, 1859, p. 3.

118 *"perfectly harmless . . ."*: Miss Tennessee's Magnetic Life Elixir label reproduced in Sachs, *The Terrible Siren: Victoria Woodhull (1838–1927)* (New York: Harper & Brothers, 1928), p. 32.

118 *"hard life"*: *The Sun* (NYC), May 17, 1871, p. 1.

118 *"humbug"*: Tilton, *BVCW*, p. 22.

120 *went into labor*: Details about VCW's second labor and its aftermath are drawn from Tilton, *BVCW*, pp. 20–21.

121 *separate from*: VCW told Tilton that a divorce was granted in Chicago, but no official record has come to light. The city's divorce records were destroyed in the Great Fire of 1871.

121 *John Bortel*: *Evening News* (Portsmouth), March 4, 1903, p. 2.

121 *"Dr. R. B. Claflin . . ."*: *Ottawa Free Trader*, June 27, 1863, p. 3.

122 *"magnetic doctress . . ."*: *Joliet Signal*, May 17, 1864, p. 3.

122 *Rebecca Howe*: The statement of Rebecca Howe, published in *The Ottawa Republican* on June 4, 1864, is reproduced in Sachs, *The Terrible Siren*, pp. 35–36.

122 Circuit Court: The judgment of the La Salle County Circuit Court is reproduced in Sachs, *The Terrible Siren*, pp. 36–37.

123 *"She straightened the feet . . ."*: Tilton, *BVCW*, p. 19.

123 *partially paralyzed arm . . .*: Details about James Harvey Blood's wartime injuries are drawn from James H. Blood pension records, file #459314. National Archives and Records Administration, Washington, D.C./Robbins Hunter Museum (Granville, OH) copies.

123 *Some said*: *New York Times*, July 4, 1866, p. 2.

123 *endorsed by Victoria*: Details in this scene, including the quotations, are drawn from Tilton, *BVCW*, pp. 23–24.

A Valuable Asset

125 *"fraught with great difficulty"*: William E. Gienapp, ed., *This Fiery Trial: The Speeches and Writings of Abraham Lincoln* (New York: Oxford University Press, 2002), p. 223.

126 *"The Rebel Fiends at Work"*: *Nashville Union*, April 15, 1865 (Morning Extra edition), p. 1.

126 *"draped in mourning . . .":* *Evening Star,* April 15, 1865, p. 2.

126 *$10,000 reward:* *New York Herald,* April 15, 1865, p. 1.

126 *a premonition:* *Boston Post,* October 20, 1876, p. 8.

127 *auditor:* Tilton, *BVCW,* 23; *Daily Missouri Democrat,* April 3, 1865, p. 1.

127 *$2,500:* Lois Beachy Underhill, *The Woman Who Ran for President: The Many Lives of Victoria Woodhull* (Bridgehampton, NY: Bridge Works Publishing, 1995), p. 37.

127 *$3,000:* Details about this and James Harvey Blood's career as a magnetic and clairvoyant physician, including the quotations, are drawn from *The Weekly Ottumwa Courier,* February 23, 1865, p. 2.

127 *"Witch of Washington-avenue":* Details of the public scandal surrounding VCW and JHB's relationship, including the quotations, are drawn from an article in the *"St. Louis Democrat"* (presumably the *Daily Missouri Democrat*) reproduced in *The New York Times,* July 4, 1866, p. 2. The article refers to VCW as "Madame Holland," but it is clear from the context that this woman and VCW are one and the same.

128 *July 10, 1865:* There has been a great deal of confusion over the years about the date when VCW and James Harvey Blood were married. Researcher Mary L. Shearer is responsible for uncovering the relevant marriage certificate, which can be viewed at www.victoria-woodhull.com/marriages.htm.

128 *dissolved her marriage:* Tilton, *BVCW,* p. 21.

128 *legal separation:* *Chicago Tribune,* February 10, 1868, p.4; www.victoria-woodhull.com/marriages.htm. *The Tribune* writes that the divorce was granted "on the ground of adultery." Possible alternatives to this official reason include the state of VCW and James Harvey Blood's physical relationship, and moral grounds relating to their developing ideas about "free love."

129 *covered wagon:* Sachs, *The Terrible Siren,* p. 45.

129 *the "Prof.":* *New-Orleans Times,* December 24, 1866, p. 7.

129 *cared for Byron:* Thankful M. Claflin to Zula Maud Woodhull, June 25, 1927, box 2, folder 9, Victoria Woodhull-Martin papers, Special Collections Research Center, Southern Illinois University Carbondale; Stanley B. Davis to Sachs, August 5, [1927?], Emanie (Nahm)

Sachs Arling Philips Archive, Western Kentucky University/Robbins Hunter Museum (Granville, OH) copies.

129 *sometimes assisted her*: *Cincinnati Daily Gazette*, February 12, 1866, p. 2.

129 *"huge cancer . . ."*: *Goshen Times*, January 30, 1868, p. 3.

130 *even treated*: WCW 4, no. 4, April 27, 1872, p. 8.

130 *get Tennessee away*: *New York Herald*, May 17, 1871, p. 10.

130 *figure in white robes*: Details of this incident are drawn from Tilton, *BVCW*, p. 12.

132 *"harlots . . ."*: George Ellington, *The Women of New York; or, The Under-World of the Great City* (New York: The New York Book Company, 1869), pp. 173 and 196–97.

132 *joined by their parents*: In *The New York Herald*, May 17, 1871, p. 10, VCW mentions that her parents had lived with her at two addresses in New York City for three years.

132 *in East Coast newspapers*: *Daily Evening Traveller* (Boston), December 28, 1868, p. 1; *Philadelphia Inquirer*, September 29, 1868, p. 4.

133 *"Come! speak quick and be off!"*: W. A. Croffut, *The Vanderbilts and the Story of Their Fortune* (London: Griffith, Farran, Okeden & Welsh, 1886), p. 111.

133 *". . . battle with the world"*: WCW 9, no.18, April 3, 1875, p. 4.

133 *in fact close*: Underhill makes the point about the proximity between these two addresses in *The Woman Who Ran for President*, p. 45.

134 *". . . consult the spirits?"*: *New-York Tribune*, October 24, 1878, p. 2.

134 *"in a clairvoyant state . . ."*: *New York Times*, October 16, 1878, p. 2.

135 *". . . descended on their shoulders"*: *New York Herald*, January 22, 1870, p. 10.

135 *"old boy . . ."*: Arthur Vanderbilt II, *Fortune's Children: The Fall of the House of Vanderbilt* (London: Michael Joseph, 1990), p. 43.

136 *unpublished memoir*: Unless otherwise stated, details in this scene, including the quotations, are drawn from VCW, unpublished memoir [n.d.], box 1, folder 1, Victoria Woodhull-Martin papers, Special Collections Research Center, Southern Illinois University Carbondale.

137 *". . . clear and forcible as ever"*: *The Revolution*, January 28, 1869, p. 49.

137 *letters of regret*: Elizabeth Cady Stanton, Susan B. Anthony, and Mathilda Joslyn Gage, eds., *History of Woman Suffrage*, vol. 2, 1861–1876 (New York: Fowler & Wells, 1882), p. 357.

137 *"black and white . . ."*: The Revolution, January 28, 1869, p. 49.

138 *"claiming to be liberal . . ."*: Stanton, Anthony, and Gage, *History of Woman Suffrage*, vol. 2, 1861–1876, pp. 354–55.

138 *"as sacred . . ."*: William S. McFeely, *Frederick Douglass* (New York: W. W. Norton & Company, 1991), pp. 268–69.

139 *Victoria "was destined . . ."*: The World (NYC), January 28, 1869, p. 7.

140 *simple ceremony*: New York Herald, August 22, 1869, p. 7.

141 *Jay Gould*: For an overview of the career of Jay Gould and the events leading up to Black Friday, see Charles R. Geisst, *Wall Street: A History from Its Beginnings to the Fall of Enron* (New York: Oxford University Press, 2004), pp. 58–61.

141 *"wildest confusion and excitement"*: The Sun (NYC), September 23, 1869, p. 1.

141 *"a shouting mass of brokers"*: New York Herald, September 24, 1869, p. 8.

141 *"Bedlam in the Gold Room . . ."*: New York Herald, September 25, 1869, p. 3.

142 *"operating heavily"*: New York Herald, January 22, 1870, p. 10.

The Devil's Wife

144 *yet simply dressed*: The intentional plainness of VCW and Tennessee Claflin's dress struck an early reporter who called at Woodhull, Claflin & Co: New York Herald, January 22, 1870, p. 4.

144 *hovering journalist*: New York Herald, January 20, 1870, p. 9.

145 *"should be glad . . ."*: Details of the business cards and note, and the description of the *Herald* reporter's visit to Hoffman House, are drawn from *The New York Herald*, January 22, 1870, p. 4.

147 *"The Bewitching Brokers"*: New York Herald, February 10, 1870, p. 9.

147 *"The Petticoat Financiers"*: The Sun (NYC), March 26, 1870, p. 3.

147 *One caricature*: Harper's Weekly, March 5, 1870, p. 160.

147 *Another parody*: Evening Telegram, February 18, 1870, reprinted in

M. F. Darwin, *One Moral Standard for All: Extracts from the Lives of Victoria Claflin Woodhull and Tennessee Claflin* (New York: Caulon Press, n.d.), p. 10. This book incorrectly gives the name of the paper as the *Evening Telegraph*.

147 *"a very good doctor . . .":* *The Revolution* 5, no. 10, March 10, 1870, p. 155.

147 *private room*: *New York Herald*, February 10, 1870, p. 9.

147 *Some men called . . .*: *The Sun* (NYC), February 7, 1870, p. 1.

147 *lisping tone*: *Camden Daily Telegram* (NJ), March 28, 1887, p. 1.

148 *seeking an interview*: Details of Susan B. Anthony's visit to Woodhull, Claflin & Co. are drawn from *The Revolution* 5, no. 10, March 10, 1870, pp. 154–55.

149 *"lady broker of Broad street"*: *New York Herald*, April 2, 1870, p. 6.

149 *Victoria's message*: Details of Victoria's announcement that she planned to run for president are drawn from *The New York Herald*, April 2, 1870, pp. 6 and 8.

150 *Daniel Pratt Jr.*: *New York Herald*, April 3, 1870, p. 6.

151 *"a curiosity"*: *Maryland Union*, April 21, 1870, p. 2.

151 *her writing style*: *Alexandria Gazette*, April 21, 1870, p. 2.

151 *"without sufficient intellect . . ."*: *Providence Evening Press*, April 19, 1870, p. 3.

151 *"excellent"*: *New York Herald*, May 18, 1870, p. 6.

151 *"a well-edited . . ."*: *Banner of Light* 27, no. 23, August 20, 1870, p. 5.

151 *"the vital interests . . ."*: WCW 1, no. 1, May 14, 1870, p. 8.

152 The Communist Manifesto: WCW 4, no. 7, December 30, 1871, pp. 3–7 and 12–13.

152 *mutterings and moans*: Tilton, BVCW, p. 16, describes Byron Woodhull's vocalizations as "sepulchral."

153 The World: *The World* (NYC), September 24, 1870, p. 5.

153 *"one of the most virtuous acts of my life"*: *New York Times*, May 22, 1871, p. 5.

154 *"praying for . . . "*: *Cong. Globe* , 41st Cong., 3d Sess. (1870), p. 218.

154 *put in considerable time*: *New-York Tribune*, January 12, 1871, p. 1, reported that VCW and Tennessee Claflin had been "industriously pulling wires."

154 *address to Congress*: Details about VCW's address to Congress, in-

cluding the quotations, are drawn from *The Evening Telegraph* (Philadelphia), January 11, 1871, p. 1; *New-York Tribune*, January 12, 1871, p. 1; *The Press* (Philadelphia), January 13, 1871, p. 6.

155 *at the Cooper Union*: *New York Herald*, May 9, 1871, p. 7, referred to this speech as an "admirable production." The paper incorrectly gave Victoria's first name as Virginia.

155 *headline billing alongside*: *New York Times*, May 12, 1871, p. 8.

155 *"all love . . ."*: *New-York Tribune*, May 10, 1871, p. 5.

156 *"any pure wife . . ."*: *New-York Tribune*, May 13, 1871, p. 5.

156 *issued a warrant*: Details of James Harvey Blood's arrest and the ensuing court appearances of Claflin family members, Canning Woodhull, and VCW, and the quotations, are drawn from *The New York Herald*, May 6, 1871, p. 8; May 16, 1871, p. 3; May 17, 1871, p. 10; *The Sun* (NYC), May 17, 1871, p. 1.

156 *On May 15*: Details of the court proceedings, including the quotations, are drawn from *The New York Herald*, May 16, 1871, p. 3; May 17, 1871, p. 10; *The Sun* (NYC), May 17, 1871, p. 1.

156 *in her sixties*: As with several other individuals featured in this book, conflicting information surrounds Roxanna Claflin's exact date of birth. The 1850 U.S. Census gives her age as forty-three, making her about sixty-four in 1871. On the other hand, *The Morning Post* (London), June 14, 1889, p. 5, which recorded her death, states that she was "in her 85th year," which would have made her about sixty-seven in 1871.

160 *and* The World: *The World* (NYC), May 22, 1871, p. 3.

160 *"because I am a woman . . ."*: *New York Times*, May 22, 1871, p. 5.

161 *confront Victoria*: Unless otherwise stated, details of Tilton's visit to Woodhull, Claflin & Co., including the quotations, are drawn from *WCW* 5, no. 24, May 17, 1873, pp. 5–6.

161 *including Elizabeth Cady Stanton*: *WCW* 5, no. 7, November 2, 1872, p. 11.

162 *attacking Henry's oldest sister*: *WCW* 2, no. 8, January 7, 1871, p. 1.

162 *for a carriage ride*: *WCW* 5, no. 24, May 17, 1873, p. 15.

163 *"one of the sincerest . . ."*: Tilton, *BVCW*, p. 35.

163 *arrange a meeting*: Details of VCW's meeting with Henry Ward Beecher are drawn from *WCW* 5, no. 7, November 2, 1872, p. 12.

163 *night of the event*: Details of VCW's Steinway Hall speech, including the quotations, are drawn from *The New York Herald*, November 21, 1871, p. 10; WCW 5, no. 24, May 17, 1873, p. 6.

165 *"Let me through . . ."*: *The Sun* (NYC), December 18, 1871, p. 1.

166 *Academy of Music*: Details of the delivery of this speech and its aftermath, including the quotations, are drawn from *The New York Herald*, February 21, 1872, p. 10; *New York Times*, February 22, 1872, p. 4; *New Orleans Republican*, February 24, 1872, p. 2; WCW 4, no. 16, March 2, 1872, pp. 9–10.

166 *"A Vanderbilt . . ."*: VCW, *A Speech on the Impending Revolution* (New York: Woodhull, Claflin & Co., 1872), p. 12.

166 *soon-to-be-infamous cartoon*: *Harper's Weekly* 16, no. 790, February 17, 1872, p. 140.

167 *his achievements*: WCW 4, no. 24, April 27, 1872, p. 8.

167 *Victoria's sister Utica*: *Chicago Tribune*, April 15, 1872, p. 5.

167 *"the old faces . . ."*: *New York Herald*, May 11, 1872, p. 10.

168 *alternative suggestions*: *Charleston Daily News*, May 14, 1872, p. 1.

168 *"Piebald Presidency"*: *New York Herald*, May 11, 1872, p. 10.

168 *"A Shameless Prostitute and a Negro"*: Quotation from *The Guard* (OR) reproduced in Amanda Frisken, *Victoria Woodhull's Sexual Revolution: Political Theater and the Popular Press in Nineteenth-Century America* (Philadelphia: University of Pennsylvania Press, 2004), p. 74.

168 *more modest dwellings*: WCW 5, no. 7, November 2, 1872, p. 8, states that, after giving up the Murray Hill property, VCW "took board at greatly reduced expense."

169 *American Association of Spiritualists*: VCW's account of her appearance at the conference, and the quotations, are drawn from WCW 5, no. 7, November 2, 1872, p. 10.

170 *"surpassed even her own indecencies"*: *Watchman and Reflector*, September 19, 1872, p. 2.

170 *"never equalled in vulgarity . . ."*: *Boston Herald*, September 30, 1872, p. 2.

170 *"most foul and indecent . . ."*: *Daily Phoenix*, September 25, 1872, p. 3.

170 *"one of the oldest . . ."*: WCW 5, no. 7, November 2, 1872, pp. 13–14.

170 *"like buttered hot cakes . . ."*: Quotation from *The Chicago Times*, July 9, 1874, reproduced in Myra MacPherson, *The Scarlet Sisters: Sex, Suffrage, and Scandal in the Gilded Age* (New York: Twelve, 2014), p. 185. This reporter's account ran two years after these events occurred.

171 *sisters claimed*: WCW 5, no. 8, December 28, 1872, p. 10.

171 *eight charges*: Lois Beachy Underhill, *The Woman Who Ran for President: The Many Lives of Victoria Woodhull* (Bridgehampton, NY: Bridge Works Publishing, 1995), p. 233.

172 *"so sweet & perfect"*: Harriet Beecher Stowe to George Eliot, March 18, 1876, Harriet Beecher Stowe Collection of Papers, 1847–1895, The Henry W. and Albert A. Berg Collection of English and American Literature, The New York Public Library, Astor, Lenox and Tilden Foundations.

172 *wife of the governor*: Harriet Beecher Stowe quotation reproduced in Underhill, *The Woman Who Ran for President*, p. 234.

172 *at any hall*: New York Herald, December 23, 1872, p. 6.

172 *negative review*: WCW 11, no. 21, April 22, 1876, pp. 5–6.

172 *divorced again*: Woodhull & Claflin's Journal 12, no. 3, January 29, 1881, p. 3.

Private Frustrations

176 *"if anything should happen . . ."*: Details about GW's family background, and the quotations, are drawn from Grierson, *Storm Bird*, pp. 9–12 and 18, based on an archive of GW's papers that is now in private ownership, and GW, *My Orphanage*, pp. 2–3.

177 *in Italy*: GW, *My Orphanage*, p. 2, states that the family moved to Italy in 1840.

177 *"the nicest, delightful book . . ."*: GW diary extract reproduced in Helen F. Nicholson, "Spirited Performances: A Critical Study of the Life of Georgina Weldon (1837–1914)" (PhD diss., University of Manchester, 2000), p. 30.

178 *returned to Britain*: GW, *My Orphanage*, p. 5.

178 Hearts and Tarts . . .: Treherne, *Plaintiff*, p. 11; GW, *My Orphanage*, p. 11.

178 *according to a nephew*: Treherne, *Plaintiff*, p. 12.

178 *"little Bambina"*: George Frederic Watts to GW ("Signor" to "Bambina"), August 5, August 25, and October 1857, Western Manuscripts, Archives and Manuscripts, British Library, copies. The artist uses the name "Bambina" repeatedly in his missives and tends to sign his letters to GW "the scolding Signor."

178 *nineteen*: Treherne, *Plaintiff*, p. 12.

179 *"Papa and Mama . . ."*: GW diary extract reproduced in Grierson, *Storm Bird*, p. 20.

179 *romance via letters*: Details of GW and Harry Weldon's romance and marriage, including the quotations, are drawn from Grierson, *Storm Bird*, pp. 20–29.

180 *married in secret*: GW and Harry Weldon's marriage entry, April 21, 1860, Church of England Marriages and Banns, 1754–1937 (Woking, Surrey: Surrey History Centre).

180 *enamored with*: "Poodle" Byng and GW moved in some of the same social circles. He had, for instance, acted as a theatrical promoter for *Hearts and Tarts* by Augustus Stafford, the lavish amateur production in which GW had appeared in 1857.

181 *"lofty pine . . ."*: This masculine and feminine imagery appeared in an anonymous poem, widely published in newspapers of the day.

181 *appeared to do just that*: In GW, *My Orphanage*, p. 9, GW claims that in the early days of her marriage she "no longer thought of the stage."

181 *Georgina enjoyed*: Grierson, *Storm Bird*, p. 33.

181 *Georgina carped privately*: Ibid., p. 37.

182 *her family's connections*: Treherne, *Plaintiff*, p. 23.

182 *Tavistock House*: Details of GW's new home are drawn from Grierson, *Storm Bird*, p. 77; GW, *The Ghastly Consequences of Living in Charles Dickens' House* (London: Tavistock House, 1882), p. 1.

182 *"finished" artists . . .*: Extract from letter by GW, reproduced in Grierson, *Storm Bird*, p. 57.

183 *drawing room performance*: Queen Victoria's journals, RA VIC/MAIN/QVJ (W), March 18, 1871 (Princess Beatrice's copies).

183 *end up remaining*: Grierson, *Storm Bird*, p. 76.

184 *"made me almost die . . ."*: GW, *My Orphanage*, p. 64.

184 *family members*: Grierson, *Storm Bird*, p. 72, says that by mid-July 1871 GW's mother had heard of the rumors.

184 *go barefoot*: GW, *The History of my Orphanage: or, The Outpourings of an Alleged Lunatic* (London: self-published, 1878), pp. 25 and 28–29.

184 *quarter hour*: Grierson, *Storm Bird*, p. 148.

184 *rip skeins of cloth*: *The Spiritualist* 12, no. 20, May 17, 1878, p. 237.

184 *"horrible . . ."*: GW, *The History of my Orphanage*, pp. 26 and 32.

185 *dusting some books*: *The Spiritualist* 12, no. 20, May 17, 1878, p. 236.

185 *scandalized the local gentry*: GW as quoted in Grierson, *Storm Bird*, p. 49.

185 *troubling letter*: Unless otherwise stated, details of GW's homecoming are drawn from Grierson, *Storm Bird*, pp. 158–62.

185 *partially in charge*: *Pall Mall Gazette*, April 15, 1878, p. 6.

186 *James Samuel Bell*: Most accounts give his name only as Mr. Bell, but his full name appears in an account of the case of *Weldon v. Winslow*, in *Reynolds's Newspaper*, March 16, 1884, p. 5.

186 *Elizabeth Villiers*: As revealed in GW's account of the attempt to capture her in *The Spiritualist* 12, no. 20, May 17, 1878, p. 236, she called her maid by her surname, but her full name appears in *Social Salvation* 1, no.1, May 1883, p. 2.

186 *two gentlemen*: Unless otherwise stated, details in the following scenes of April 14–15, 1878, including the quotations, are drawn from *The London Figaro*, December 4, 1878, pp. 11–12; *The Spiritualist* 12, no. 20, May 17, 1878, pp. 236–37; Visitors' book originally used at Tavistock House, 1871–1913, MSL/1952/1618, National Art Library (UK); GW, *How I Escaped the Mad Doctors* (London: self-published, 1882), pp. 9–16.

186 *a pamphlet on the subject*: GW, *The Ghastly Consequences of Living in Charles Dickens' House.*

189 *"full consent . . ."*: *London Figaro*, January 15, 1879, p. 4.

190 *"the curse of our age . . ."*: L. S. Forbes Winslow, *Spiritualistic Madness* (London: Baillière, Tindall, and Cox, 1877), pp. 5 and 28–29.

191 *Anacharsis Ménier's appearance*: In *The Standard*, April 15, 1878, p. 2, the defendant is referred to by his real first name, Jean.

Ghastly Consequences

194 *own husband*: For an overview of Louisa Lowe's life, see Alex Owen, *The Darkened Room: Women, Power and Spiritualism in Late Victorian England* (London: Virago Press, 1989), pp. 168–201; Roy Porter, Helen Nicholson, and Bridget Bennett, *Women, Madness and Spiritualism*, vol. 1 (London: Routledge, 2003), pp. 139–50; Sarah Wise, *Inconvenient People: Lunacy, Liberty and the Mad-Doctors in Victorian England* (London: Vintage, 2013), pp. 291–324.

194 *in her late fifties*: The 1871 England Census gives Louisa Lowe's age as fifty, making her about fifty-seven in 1878.

194 *"in a wonderful way"*: From Louisa Lowe, *Quis Custodiet Ipsos Custodes? No. 3, How an Old Woman Obtained Passive Writing, and the Outcome Thereof* (London: J. Burns, 1873), p. 1.

195 *bring a case*: For a contemporary account of the lawsuit see *The Spiritualist* 3, no. 2, December 1, 1872, pp. 22–23.

196 *"many sane . . ."*: Louisa Lowe, *Quis Custodiet Ipsos Custodes? No. 1, Report of a Case Heard in Queen's Bench* (London: J. Burns, 1872), p. 4.

197 *She advised*: Unless otherwise stated, details in the following scene, including the quotations, are drawn from *The Spiritualist* 12, no. 20, May 17, 1878, pp. 237–38; *The Times* (London), July 11, 1884, p. 2, and July 17, 1884, p. 3; GW, *How I Escaped the Mad Doctors*, pp. 16–19.

197 *"dear old friend"*: GW to William Ewart Gladstone, March 24, 1871, Gladstone Papers, Western Manuscripts, Archives and Manuscripts, British Library.

197 *that "reptile . . ."*: GW to William Ewart Gladstone, April 15, 1878, Gladstone Papers, Western Manuscripts, Archives and Manuscripts, British Library. Over the years, GW's accounts varied as to the exact point in the day when she wrote to the former prime minister. However, her letter makes clear that it was while Louisa Lowe was on her way to the police station and while Georgina was barricaded inside the library of Tavistock House.

198 *Sarah Southey*: Contemporary news reports tend to refer to the women, if at all, by their surnames only, but Lyttleton Stewart Forbes Winslow's biographer, Molly Whittington Egan, points out that Sarah Southey and Mary Anne Tomkins were both listed at the doctor's Brandenburgh House asylum three years later, in 1881: Molly Whittington-Egan, *Doctor Forbes Winslow: Defender of the Insane* (Great Malvern: Cappella Archive, 2000), p. 123.

200 *another party*: *The Spiritualist* 12, no. 20, May 17, 1878, p. 238.

200 *on the run*: Details of GW's time in hiding are drawn from Grierson, *Storm Bird*, p. 170.

200 *two separate doctors*: GW named these men as Dr. George Wyld and Dr. James Edmunds in *The Spiritualist* 12, no. 20, May 17, 1878, p. 238.

200 *"On condition of Mr. Weldon . . ."*: GW's statement reproduced in Grierson, *Storm Bird*, p. 171.

200 *Harry's co-conspirator*: Details of the scene between the de Bathes and GW, including the quotations, are drawn from an extract from GW's diary, reproduced in Grierson, *Storm Bird*, p. 172.

202 *". . . woefully mismanaged"*: William Henry "Harry" Weldon's words were recalled by Lyttleton Stewart Forbes Winslow during an 1884 court appearance and reported in *The Times* (London), March 17, 1884, p. 4.

202 *"always thought . . ."*: Emily Louisa Williams to William Ewart Gladstone, April 24, 1878, Gladstone Papers, Western Manuscripts, Archives and Manuscripts, British Library.

202 *"What reason . . ."*: *London Figaro*, January 15, 1879, p. 4.

202 *before Frederick Flowers*: Details of GW's October 1878 court appearance, including the quotations, are drawn from *The Spiritualist* 13, no. 16, October 18, 1878, p. 183. Related press reports consistently refer to a Mr. Flowers, with no first name mentioned. However, his first name appears in a brief notice announcing his death, published in the *Cambridge Independent Press*, January 30, 1886, p. 3.

203 *"in every phase of her life . . ."*: *Illustrated Sporting and Dramatic News*, November 2, 1878, p. 151.

204 *One journalist*: Details in the following scene, including the quota-

tions, are drawn from *The Illustrated Police News*, November 16, 1878, p. 2.

205 *"strictly according to the law . . .":* British Medical Journal 2, no. 932, November 9, 1878, p. 700.

206 *"behaviour and manners . . .":* Louisa Lowe, *Quis Custodiet Ipsos Custodes? No. 1, Report of a Case Heard in Queen's Bench* (London: J. Burns, 1872), p. 24.

206 *one of their number:* Details of this episode are drawn from *Social Salvation* 2, nos. 15–18, July/August/September/October 1884, p. 6.

207 *". . . prefer a lunatic asylum . . .":* Ibid.

207 The Medium and Daybreak *reported:* Details of GW's Langham Hall appearance on October 24, 1878, including the quotation, are drawn from *The Medium and Daybreak* 4, no. 448, November 1, 1878, p. 699.

208 *at homes:* Ticket from GW's at homes, reproduced in Grierson, *Storm Bird*, p. 176.

208 *as a pamphlet:* GW, *How I Escaped the Mad Doctors.*

208 *"most people who read . . .":* Medium and Daybreak 10, no. 490, August 22, 1879, p. 522.

209 *"almost American":* Treherne, *Plaintiff*, p.119.

Public Triumph

210 *sandwich-board men:* Yorkshire Post, March 17, 1884, p. 5.

210 *hot-air balloon:* Hastings and St. Leonard's Observer, September 15, 1883, p. 3; *Social Salvation* 1, no. 6, October 1883, p. 1.

211 *"book, pamphlet, or letter . . .":* Details of GW's "The Story of Mrs. Weldon Written by Herself," including the quotations, are drawn from *The London Figaro*, December 4, 1878, p. 11; December 11, 1878, p. 5; December 25, 1878, p. 4; January 15, 1879, p. 4; January 22, 1879, p. 3.

211 *whether "it was right . . .":* British Medical Journal 1, no. 943, January 25, 1879, p. 129.

212 *"a lady of world-wide celebrity":* London Figaro, January 22, 1879, p. 11.

212 *multiple grievances:* Further details of GW's other allegations are

drawn from *The London Figaro*, January 22, 1879, pp. 3–4; *The Spiritualist* 15, no. 1, July 4, 1879, p. 4.

212 *"no Valentine for me . . .":* Treherne, *Plaintiff,* p. 78.

213 *vivid picture*: Details of the libel case against James Mortimer, including the quotations, are drawn from *The Spiritualist* 15, no. 1, July 4, 1879, p. 4.

214 *seven affidavits: Illustrated Police News,* November 22, 1879, p. 2.

215 *Rivière's Promenade Concerts: The Standard* (London), October 6, 1879, p. 4.

215 *both had strong opinions*: Details about GW and Jules Rivière's discussions, including the quotations, are drawn from extracts from their letters in Grierson, *Storm Bird,* pp. 180–81.

216 *came to a head*: Details about the Balaclava Night benefit and GW's return to the Theatre Royal on October 29, 1879, including the quotations, are drawn from Grierson, *Storm Bird,* pp. 188–89, and *The Globe,* November 7, 1879, p. 2.

217 *Bow Street Police Court*: Unless otherwise stated, details of GW's November 6, 1879, court appearance are drawn from *The Globe,* November 7, 1879, p. 2; *The Era,* November 9, 1879, p. 3.

217 *"the irrepressible lady . . .": The Graphic,* November 15, 1879, p. 483.

218 *back in the dock*: Details of GW's December 11, 1879, appearance at Clerkenwell Police Court are drawn from *The Morning Post* (London), December 12, 1879, p. 3.

218 *appeared in court*: Details of GW's March 1880 appearance at the Central Criminal Court, including the quotations, are drawn from *The Globe,* December 15, 1879, p. 5; *Pall Mall Gazette,* March 3, 1880, p. 8; *Daily Telegraph,* March 6, 1880, p. 5.

219 *evict Angèle Ménier: Lloyd's Weekly Newspaper,* May 30, 1880, p. 7.

219 *From Newgate Prison*: Unless otherwise stated, details of GW's time in Newgate Prison, including the quotations of GW's words, are drawn from Grierson, *Storm Bird,* pp. 192–93.

220 *June 30, 1880*: Details of GW's 1880 departure from prison are drawn from *Reynold's Newspaper,* July 4, 1880, p. 5.

220 *"if I can get a chance . . .": The Referee,* July 4, 1880, p. 3.

220 *Great Central Hall*: Details of GW's July 13 appearance are drawn from an extract from *The People's Cross* reproduced in Grierson, *Storm Bird*, p. 193, and *Reynold's Newspaper*, July 18, 1880, p. 5.

221 *"All you have done . . ."*: Dalrymple Treherne to GW, [n.d.], reproduced in Treherne, *Plaintiff*, p. 90.

222 Weldon v. Weldon: Details of GW's July 13, 1882, court appearance, including the quotations, are drawn from *The Globe*, July 14, 1882, p. 2, and *The Standard* (London), July 14, 1882, p. 3.

223 *"bow to the inevitable . . ."*: Extract from GW to Harry Weldon, [n.d.], reproduced in Grierson, *Storm Bird*, p. 199.

223 *"amid a chaos . . ."*: Francis Charles Philips quoted in Treherne, *Plaintiff*, pp. 92–93.

224 Weldon v. Winslow: Details of GW's March 1884 court appearance, including the quotations, are drawn from *The St. James's Gazette*, March 14, 1884, p. 12; *Reynolds's Newspaper*, March 16, 1884, p. 2; *The Globe*, March 18, 1884, p. 2; *Morning Post* (London), March 19, 1884, p. 3; extracts of court transcripts reproduced in Grierson, *Storm Bird*, pp. 208–12.

227 *a new trial*: Grierson, *Storm Bird*, p. 212.

227 *emotional missive*: *Morning Post* (London), July 14, 1884, p. 6.

227 *". . . upset water . . ."*: Court transcript reproduced in Grierson, *Storm Bird*, p. 215.

227 *"but to the public generally . . ."*: *The Standard* (London), July 29, 1884, p. 6.

229 *"every reason to hope . . ."*: *Medium and Daybreak* 15, no. 755, September 19, 1884, p. 605.

229 *Serjeant Buzfuz*: *The Entr'acte*, September 20, 1884, p. 4.

229 *awarding her £500*: *West London Observer*, December 6, 1884, p. 5.

230 *"she passes muster . . ."*: *Islington Gazette*, October 16, 1885, p. 3.

230 *"sufficiently serves . . ."*: *The Era*, October 17, 1885, p. 14.

230 *"first-class misdemeanant"*: Details of GW's departure from Holloway Gaol, including the quotations, are drawn from *The Witney Express*, October 1, 1885, p. 7.

230 *seventeen thousand people*: Grierson, *Storm Bird*, p. 247.

231 *temporarily moved into*: Ibid., p. 254.

231 *the chair*: *Witney Express*, October 1, 1885, p. 7.

231 *"My dear Lunie . . ."*: Lyttleton Stewart Forbes Winslow to GW, October 16, 1901, reproduced in Molly Whittington-Egan, *Doctor Forbes Winslow: Defender of the Insane* (Great Malvern: Cappella Archive, 2000), p. 144.

231 *"marvelled at . . ."*: *Light* 33, no. 1,695, July 5, 1913, p. 345.

232 *uncover clues*: *Light* 8, no. 405, October 6, 1888, has several articles that deal with the place of clairvoyance in the hunt for the murderer. It is worth noting that Winslow also featured extensively in the related national press coverage, thanks to his attempts to provide an early example of a criminal profile of the killer. His memoirs devote a chapter to his hypotheses on the Ripper's identity: L. Forbes Winslow, *Recollections of Forty Years* (London: John Ouseley Ltd., 1910), pp. 251–83.

End of an Era?

233 *"DEATH OF SPIRITUALISM"*: *The Sun* (NYC), October 21, 1888, p. 19. This advertisement, published in many of the city's papers, referred to MFK as "Margaret," not "Margaretta." MFK was sometimes known by this name, but I have called her Margaretta here for reasons of consistency, and to avoid unnecessary confusion with her mother, Margaret Fox.

233 *That night*: Unless otherwise stated, details about MFK's appearance at the Academy of Music, including the quotations, are drawn from *The New York Herald*, October 22, 1888, p. 5; *New-York Daily Tribune*, October 22, 1888, p. 7; *The World* (Evening Edition, NYC), October 22, 1888, p. 2.

234 *midfifties*: MFK's given age here is based on my reckoning of her year of birth outlined in the notes to chapter 1.

236 *her relationship with*: Unless otherwise stated, details of MFK's relationship with Elisha Kent Kane, including the quotations, are drawn from EKK and MFK, *The Love-Life of Dr. Kane* (New York: Carleton, 1866), pp. 21–28, 35, 38, 108, 148–49, and "A friend to both parties" to Jane Duval Leiper Kane, January 3, n.y., Elisha Kent Kane Papers, American Philosophical Society, Philadelphia.

237 *". . . all over the world . . ."*: MFK to EKK, n.d., Elisha Kent Kane Papers, American Philosophical Society, Philadelphia.

238 *in an ice floe*: Details of the fate of the USS *Advance* and EKK's on-ward journey are drawn from *The New York Herald*, October 12, 1855, p. 1.

238 "*. . . lead to the altar . . .*": Quotation reproduced in EKK and MFK, *The Love-Life of Dr. Kane*, p. 190.

238 *later recollections*: EKK and MFK, *The Love-Life of Dr. Kane*, p. 228.

238 *new book*: EKK, *Arctic Explorations: The Second Grinnell Expedition in Search of Sir John Franklin, 1853, '54, '55* (Philadelphia: Childs & Peterson, 1857).

239 *had urged her*: EKK to MFK, *The Love-Life of Dr. Kane*, p. 284.

239 "*a relative*": Ibid., p. 28.

240 *baskets of champagne*: Article from *The World* (NYC), May 6, 1888, reproduced in Herbert G. Jackson Jr., *The Spirit Rappers* (New York: Doubleday & Co., 1972), p. 198.

240 "*crazy with brandy . . .*': W. G. Langworthy Taylor, *Katie Fox: Epochmaking Medium and the Making of the Fox-Taylor Record* (Boston: Bruce Humphries, 1936), pp. 154 and 157.

241 *chorus of raps*: *New York Herald*, February 2, 1873, p. 6.

241 *biblical line*: In the King James Version, John 11:25, this appears as "he that believeth in me, though he were dead, yet shall he live."

241 *article about Ferdie*: ALU, *Missing Link*, pp. 465–70.

241 *part-memoir*: Although ALU claimed that her book was not an autobiography, this element to the work feels undeniable.

241 *in purple velvet*: *Golden Gate* 1, no. 3, August 1, 1885, p. 5.

241 *flurry of rumors*: The British Spiritualist magazine *Light* addressed these rumors after the death of Queen Victoria in 1901. *Light* 21, no. 1,056, April 6, 1901, p. 158, concluded that "Her Majesty firmly believed in the continuance of life after death, and was fully persuaded in her own mind that Prince Albert was frequently with her, guiding, protecting, and sustaining her—but this was belief only, not knowledge. In Spiritualism as we know it she took no interest whatever. We may wish it had been otherwise—but it is well to know the truth."

242 "*The Spirits Too Much for Her . . .*": *New York Herald*, May 5, 1888, p. 4.

242 *Kate suspected*: *New York Herald*, October 10, 1888, p. 3.

242 *aged fourteen*: The baptismal records for Ferdinand Dietrich Lowenstein Jencken and Henry Dietrich Lowenstein Jencken give their dates of birth as September 19, 1873, and December 3, 1874, respectively: London Metropolitan Archives.

242 *"darling sister's . . ."*: *New York Herald*, May 27, 1888, p. 15.

243 *an interview*: Details of MFK's conversation with the reporter, including the quotations, are drawn from *The New York Herald*, September 24, 1888, p. 10.

244 *"got their money's worth . . ."*: *New-York Tribune*, October 22, 1888, p. 7.

244 *". . . follies . . ."*: *Sacramento Daily Record-Union*, October 27, 1888, p. 4.

244 *"if any further proofs . . ."*: *Lloyd's Weekly London Newspaper*, November 4, 1888, p. 7.

244 *"ignorance and misconception . . ."*: *Banner of Light* 64, no. 16, December 29, 1888, p. 4; vol. 64, no.13, December 8, 1888, p. 5.

245 *"Painful, therefore . . ."*: *Light* 8, no. 409, November 3, 1888, p. 543.

245 *". . . public or private"*: *Two Worlds* 2, no.53, November 16, 1888, p. 7.

246 *". . . under spiritual guidance . . ."*: *London Figaro*, January 22, 1879, p. 11.

247 *pastimes like these*: VCW was also a proficient cyclist. The author of the following typescript refers to VCW and Zula Maud Woodhull as "first-rate bikists'": "Call for a revision of the constitution of the United States," n.d., p. 6, MS 2001, box 2, folder 30, Victoria Woodhull Martin Papers, 1883–1927, Rare Books Department, Boston Public Library.

247 *"noble magazine"*: EHB to VW, September 1 [?], 1897, box 1, folder 13, Victoria Woodhull-Martin papers, Special Collections Research Center, Southern Illinois University Carbondale.

248 *chief beneficiary*: VCW will, August 9, 1927, Emanie (Nahm) Sachs Arling Philips Archive, Western Kentucky University/Robbins Hunter Museum (Granville, OH), copies. The will also made substantial provision for the care of Byron Woodhull.

249 *address the crowd*: *Light* 8, no. 412, November 24, 1888, p. 583; vol. 8, no. 413, December 1, 1888, p. 589.

249 *moving saucers*: Details of Charles Gounod's supposed communications to GW are drawn from Grierson, *Storm Bird*, pp. 262–65.

249 *ideally placed*: *Banner of Light* 64, no. 8, November 3, 1888, p. 5.

249 "... *made such statements* ...": Both ALU's statement and MFK's reply appear in *The Indiana State Sentinel*, May 1, 1889, p. 5.

250 *Grand Opera House*: *New York Herald*, October 28, 1888, p. 9.

250 *"thoroughly explain* ...": *Boston Herald*, November 1, 1888, p. 2.

250 *a "committee"*: Details of MFK's appearance in New Haven, including the quotations, are drawn from the *Morning Journal and Courier* (New Haven, CT), December 10, 1888, p. 2.

250 *"a humbug* ...": *New York Herald*, November 11, 1888, p. 11.

251 Death-Blow to Spiritualism—Is It?: GW, *Death-Blow to Spiritualism—Is It? Dr. Slade, Messrs. Maskeylyne & Cooke, and Mr. W. Morton* (London: Music and Art Association, 1882).

251 *November 17*: *New York Herald*, November 17, 1888, p. 7.

251 *"written in extreme haste* ...": Reuben Briggs Davenport, *The Death-Blow to Spiritualism: Being the True Story of the Fox Sisters, as Revealed by Authority of Margaret Fox Kane and Catherine Fox Jencken* (New York: G. W. Dillingham, 1888), pp. v–vii.

252 *"if I had the means* ...": *Light* 8, no. 415, December 15, 1888, p. 619.

252 *resume her career*: *Boston Herald*, October 29, 1889, p. 2.

252 *"false in every particular* ...": Interview originally published in *The Press* (NYC), reproduced in *The Two Worlds* 3, no. 110, December 20, 1889, p. 58.

252 *Maggie's recantation*: *New-York Tribune*, December 20, 1889, p. 9.

253 *"Who can trust her* ...": *Banner of Light* 66, no. 12, November 30, 1889, p. 4.

253 *"to unsay* ...": *Two Worlds* 3, no. 110, December 20, 1889, pp. 57 and 59.

254 "... *hour after hour* ...": Arthur Conan Doyle, *The History of Spiritualism*, vol. 1 (London: Cassell and Company, 1926), pp. 87–88.

254 *". . . to the end"*: *Banner of Light* 68, no. 10, November 15, 1890, p. 4.

254 *"she played . . ."*: *Light* 10, no. 518, December 6, 1890, p. 590.

254 *established a fund*: *Banner of Light* 73, no. 1, March 11, 1893, p. 4.

254 *"transition . . ."*: *Banner of Light* 73, no. 2, March 18, 1893, p. 4.

SELECT BIBLIOGRAPHY

In addition to the original diaries, letters, and newspaper articles detailed in the notes, the following books and pamphlets were the most helpful to my research.

Primary Sources

~ associated with the Fox sisters

Capron, E. W. *Modern Spiritualism, Its Facts and Fanaticisms, Its Consistencies and Contradictions. With an Appendix*. Boston: Bela Marsh, 1855.

Capron, E. W., and Henry D. Barron. *Singular Revelations: Explanation and History of the Mysterious Communion with Spirits, Comprehending the Rise and Progress of the Mysterious Noises in Western New-York, Generally Received as Spiritual Communications*. Auburn, NY: Capron and Barron, 1850.

Davenport, Reuben Briggs. *The Death-Blow to Spiritualism: Be-*

ing the True Story of the Fox Sisters, as Revealed by Authority of Margaret Fox Kane and Catherine Fox Jencken. New York: G. W. Dillingham, 1888.

Dewey, D. M. *History of the Strange Sounds or Rappings, Heard in Rochester and Western New-York, and usually called The Mysterious Noises! Which Are Supposed by Many to Be Communications from the Spirit World, Together with All the Explanation That Can Yet Be Given of the Matter*. Rochester: D. M. Dewey, 1850.

Elwood, George M. *Some Earlier Public Amusements of Rochester*. Rochester, NY: Democrat and Chronicle Print, 1894.

Greeley, Horace. *The Autobiography of Horace Greeley, or Recollections of a Busy Life*. New York: E. B. Treat, 1872.

Kane, Elisha K., and Margaret Fox. *The Love-Life of Dr. Kane*. New York: Carleton, 1866.

Lewis, E. E. *A Report of the Mysterious Noises Heard in the House of Mr. John D. Fox, In Hydesville, Arcadia, Wayne County, N.Y. Authenticated by the Certificates, and Confirmed by the Statements of the Citizens of That Place and Vicinity*. Shelburne Falls, MA: J. L. Wade & Co., 1887.

Podmore, Frank. *Modern Spiritualism: A History and Criticism*. London: Methuen & Co., 1902.

Taylor, W. G. Langworthy. *Katie Fox: Epochmaking Medium and the Making of the Fox-Taylor Record*. Boston: Bruce Humphries, 1936.

Underhill, A. Leah. *The Missing Link in Modern Spiritualism*. New York: Thomas R. Knox & Co., 1885.

~ associated with Emma Hardinge Britten

Britten, Emma Hardinge [Published as Emma Hardinge]. *America and Her Destiny: Inspirational Discourse Given Extempora-*

neously at Dodworth's Hall, New York, on Sunday Evening, August 25, 1861, Through Emma Hardinge, by the Spirits. 2nd ed. New York: Robert M. De Witt, 1861.

——. *Autobiography of Emma Hardinge Britten*, London: J. Heywood, 1900.

——. *Extemporaneous Addresses by Emma Hardinge. Spoken at the Winter Soirées Held at Harley Street, London, 1865.* London: Thomas Scott, 1865.

——. *The Faiths, Facts, and Frauds of Religious History.* Manchester: John Heywood, n.d.

——. *The Great Funeral Oration on Abraham Lincoln.* New York: American News Company, n.d.

—— [Published as Emma Hardinge]. *Miss Emma Hardinge's Political Campaign in Favour of the Union Party of America, on the Occasion of the Last Presidential Election of 1864.* London: Thomas Scott, n.d.

——. *Modern American Spiritualism: A Twenty Years' Record of the Communion Between Earth and the World of the Spirits.* New York: self-published, 1870.

——. *Modern American Spiritualism: A Twenty Years' Record of the Communion Between Earth and the World of the Spirits.* New Hyde Park, NY: University Books, 1970.

——. *Nineteenth Century Miracles; or, Spirits and Their Work in Every Country of the Earth.* New York: Lovell & Co., 1884.

—— [Published as Emma Hardinge]. *The Place and Mission of Woman: An Inspirational Discourse.* Boston: Hubbard W. Swett, 1859.

—— [Published as Emma Hardinge]. *Six Lectures on Theology and Nature,* n.p., 1860.

—— [Published as Emma Hardinge]. *The Wildfire Club.* Boston: Berry, Colby, & Company, 1861.

Britten, Emma Hardinge, ed. *Art Magic, or Mundane, Sub-Mundane and Super-Mundane Spiritism*. Chicago: Progressive Thinker Publishing House, 1909.

———. *Ghost Land; or Researches into the Mysteries of Occultism*. Boston: self-published, 1876.

Crosland, Mrs. Newton (Camilla Toulmin). *Landmarks of a Literary Life, 1820–1892*. London: Sampson Low, Marston & Company, 1893.

Dall, Caroline H. *A Woman's Right to Labor, or, Low Wages and Hard Work*. Boston: Walker, Wise, and Company, 1860.

Lemon, Mark, and G. A. A'Beckett. *The Chimes; or, Some Bells That Rang an Old Year Out and a New Year In: A Goblin Drama in Four Quarters, Dramatised by Mark Lemon and G. A. a'Beckett from the Story by Charles Dickens*. London: John Dicks, n.d.

Mayhew, Henry. *London Labour and the London Poor; A Cyclopaedia of the Condition and Earnings of Those That Will Work, Those That Cannot Work, and Those That Will Not Work*, vol. 1. London: Griffin, Bone, and Company, 1861.

Robertson, James. *A Noble Pioneer: The Life Story of Emma Hardinge Britten*. Manchester: Two Worlds' Publishing Co., n.d.

~ associated with Victoria Woodhull

Darwin, M. F. *One Moral Standard for All: Extracts from the Lives of Victoria Claflin Woodhull and Tennessee Claflin*. New York: Caulon Press, n.d.

Ellington, George. *The Women of New York; or, The Under-World of the Great City*. New York: The New York Book Company, 1869.

Foster, George G. *New York by Gas-light: With Here and There a Streak of Sunshine*. New York: Dewitt & Davenport, 1850.

Stanton, Elizabeth Cady, Susan B. Anthony, and Mathilda Joslyn

Gage, eds. *History of Woman Suffrage*, vols. 1–2. New York: Fowler & Wells, 1881–82.

Stowe, Harriet Beecher. *My Wife and I: or, Harry Henderson's History*. New York: J. B. Ford and Company, 1872.

Tilton, Theodore. *Biography of Victoria C. Woodhull*. New York: The Golden Age, 1871.

Woodhull, Victoria Claflin. *Autobiography of Victoria Chaflin* [sic] *Woodhull*. Bredons Norton, U.K.: self-published, 1895.

—— [Published as Victoria C. Woodhull Martin]. *The Rapid Multiplication of the Unfit*. London: Hyde Park Gate, 1891.

——. *A Speech on the Impending Revolution*. New York: Woodhull, Claflin & Co., 1872.

~ associated with Georgina Weldon

Braddon, M. E. *Lady Audley's Secret*. London: Tinsley Bros., 1862.

Collins, Wilkie. *The Woman in White*. London: Sampson Low, Son & Co., 1860.

Lowe, Louisa. *Quis Custodiet Ipsos Custodes? No. 1, Report of a Case Heard in Queen's Bench*. London: J. Burns, 1872.

——. *Quis Custodiet Ipsos Custodes? No. 3, How an Old Woman Obtained Passive Writing, and the Outcome Thereof*. London: J. Burns, 1873.

Reade, Charles. *Hard Cash: A Matter-of-fact Romance*. London: Sampson Low, Son & Marston, 1863.

Weldon, Georgina. *Death-Blow to Spiritualism—Is It? Dr. Slade, Messrs. Maskeylyne & Cooke, and Mr. W. Morton*. London: Music and Art Association, 1882.

——. *The Ghastly Consequences of Living in Charles Dickens' House*. London: Tavistock House, 1882.

——. *The History of my Orphanage: or, The Outpourings of an Alleged Lunatic*. London: self-published, 1878.

——. *How I Escaped the Mad Doctors*. London: self-published, 1882.

——. *My Orphanage and Gounod in England*. London: Music and Art Association, 1882.

Winslow, L. S. Forbes. *Spiritualistic Madness*. London: Baillière, Tindall, and Cox, 1877.

——. *Recollections of Forty Years*. London: John Ouseley Ltd, 1910.

Secondary Sources

Braude, Ann. *Radical Spirits: Spiritualism and Women's Rights in Nineteenth-Century America*. Boston: Beacon Press, 1989.

Croffut, W. A. *The Vanderbilts and the Story of Their Fortune*. London: Griffith, Farran, Okeden & Welsh, 1886.

Doyle, Arthur Conan. *The History of Spiritualism*. London: Cassell and Company, 1926.

Frisken, Amanda. *Victoria Woodhull's Sexual Revolution: Political Theater and the Popular Press in Nineteenth-Century America*. Philadelphia: University of Pennsylvania Press, 2004.

Gabriel, Mary. *Notorious Victoria: The Life of Victoria Woodhull, Uncensored*. Chapel Hill, NC: Algonquin Books of Chapel Hill, 1998.

Geisst, Charles R. *Wall Street: A History from Its Beginnings to the Fall of Enron*. New York: Oxford University Press, 2004.

Gienapp, William E. *This Fiery Trial: The Speeches and Writings of Abraham Lincoln*. New York: Oxford University Press, 2002.

Godwin, Joscelyn. *The Theosophical Enlightenment*. Albany: State University of New York Press, 1994.

Goldsmith, Barbara. *Other Powers: The Age of Suffrage, Scandal and the Notorious Victoria Woodhull*. London: Granta Books, 1998.

Grierson, Edward. *Storm Bird: The Strange Life of Georgina Weldon*. London: Chatto & Windus, 1959.

Hale, William Harlan. *Horace Greeley: Voice of the People*. New York: Harper & Brothers, 1950.

Howe, Lisa. "Spirited Pioneer: The Life of Emma Hardinge Britten." PhD diss. University of Florida, 2015.

Jackson, Herbert G. Jr. *The Spirit Rappers*. New York: Doubleday & Co., 1972.

Kontou, Tatiana. *Spiritualism and Women's Writing: From the Fin de Siècle to the Neo-Victorian*. Basingstoke, U.K.: Palgrave Macmillan, 2009.

Lavoie, Jeffrey D. *The Theosophical Society: The History of a Spiritualist Movement*. Boca Raton, FL: Brown Walker Press, 2012.

Lehman, Amy. *Victorian Women and the Theatre of Trance: Mediums, Spiritualists and Mesmerists in Performance*. Jefferson, NC: McFarland & Company, 2009.

Linn, William Alexander. *Horace Greeley, Founder and Editor of The New York Tribune*. New York: D. Appleton and Company, 1903.

MacPherson, Myra. *The Scarlet Sisters: Sex, Suffrage and Scandal in the Gilded Age*. New York: Twelve, 2014.

Manseau, Peter. *The Apparitionists: A Tale of Phantoms, Fraud, Photography, and the Man Who Captured Lincoln's Ghost*. Boston: Houghton Mifflin Harcourt, 2017.

McFeely, William S. *Frederick Douglass*. New York: W. W. Norton & Company, 1991.

Natale, Simone. *Supernatural Entertainments: Victorian Spiritual-*

ism and the Rise of Modern Media Culture. University Park: Pennsylvania State University Press, 1981.

Nicholson, Helen F. "Spirited Performances: A Critical Study of the Life of Georgina Weldon (1837–1914)." PhD diss. University of Manchester, 2000.

Owen, Alex. *The Darkened Room: Women, Power and Spiritualism in Late Victorian England*. London: Virago Press, 1989.

Pond, Mariam Buckner. *The Unwilling Martyrs: The Story of the Fox Family*. London: Spiritualist Press, 1947.

Porter, Roy, Helen Nicholson, and Bridget Bennett. *Women, Madness and Spiritualism*, vol. 1. London: Routledge, 2003.

Sachs, Emanie. *The Terrible Siren: Victoria Woodhull (1838–1927)*. New York: Harper & Brothers, 1928.

Stern, Madeleine B., ed. *The Victoria Woodhull Reader*. Weston, MA: M&S Press, 1974.

Thompson, Brian. *A Monkey Among Crocodiles: The Disastrous Life of Mrs Georgina Weldon*. London: Flamingo, 2000.

Tomalin, Claire. *Charles Dickens: A Life*. London: Penguin Books, 2012.

Treherne, Philip. *A Plaintiff in Person (Life of Mrs Weldon)*. London: William Heinemann Ltd., 1923.

Underhill, Lois Beachy. *The Woman Who Ran for President: The Many Lives of Victoria Woodhull*. Bridgehampton, NY: Bridge Works Publishing, 1995.

Vanderbilt, Arthur II. *Fortune's Children: The Fall of the House of Vanderbilt*. London: Michael Joseph, 1990.

Weisberg, Barbara. *Talking to the Dead: Kate and Maggie Fox and the Rise of Spiritualism*. New York: HarperOne, 2005.

Whittington-Egan, Molly. *Doctor Forbes Winslow: Defender of the Insane*. Great Malvern: Cappella Archive, 2000.

Wiley, Barry H. *The Thought Reader Craze: Victorian Science at the Enchanted Boundary.* Jefferson, NC: McFarland & Company, 2012.

Wise, Sarah. *Inconvenient People: Lunacy, Liberty and the Mad-Doctors in Victorian England.* London: Vintage, 2013.

INDEX

abolition of slavery: Emma
  Hardinge Britten, support for,
  93, 94, 97, 101; and Spiritualism, 18, 92, 94
Advance (steamship), 237, 238
African Americans, 125, 136, 137–38;
  see also slavery and slave trade
Albany (NY), 39
Albert, Prince, 3, 69, 241, 304n
alcoholism: of Canning Woodhull,
  114–15, 117, 120–21; of Kate Fox,
  79, 240, 242, 245, 254; of Maggie
  Fox, 234, 243, 245, 253, 254
Allen, Mary B., 34–35
alphabet method, 23, 32,
  44, 47, 254; *see also* spirit
  communication
American Association of Spiritualists, 165, 169–70

American Spiritualism; *see* Modern Spiritualism
American Woman Suffrage Association, 155; *see also* suffrage
Andrews, Stephen Pearl, 152, 165
Anglo-Zulu War, 215
animal magnetism, 31–32; *see also*
  trances
Anthony, Susan B., 92, 137, 148–
  49, 154, 167; *see also* women's
  rights movement
astrology, 59; *see also* spirit
  communication
asylums: for children, 242,
  243; and coercion of women,
  136, 190–91, 195–96, 206;
  private, 205, 209, 212, 232;
  unjust incarceration in, 189,
  192, 196

Autobiography of Emma Hardinge Britten, 57, 60, 76, 102, 107, 246
automobiles, 247

Balaclava, Battle of, 216
Banner of Light (Boston): Emma Hardinge Britten in, 58; on Fox sisters, 244–45, 255; on Kate Fox, 253; on Leah Underhill, 254; Maggie Fox, support for, 254; and Victoria Woodhull, 146; on *Woodhull & Claflin's Weekly*, 151
Barnes Mystery, 215
Barnum, P. T., 42, 49, 274n
Barron, Henry D., 35, 36–37
Beecher, Catharine, 162
Beecher, Henry Ward, 161, 163, 168, 169–70, 171–72
Bell, James Samuel: Georgina Weldon, support for, 197, 225; in plot to institutionalize Georgina, 186, 187, 188–89, 191, 192–93
Bell, John C., 6–7, 8, 9, 10
Bell, Mrs., 7, 8, 9
Berkeley, Francis Henry Fitzhardinge and George Charles Grantley Fitzhardinge, 61
Black Friday (September 24, 1869), 141–42; *see also* Wall Street
Blessington, Countess of (Marguerite Gardiner), 59, 61
Blood, James Harvey: about, 123; charges against, 156–60; as clairvoyant physician, 127, 128–29; and communism, 165;

and Victoria Woodhull, 124, 128–29, 172; and *Woodhull & Claflin's Weekly*, 152, 171
Blood, Mary Anna C., 128
Booth, John Wilkes, 125–26
Bortel, John, 121
Boston (MA), 39, 95, 169–70, 172
The Boston Herald, 170, 250, 252
Bristol (UK), 55–56
The Bristol Mercury, 56, 61
British Medical Journal, 204, 211–12
British Spiritualism; *see* Modern Spiritualism
Britten, Emma Hardinge (née Floyd): and abolition of slavery, 93, 94, 97, 101; age, 276n, 277n, 278n; *Autobiography*, 57, 60, 76, 102, 107, 246; birth and childhood, 54–55; and Fox sisters, 79–80, 83, 240, 245, 246, 253; on free love, 92; as historian of Spiritualism, 106–107; in later life, 245–46; on Lincoln, 101, 102, 126, 256; and Lincoln campaign, 99–101; magnetic abilities, 54, 57–58, 63; marriages and name changes, 60–61, 80–81, 106–107, 278n; media opinions, 64, 86, 93, 97, 102, 105–106; music and theater career, 56–57, 58, 61–64; and Orphic Circle, 58–60, 65, 70, 277n; political context, 55–56; public testing of, 83–86; and religion, 87–88,

104–105; and SDSK, 77, 78, 80; Spiritualism, conversion to, 66–67, 70–74; and SS *Pacific*, 75–76; stalkers and harassment of, 88–91, 257; tours and talks, 76–77, 81–83, 87, 91, 93, 94–95, 96–99, 102–105; trance lecturing, 82, 84–85, 97, 103–104, 134, 256–57; on Victoria Woodhull, 172, 247–48; and women's movement, 82, 91–92, 95–97

Britten, William, 106–107
Brooker, Utica, 163, 164, 165, 167
Brown, Calvin, 15, 16, 38, 79
Buchanan, James, 78
Buffalo Commercial Advertiser, 66
Bullard, Edward F., 81, 82
Burns, James, 175
Burns, Robert (spirit of), 47
Byng, Frederick Gerald (Poodle), 180

Capron, Eliab Wilkinson: demotion of, 38, 39; on Fox sisters, attacks on, 53; Fox sisters, management of, 27–28, 30, 35–36; and Kate Fox, testing of, 23–24; media opinions, 38; on spirit rapping, 36–37; on Spiritualism, 66
Challis, Luther C., 170, 171
Christianity, 104–105
Christian Spiritualist, 75, 77
civil rights movement; *see* slavery and slave trade; suffrage
Civil War (U.S.): aftermath of,

101, 125, 131; Emma Hardinge Britten's prophecy of, 94; and Spiritualism, 121, 123; tensions before, 46, 93, 96
Claflin, Reuben Buckman (Buck): medical and criminal schemes of, 109, 112, 118, 121–22; Tennessee Claflin, control of, 118, 122–23, 130, 139–40, 159; Victoria Woodhull on, 108, 109–111, 113, 285n; in Victoria Woodhull's home, 132, 140, 152
Claflin, Roxanna Hummel (Annie): James Blood, charges against, 156–60; and Tennessee Claflin, 130, 159–60; and Victoria Woodhull, 108–109, 111, 113, 163, 173; in Victoria Woodhull's home, 132, 139–40, 152
Claflin, Tennessee: birth, 287n; brokerage firm of, 144, 146–49; charges against, 122, 147, 171; as clairvoyant healer, 118, 121, 122–23, 129, 132, 159; and Cornelius Vanderbilt, 133, 135, 136, 140, 246; father's control of, 118, 122–23, 130, 139–40, 159; at James Blood hearing, 159–60; and Lincoln's death, 126; marriages, 121, 246–47; media opinions, 145–47, 149, 154–55, 165; news publication of, 151–52, 170–71; Victoria Woodhull's vision of, 119; and women's movement, 153–55
Claflin, Thankful, 129

clairvoyance; *see* spirit
communication
Clark, Lemuel, 18–19
Clarke, Edward, 224, 225
class, 55–56, 95, 97
Cleveland (OH), 114
Cogswell, Anna, 116–17
Collins, Wilkie, 192, 209
Commissioners in Lunacy, 196,
203; *see also* lunacy laws
communism, 165–66
The Communist Manifesto
(Marx), 152
Compromise of 1850, 46, 51, 78;
see also slavery and slave trade
conjugal rights, 221–22, 223; *see*
also women
Cooper, James Fenimore, 46, 83
Corinthian Hall (Rochester), 25,
26–29, 65, 85, 250
Crawford, Frank Armstrong, 140–41
Crimean War, 216
crystal gazing, 59, 60; *see also*
spirit communication

Dall, Caroline Healey, 95–96, 137
Davenport, Reuben Briggs, 251
Day, Horace H., 77, 78, 281n
The Death-Blow to Spiritualism
(Davenport), 251
de Bathe, Henry: Georgina Wel-
don, plot to institutionalize,
187, 190, 196, 199, 200–201;
Georgina Weldon's campaign
against, 204, 211, 212–13, 223
de Bathe, Kate, 212, 213
Dewey, D. M., 37

Dickens, Charles, 70, 182, 186, 208
d'Orsay, Alfred, 177
double standards, 132, 161; *see*
also women
Douglass, Frederick: and Fox
sisters, 23, 24, 34; and Underground Railroad, 16; and Victoria Woodhull, 168; and women's
movement, 22, 92, 137, 138
Doyle, Arthur Conan, 253–54
Draper, Nathaniel and Rachel, 31–33
Drew, Daniel, 141, 142, 148
Duesler, William, 6, 7

Edmunds, James, 225, 299n
elections: and Emma Hardinge
Britten, 99–101; and Spiritual-
ism, 77–78; Victoria Woodhull's
campaign, 149–51, 155, 162–63,
167–69, 171, 257; *see also* suffrage
Eliot, George, 70, 172
Ellington, George, 131–32
epilepsy, 211; *see also* lunacy
Equal Rights Party, 167; *see also*
Woodhull, Victoria
Erard, Pierre, 57
Erie Canal, 131
eugenics, 115, 247
The Evening Star (Washington,
D.C.), 126, 139

fallen women, 82, 96, 102, 137;
see also women; women's rights
movement
Fenno, Augustus, 65, 71, 72
Fifteenth Amendment, 136; *see*
also suffrage

Fish, Elisabeth (Lizzie): birth, 269n; and Hydesville rapping, 12, 14; Leah Underhill's removal of, 19, 36, 51, 270–71n; Leah Underhill's support for, 11; spirit rapping, protest against, 18–19; *see also* Underhill, Ann Leah

Fisk, James, 141, 142

Flowers, Frederick, 202–203

Floyd, Ann Sophia: Emma Hardinge Britten, concerns for, 54, 57–58; Emma Hardinge Britten's support for, 76, 83, 103; and Emma Hardinge Britten's theater career, 63–64, 65; spirit communication, opinions on, 73–74

Floyd, Ebenezer, 55, 82

Floyd, Tom, 72–73

Foster, George G., 117

Fourteenth Amendment, 136; *see also* African Americans

Fox, Catherine (Kate): alcoholism of, 79, 240, 242, 245, 254; death, 254; descriptions of, 5, 43, 47; early career, 18, 30, 31–32, 33, 35–36, 48–50; education, 35, 48; Eliab Capron's testing of, 23–24, 26, 27; and Hydesville rapping, 5–6, 7, 10–11, 12, 13–17; in Maggie Fox's writings, 239; marriage, 195, 240–41; name and age, 268n; pressure of work and family, 49–50, 78, 79, 207, 237, 240, 253, 256; professional readings, 77; public talks of, 207;

and Robert Dale Owen, 69; sons of, 241, 242, 243; Spiritualism, disenchantment with, 233–34, 235, 250–51, 258; Spiritualism, return to, 251–52, 253; *see also* Fox sisters

Fox, David, 11, 12, 20, 21–22

Fox, John D., 5, 6, 7, 10, 12–13, 16

Fox, Margaret: age, 268n; description of, 47; and Fox sisters' early career, 22, 30, 32, 35–36, 38, 45; and Hydesville rapping, 5–6, 7–8, 10, 12, 15–16; Leah Underhill's influence on, 36; social stigma, fear of, 13, 45, 236

Fox, Margaretta (Maggie): age, 268n; alcoholism of, 234, 243, 245, 253, 254; Catholicism, conversion to, 239; Corinthian Hall demonstration, 26–27, 28–30, 36, 85; death, 254; descriptions of, 5, 27, 43, 47; early career, 18, 24–25, 31–32, 33; education, 35, 237; and Elisha Kent Kane, 78, 236–39; financial difficulties, 239–40, 254; and Hydesville rapping, 5–6, 7, 10–11, 12, 13, 15, 16–17; illness, 45; Kate Fox and sons, support for, 243; Leah Underhill, anger with, 240, 243, 249; media opinions, 238, 244, 248, 250, 252–53, 254; Spiritualism, disenchantment with, 78, 79, 236, 237, 256, 258; Spiritualism, return to, 252–53; on Spiritualism as fraud, 233–36, 242–44, 249–51; *see also* Fox sisters

Fox sisters (collective career): Leah
    Underhill's influence on, 11, 36,
    38, 45, 51, 79, 237–38, 239,
    243, 250, 251, 255–56; media
    opinions, 30–31, 36–38, 42,
    45–46, 48, 58, 65–66, 190,
    244–45; public demonstrations,
    25, 26–29, 38–39, 85; radical
    mission of, 23, 25; Spiritual-
    ism, influence on, 22, 23, 32,
    53, 65, 69, 74, 106, 118, 254;
    Spiritualism and empowerment
    of, 22, 24, 255–56, 258–59;
    support for, 23, 24, 34, 39, 53,
    66; threats and violence against,
    21–22, 29, 30, 51–53; touring,
    35–36, 38–40; *see also specific
    sisters*
Foye, Ada, 71–73
Franklin, Benjamin (spirit of),
    32–33, 76, 81
Franklin, John and Jane, 237, 238
free love: Emma Hardinge Britten
    on, 92; and James Blood, 128;
    Victoria Woodhull's endorsement
    of, 155, 157, 163–65, 246, 257
French, E. J., 76, 81, 88
Fugitive Slave Act (1850), 51; *see
    also* slavery and slave trade

Gallagher, John, 88, 89–90
Gardiner, Marguerite (Countess of
    Blessington) 59, 61
Ghost Land (Britten), 60
ghosts; *see* Hydesville rapping;
    spirit communication

Gladstone, Catherine, 181
Gladstone, William Ewart, 181,
    197, 202
gold market crash, 141–42; *see
    also* Wall Street
Gore House, 59, 61, 70, 177
Gould, Jay, 141, 142
Gounod, Charles, 183–84, 208,
    215, 249
Granger, Lyman and Elisabeth,
    16–17, 26, 270n
Great Police Riot (NYC, 1857), 88
Great Reform Act (UK, 1832), 56
Great Western Railway, 55
Greeley, Horace, 42–45, 46,
    48–49, 50, 83, 169
Greeley, Mary, 42, 46, 48–49, 50
Guppy, Agnes, 175, 188

Hannen, James, 222–23
Hard Cash (Reade), 209
Harper's Weekly, 147, 166
Hartford Female Seminary, 162
Hawkins, Henry, 227–28
Hayden, Maria and William R.,
    68–69, 70
Hayes, Samuel, 217, 218
Henry, Philip (Earl Stanhope), 59,
    61
The History of Spiritualism
    (Doyle), 253–54
*History of the Strange Sounds or
    Rappings* (Dewey), 37
Hitler, Adolf, 247
Holland House Circle, 178
Home, Daniel Dunglas, 207

Homer (OH), 108, 112
Hooker, Isabella Beecher, 154, 155
Howe, Rebecca, 122–23
Huddleston, John Walter, 224, 225, 226
The Humanitarian (Woodhull), 247
Hydesville rapping: anniversary celebrations of, 255; body, search for, 19–21; community backlash, 21–22; early appearances, 4–15; public interest in, 16–19; in Rochester, 14–16; *see also* Fox sisters
hysteria, 13, 190, 195; *see also* lunacy laws

Ingham, James, 217–18
insanity; *see* lunacy laws
International Workingmen's Association (IWA), 165–66, 168

Jack the Ripper, 232, 303n
Jencken, Ferdinand Dietrich Lowenstein, 241, 242, 243, 305
Jencken, Henry Diedrich (father), 195, 240, 242
Jencken, Henry Dietrich Lowenstein (son), 242, 243
Jones, Wallace A., 198
Juvenile Asylum (NYC), 242, 243; *see also* asylums

Kane, Elisha Kent, 78, 79, 236–39, 241, 243
Keighley (UK), 69

Labor Reform League, 155
Ladies' Automobile Club, 247
Lander, George, 229
Lape, Jane, 9
Lester, Charles Edwards, 58
Lewes, George Henry, 69–70
Lewis, E. E., 9, 10, 12, 24
Light (magazine), 231, 245, 248, 251, 254, 304n
Lincoln, Abraham, 99–101, 102, 119–20, 125–26, 256
Lincoln, Mary Todd, 101–102
Lind, Jenny, 49–50, 181–82, 275n
The London Figaro, 202, 210–11, 212–14, 246
London Spiritualist Federation, 248
The Love-Life of Dr. Kane (Margaretta Fox), 239
Lowe, Annie, 184, 191, 222
Lowe, George, 195
Lowe, Louisa, 192, 194–97, 198, 205–206, 225, 248
lunacy, 190, 195, 208, 211, 258
Lunacy Act (1890), 232
Lunacy Law Reform Association (LLRA), 196
lunacy laws: in court proceedings, 225–28; Georgina Weldon's campaign for reform of, 203–205, 208–209, 210, 220, 231–32, 248; Louisa Lowe's campaign for reform of, 195–96; men's power in, 189, 195, 203, 206

madness; *see* lunacy
Magnetic Healing Institute, 132, 159

magnetism, 4, 31–32, 57, 63,
80, 105, 135; *see also* spirit
communication
Mansfield, J. V., 98
Married Women's Property Act
(1882), 223; *see also* women
Marshall, E. A., 63, 64, 65
Martin, John Biddulph, 246, 247
Marx, Karl, 166, 168
The Medium and Daybreak: and
Georgina Weldon, 191, 207,
208, 216, 229; Leah Underhill's
reproduction of, 241; popularity of, 175
Ménier, Anacharsis, 185–86, 187,
188, 191–92, 197
Ménier, Angèle, 185, 217, 219
Mesmer, Franz, 31–32
mesmerism, 31–32, 59, 70; *see also*
trances
*The Missing Link in Modern Spiri-
tualism* (Underhill), 241, 249
Modern American Spiritualism
(Britten), 106–107, 245, 253
Modern Spiritualism: in Britain,
68, 69–70, 103–104, 174–75;
in California, 98; and Christianity, 104–105; and Civil
War, 121, 123; debunking of,
233–36, 242–43, 244–45,
249–51; decline of movement,
255, 258; demographics, 276n;
Fox sisters' influence on, 22,
23, 32, 53, 65, 69, 74, 106, 118,
254; and free love movement,
92, 257; historians of, 106–107,

253–54; and lunacy, 190, 195,
208, 258; media opinions on,
30–31, 37, 69–70, 80, 86,
102, 244–45; and medical
techniques, 68, 70, 112–13,
121–22, 127, 159; popularity
and growth of, 65, 66, 74,
75; respectability of, 91; and
slavery, abolition of, 18, 92, 94;
in southern U.S., 93–94; and
women's empowerment, 22,
77, 82, 85, 97, 134, 176, 246,
258–59; and women's move-
ment, 18, 23, 91–92
Morrison, Richard James (Zadkiel), 59
Morse, Samuel, 17
Mortimer, James, 213–14, 215
motoring, 247
Mott, Lucretia, 22, 92, 137; *see
also* women's rights movement
Mount Gilead (OH), 112–13
Mrs. Weldon Relief Committee,
231; *see also* Weldon, Georgina
Mumler, William H., 102
Mysterious Knockings (theater
performance), 45
My Wife and I (Stowe), 162

Nast, Thomas, 166
National Society for Women's
Suffrage (UK), 174
National Training School of Mu-
sic, 182–83, 184
National Woman Suffrage Associa-
tion (NWSA), 155, 156, 165, 167

National Women's Rights Convention, 50–51, 136–38
Nevada, 99
Newgate Prison, 219–20
Newton, Isaac, 225
New York City, 74, 131–32
New-York Commercial Advertiser, 37–38
The New York Herald: on Emma Hardinge Britten, 64, 80, 87–88, 102; on gold market crash, 141; on Kate Fox, 240–41, 242–43; on Lincoln assassination, 126; on Maggie Fox, 233, 235–36, 244; on presidential election (1872), 150–51, 168; on SS *Pacific*, 75; on Victoria and Tennessee, 144–46, 158; on Victoria Woodhull, 149, 165, 167
New York Spiritualists' choir, 80
The New York Times, 155, 160, 166
New-York Tribune: on Emma Hardinge Britten, 64; on Fox sisters, 30–31, 46, 47–48, 244, 252; on free love, 155; on women's movement, 154
Nineteenth Century Miracles (Britten), 107
Not Alone (Lander), 229–30

Orphic Circle, 59–60, 61, 65, 277n
Owen, Robert Dale, 69, 168

Pacific (steamship), 63, 74–76
The Pall Mall Gazette, 213, 214, 218

Paris Commune massacre (1871), 165
Pears soap brand, 229
Philips, Francis Charles, 223–24
The Pickwick Papers (Dickens), 229
The Place and Mission of Woman (Britten), 91, 95
Platt's Hall (San Francisco), 98, 99
police riots, 88
Pomeroy, Samuel C., 137
Post, Amy, 16, 23, 29, 30, 34
Post, Isaac, 16, 23, 30, 33, 34
poverty, 95, 97, 131–32
Progressive Library and Spiritual Institution, 175
Promenade Concerts, 215–17
property rights, 223; *see also* women
prostitution, 95–97, 131–32, 155
publishing industry, 39
Pulver, Lucretia, 8–9

Queen Square riots (1831), 55–56
The Queen v. Mortimer, 213–214

The Rapid Multiplication of the Unfit (Woodhull), 247
rapping; *see* Hydesville rapping
Reade, Charles, 209
Reconstruction, 136
Redfield, Mary and Charles, 4–6, 7, 10
Reinhold, Ernest, 58, 61
Report of the Mysterious Noises Heard in the House of Mr. John D. Fox (Lewis), 12, 24

The Revolution, 148; *see also* women's rights movement
Richmond, Cassius M., 234, 249–50
Ripley, George, 46, 47–48
Rivière, Jules, 215–16, 218–19, 230
Rochester (NY), 11, 25
Rudderforth, John, 199, 204

Salem witch trials, 13
San Francisco, 98, 116, 117
Schell, Richard, 147
science, advances in, 17–18, 37, 258
scrying, 59, 60; *see also* spirit communication
seamstress work, 117, 287n
séances; *see* spirit communication
Second Reform Act (UK, 1867), 174
Semple, C. E. Armand, 199, 204, 223, 227–28, 230–31
sex work, 95–97, 131–32, 155
Sidney, James, 217, 218
Singular Revelations (Capron and Barron), 36–37
slavery and slave trade: in 1856 presidential election, 78; abolition, Emma Hardinge Britten's support for, 93, 94, 97, 101; Bristol and wealth from, 55; Compromise of 1850, 46, 51; and Spiritualism, 18, 92, 94; and suffrage, 138; Underground Railroad, 16, 51

Society for the Diffusion of Spiritual Knowledge (SDSK), 77, 78, 80
Society for Psychical Research, 248
somnambulism, 59, 70, 82; *see also* trances
Southey, Sarah, 198, 299n
Sparr, Mary (née Claflin), 157
spirit communication: alphabet method, 23, 32, 44, 47, 254; context for belief in, 17; debunking of, 233–36, 249–51; developments in, 175; popularity of, 53, 65, 69; profits from, 36, 37–38, 39–40, 69, 77; table turning, 3–4, 69, 175; in writing, 4, 195; *see also* Hydesville rapping; Modern Spiritualism; trances
The Spiritualist, 175, 186, 191, 213
Spiritualistic Madness, 190
The Spiritual Magazine, 105
Spiritual Telegraph, 75, 86
spirit writing, 4, 195
The Standard (London), 191–92
Stanhope, Earl (Philip Henry), 59, 61
Stanton, Elizabeth Cady: and spirit rapping, 23; and Victoria Woodhull, 148, 154, 161, 167; in women's movement, 22, 137–38, 155
steamboat travel, 41
St. Louis (MO), 123, 127
stock market, 141–42; *see also* Wall Street
Stone, George W., 68–69

Stowe, Harriet Beecher, 137, 154, 162, 172
suffrage: of African Americans, 125, 136, 137–38; and Spiritualism, 18; of women, 22, 92, 136–38, 149, 153–55, 174, 257; of working classes, 55–56; *see also* elections

table turning, 3–4, 69, 175; *see also* spirit communication
Tallmadge, Nathaniel P., 66, 78
Tavistock House, 182–83, 184, 185–86, 200, 208
Taylor, Zachary, 46
technology, advances in, 17–18, 37, 39, 258
Thackeray, William Makepeace, 180
Thomas, Julia Martha, 215
Tilton, Theodore: in Beecher-Tilton scandal, 160–61, 169–70, 172; and communism, 165; Victoria Woodhull, desertion of, 169; Victoria Woodhull, support for, 162–63, 164, 168
Tomkins, Mary Anne, 198, 299n
The Tragedy Queen (play), 64, 277n
trances: and Charles Dickens, 70; and crystal gazing, 59; Emma Hardinge Britten's lectures in, 82, 84–85, 97, 103–104, 134, 256–57; Franz Mesmer on, 31–32; and Lyttleton Stewart Forbes Winslow, 231; as medical technique, 68, 112–13; and Orphic Circle, 60; and Victoria Woodhull, 124

Treherne, Dalrymple, 189, 221
Treherne, Louisa (Thomas, née Dalrymple), 177
Treherne, Morgan (Thomas), 176–77, 179, 180–81, 182, 189
Troy (NY), 40, 51–53, 81–83
The True Witness and Catholic Chronicle, 86
Truth, Sojourner, 92
The Two Worlds (Manchester), 245, 246, 253

Uncle Tom's Cabin (Stowe), 137, 177
Underground Railroad, 16, 51
Underhill, Ann Leah (Fox, Fish): age, 269n, 274n; Corinthian Hall demonstration, 26–27, 28–30, 36, 85; daughter, sending away of, 19, 36, 51, 270–71n; death, 254; descriptions of, 27, 43, 47; early career, 18–19, 24–25, 34; and Hydesville rapping, 10–11, 12, 13–15, 16–17, 19–21; and Maggie Fox's marriage, 79, 236–38; marriages, 79, 81, 83, 269n; media opinions, 245, 253, 254; *Missing Link in Modern Spiritualism*, 241, 249; sisters, control of, 11, 36, 38, 45, 51, 79, 237–38, 239, 243, 250, 251, 255–56; sisters, strained relationship with, 78, 234, 239–40, 242, 243, 249; wealth of, 30, 40, 83, 91, 239–40; *see also* Fox sisters

Underhill, Daniel, 83, 240
United States Sanitary Commission
  (USSC), 99

Vanderbilt, Cornelius (Commodore), 97–98, 132–36, 140–42,
  146, 166, 168, 246
Vanderbilt, Sophia, 135–36
vegetarianism, 182
Victoria, Queen, 3–4, 49, 110,
  176, 183, 241, 304n
Villiers, Elizabeth, 186, 187, 191,
  199
Voices from the Spirit World
  (Post), 34
voters' rights; *see* suffrage;
  women's rights movement

Wallack Company, 62–63
Wall Street, 141–42, 144, 147–49,
  168, 257
Watts, George Frederic, 178
Webster, Kate, 215
Weekly Argus (Albany), 39,
  273–74n
Weldon, Georgina: birth and upbringing, 176–77; charges and
  prison sentences, 218–20, 230,
  257–58; and Charles Gounod,
  183–84; courtship and marriage, 179–81, 182, 184;
  descriptions of, 177, 223–24;
  Harry Weldon, campaign
  against, 201–203, 210–12,
  214–15, 221–23; Harry Wel-

don's plot to institutionalize,
  186–93, 196, 198–201, 257–
  58; legal actions of, 221–29;
  and Louisa Lowe, 196–200,
  205–207; lunacy laws, reform
  of, 203–205, 208–209, 210,
  220, 231–32, 248; media
  attention, desire for, 210–11,
  212–13, 214, 216–17; media
  opinions, 203–204, 208, 217,
  218, 219, 220, 229–30; miscarriage, 181; musical ability,
  177, 178, 181; musical academy of, 182–83, 184–86, 219–
  20; Promenade Concerts court
  case, 215–18; radical views
  and qualities, 182, 184, 185;
  social circles, 178, 180, 296n;
  and Spiritualism, 176, 184,
  207, 248–49; stage career,
  178–79, 181, 209, 229–30,
  296n; talks and performances,
  203–204, 207–208, 210,
  220–21, 229, 230, 248, 257;
  Winslow and Semple's support
  for, 230–31
Weldon, William Henry (Harry):
  courtship and marriage,
  179–81; employment and
  finances, 182; *Figaro* legal case,
  213–14; Georgina Weldon, plot
  to institutionalize, 186–93, 196,
  198–201, 257–58; Georgina
  Weldon's campaign against,
  201–203, 210–12, 214–15,

221–23; and Georgina Weldon's
musical academy, 182–83, 184,
219
Weldon v. Semple, 227–29
Weldon v. Weldon, 221–23
Weldon v. Winslow, 223–27,
229
Welsh, Thomas, 57
The Western Argus (Lyons), 11
The White Cat (play), 56–57
Willets, George, 30, 42
Williams, Emily Louisa, 202
Williams, William Rhys, 206
Winn, James Michell, 186–87, 189,
204, 228
Winslow, Lyttleton Stewart
Forbes: Georgina Weldon,
plot to institutionalize, 186–
87, 189, 190–91, 196; Georgina Weldon, support for,
230–31; Georgina Weldon's
campaign against, 201–202,
204–205, 210–12, 223,
224–29; and Jack the Ripper,
303n; on Spiritualism, 190,
201, 231
The Woman in White (Collins),
192, 209
women: asylums and coercion of,
136, 190–91, 195–96, 206;
and hysteria, 13, 190, 195;
legal rights and opportunities, 131–32, 203, 221–22,
223, 243, 255–56; marriage
and status of, 79, 80–81;

in scrying experiments,
59–60; social constraints, 93,
205–206, 220; Spiritualism
and empowerment of, 22, 77,
82, 85, 97, 134, 176, 246,
258–59; written testimonies
of, 32, 37
The Women of New York (Ellington), 131–32
women's rights movement: and
class, 95, 97; conventions,
22–23, 50–51, 136–38; and
Emma Hardinge Britten, 82,
91–92, 95–97; growth of, 92;
and prostitution, 132; and
Spiritualism, 18, 23, 91–92;
suffrage, 22, 92, 136–38, 149,
153–55, 174, 257; and Victoria Woodhull, 136–39, 148,
149–50, 153–56; and Wall
Street, 148–49
Woodhull, Byron, 115, 117, 129,
152, 158, 247
Woodhull, Canning: age, 286n;
alcoholism of, 114–15, 117,
120–21; children of, 129,
152; as clairvoyant healer,
132; courtship and marriage,
113–14; death, 167; medical
career of, 112–13, 129–30;
in Victoria Woodhull's
home, 152, 153, 157–58,
160
Woodhull, Claflin & Co., 144,
146–49, 168, 257

Woodhull, Victoria: acting career, 116–17; age, 287n; ambition and plans, 110, 113, 115–16, 131, 132–34, 137, 162; arrest and charges against, 171; and Beecher family, 160–62, 169–70, 172, 246; birth and childhood, 108, 110–12; in Britain, 173–74; brokerage firm of, 144, 146–49, 168, 257; and Canning Woodhull, 112–15, 120–21, 152, 153, 157–58, 160; childbirth, 115, 120–21; children of, 129, 152, 247; as clairvoyant healer, 119–20, 123, 129, 132, 146; and communism, 165–66, 168; and Cornelius Vanderbilt, 132–36, 140, 146, 166, 168, 246; death, 248; declining support for, 172; descriptions of, 110, 111, 139; education of, 110; and Emma Hardinge Britten, 172, 247–48; and eugenics, 115, 247; financial independence, 135, 140, 151; and free love movement, 157, 160, 160–61, 163–65, 246, 257; and gold market crash, 142–43, 146; house of, 151, 152–53, 157, 168; and James Harvey Blood, 123–24, 127–29, 156, 158–59, 172; and Lincoln's death, 126; marriages, 114, 128, 246–47, 286n, 287n; media opinions, 127, 128, 139, 145–47, 149, 150–51, 154–55, 165, 166, 167, 170, 212; motoring and cycling, 247, 305n; news publication of, 151–52, 155, 162, 167, 168–69, 170–71, 172, 257; poverty and financial troubles, 115, 116, 168–69; presidential campaign, 149–51, 155, 162–63, 167–69, 171, 257; speeches of, 154–55, 163–65, 166; and Spiritualism, 159, 165, 169–70, 246–47, 248; and Tennessee Claflin, closeness, 117–18; visions and prophecies, 111, 118–19, 130; and women's movement, 136–39, 148, 149–50, 153–56

Woodhull, Zula (Zulu), 120–21, 129, 152, 248, 305n

Woodhull & Claflin's Weekly: Canning Woodhull obituary, 167; Catharine Beecher, attack on, 162; *Communist Manifesto*, publication of, 151–52; Emma Hardinge Britten's book, review of, 172; free love in, 155; on hypocrisy of well-connected men, 170–71; launch of, 151, 257; staff, 152; suspension of publication, 168–69

working classes, 55–56, 95, 97

The World (NYC), 139, 153, 160, 236

© Rosalind Hobley

EMILY MIDORIKAWA is the coauthor of *A Secret Sisterhood: The Literary Friendships of Jane Austen, Charlotte Brontë, George Eliot, and Virginia Woolf*. Her work has been published in *The Washington Post*, *The Paris Review*, *Lapham's Quarterly*, *Time*, and elsewhere. She is a winner of the Lucy Cavendish Fiction Prize and was a runner-up for the SI Leeds Literary Prize and the Yeovil Literary Prize. She teaches at New York University London. Find out more at emilymidorikawa.com.